CURTAIN GOING UP

22 SHORT PLAYS

by

STEWART H. BENEDICT

New Paltz, NY   FATA   *2002*

INTRODUCTION

The short plays in this collection reflect life in the United States during the 20th century. It was a period of great change. The nation become a major power, a strong middle class emerged, and some became enormously rich, amassing fortunes that would last for generations. The poor were most frequently the recent immigrants (of whom there were tens of millions in the 100-year period), the African-Americans and the residents of those areas of the South and the Border States slowest to recover from the Civil War.

The most remarkable change, however, was the increasing urbanization of the population. In 1910 about half of the people were classified as living in rural areas, while by the century's end, more than 70 percent were dwellers in large or small cities. The forty largest had more than a million residents each, and so it is no surprise that drama became increasingly concerned with city life as the century advanced.

Playwrights found subjects for the drama in the social and psychological adjustment to close-in living, in the drive for upward mobility, the adjustment of families to economic shifts and in racial and religious discrimination.

In these plays a reader will recognize characters drawn from the life of the time: middle-class office workers, wealthy dilettantes on the fringes of the arts, the aggressive salesman — the list is a long one, including political as well as social types. Popular notions, fads and foibles are scrutinized — even popular entertainment is parodied.

As always in the theater, the focus remains on people, viewed sentimentally, realistically, or even cynically, but invariably as individuals worthy of attention.

CURTAIN GOING UP

ONE DAY IN THE LIFE OF IVY DENNISON

CAST OF CHARACTERS

Ivy Dennison
The Men in Her Day
The Women in Her Day

The time of the play is a day in summer.

The entire play is performed without scenery, although a back-drop, either plain or suggestive of a deglamorized New York sky-line, may be used. Tables and chairs are used where necessary, but there should be no other props: eating, straphanging on the sub-way, etc. should all be pantomimed. Only three actors are required: Ivy, a female to play all the other female parts (she can use wigs and costume changes to suggest different characters), and a male to play all the male parts (he can do likewise). Ivy is in her early twenties; her chief characteristic is a very strong Metropolitan New York area accent.

ONE DAY IN THE LIFE OF IVY DENNISON

Scene 1

Ivy's mother is seated at the table eating as Ivy enters. Ivy gives her mother a perfunctory kiss on the cheek.

IVY. Hullo, Ma.

MOTHER. Morning.

IVY. Another scorcher. (She sits down and starts eating)

MOTHER. It's not gonna get too hot, but it's so sticky.

IVY. Yeah. Humidity gets you every time.

MOTHER. I wish we'd get some relief.

IVY. Yeah. Funny how the concrete holds the heat.

MOTHER. Mm. City gets like an oven after a couple of days. (Really looking at Ivy for the first time, aware that she is going to produce a strong reaction, but determined to plunge in anyway.) But even if it is hot, there's still no excuse for wearing that dress to the office. It's just not - - not nice.

IVY. (Eyes heavenward) Oh, Ma!

MOTHER. I mean it, Ivy. Well-brought-up young girls don't wear dresses that make them look, well, cheap.

IVY. Ma, they said on the radio that it's gonna get up to 95 today. I gotta wear the coolest thing I got. I'm gonna die if I have to wear some old thing with sleeves and the neck up to here!

MOTHER. Now, Ivy. You know that I don't want you to suffer. I'm only asking myself what people are going to say.

IVY. Well, they'll just have to say it.

MOTHER. (Slightly pouty) In my day I would no more have worn a dress like that to the office than I'd have flied to the moon.

IVY. Yeah, Ma. (She pushes her plate away.)

MOTHER. You didn't eat your breakfast. (She pushes it back)

IVY. Most of it.

MOTHER. It's a crime to waste good food.

IVY. I'm not hungry, Ma.

MOTHER. Waste not, want not.

IVY. I'm just not hungry, Ma.

MOTHER. A willful waste makes a woeful want.

IVY. Look, Ma, I don't want anymore.

MOTHER. It says in the paper that breakfast is the most important meal of the day.

IVY. Please, Ma, let's not get into an argument. (Consults her watch.) I gotta go now, anyway. (Rises.)

MOTHER. Oh, Ivy.

IVY. Yes?

MOTHER. Ivy, if you get a chance, would you just run into Korvette's and pick me up about four yards more of that cotton print for the bedroom curtains?

IVY. Oh Ma, I've only got half an hour for lunch. And Korvette's is six blocks.

MOTHER. Now, dear, it seems to me that you could make the effort. After all, it isn't as if I ask you to do a little errand for me every day.

IVY. Gee, Ma---

MOTHER. And you can save me a trip into the city.

IVY. I'll try. But I'm not making any promises. (Moves toward the door.)

MOTHER. Do try, dear.

IVY. (Partly to herself) Gee, how I hate the thoughts of that subway. It's like a turkish bath.

MOTHER. See you tonight, dear. I'll make a chicken salad. That'll be nice and cool. O.K.?

IVY. Sounds swell. Bye, Ma. (Exits.)

.MOTHER. Bye, honey. Have a nice day.

Blackout

SCENE 2

Ivy approaches Mr. Green, who is seated behind the counter of his candy store.

IVY. Morning, Mr. Green.

GREEN. Morning, Ivy.

IVY. (She looks over the counter, reaches out and takes a roll of lifesavers.) Guess I'll take peppermint. Hot day, isn't it?

GREEN. A person could die from the heat.

IVY. Mm. So how are you?

GREEN. How should I be in this business? Terrible.

IVY. (She has expected this answer, which is evidently a stock response. She speaks this next in a light, joshing tone.) Oh, Mr. Green, come on. Boy, that'll be the day when you say that you're doing all right.

GREEN. All right? Hah! In the candy store business?

IVY. Well, you've been in it for--for as long as I can remember.

GREEN. That only proves what a dope I am. I'm telling you: in the winter this business is hopeless; in the summer it's only miserable. And to think when I started out I figured I was going to get rich!

IVY. Gee, money isn't everything.

GREEN. It's plenty. Like the guy says, will happiness buy money?

IVY. Oh, Mr. Green, You know you don't really think that. There's lots of things more important than money.

GREEN. Like for instance?

IVY. Like health, for instance. After all, you got your health and that's something money can't buy.

GREEN. Eh.

IVY. And peace of mind. That's the best thing of all, right?

GREEN. Eh.

IVY. Come on, you know a person could have a million dollars and still not have peace of mind.

GREEN. I'll take my chances with the million dollars.

IVY. Oh, you're only saying that. And friends! What about friends? You could also have a million dollars and not have a single friend.

GREEN. Well, I'll admit that's true.

IVY. Sure it's true. Money can't buy true friendship.

GREEN. So O.K., O.K. You convinced me. But what about the subway? You want to be late for work?

IVY. Gee, yeah! (Running off) So long, Mr. Green. See you!

Blackout

SCENE 3

Ivy and her friend Peggy face the audience, each with an arm upraised hanging onto a strap. Peggy is chewing gum.

IVY. Some hot day, huh?

PEGGY. Yeah.

IVY. But it's the humidity that gets you more than the heat.

PEGGY. Yeah. Subway's fulla gentlemen, as usual.

IVY. I never expect to get a seat anymore,

PEGGY. Me neither. Hey, dja watch T.V. last night?

IVY. Mm.

PEGGY. *Undercover Agent?*

IVY. What else?

PEGGY. How about that Lance?

IVY. Boy, yeah. Is he cute!

PEGGY. Mm. How about a date with him!

IVY. I guess. Wonder what he's really like. In real life, I mean.

PEGGY. He's married, you know.

IVY. Yeah. But I mean before he was married.

PEGGY. I'll bet he was some operator, you know?

IVY. In real life, I mean.

Mm. Ma wanted to go to the Loew's, but I said to her, "Wild horses couldn't drag me out on a Thursday."

PEGGY. Me neither. (Pause) What was playing?

IVY. I don't even know. I just said, "So, O.K., Ma., if you wanna go, then go. I'm gonna watch T.V." So she said, "All right, if that's the way you feel, then all right."

PEGGY. Gee, what a drag, huh?

IVY. Yeah, I guess. But you know how it is. I mean, like it says in the Bible, you gotta honor thy father and thy mother.

PEGGY. (Sobered) Yeah. That's true.

IVY. I mean, even if it is a drag.

PEGGY. Uh-huh. (Pause) George ask you out for Saturday?

IVY. No, but I expect he will today.

PEGGY. Bill didn't ask either. But he usually waits until Friday -- It's just like, you know, he wants to keep me in suspense all week. So let him.

IVY. Boy, they're like little kids, you know.

PEGGY. Yeah.(With a start) Hey, we're at 50th. (Both start to leave, elbowing their way.) Meetcha tonight by Radio City.

IVY. S'long. See you. Take care.

Blackout

SCENE 4

Ivy is seated at her desk typing. George approaches.

GEORGE. Do my eyes deceive me, or is it the most gorgeous girl at the first desk in the typing pool?

IVY. Do my eyes deceive me, or is it the wisest guy in the shipping department?

GEORGE. Workin' hard?

IVY. Pretty hard.

GEORGE. Us too.

IVY. (Stops typing) But not that hard.

GEORGE. Why don't you let me take you away from all this? How about a trip to the Riviera on my yacht? Or how about I set you up in a penthouse on Park Avenue?

IVY. Hah!

GEORGE. Or in my furnished room on 18th street?

IVY. Watch your step, Mr. Wiseguy. You're skating on thin ice.

GEORGE. Ah, you know you love it!

IVY. George, sometimes I think you only think of one thing.

GEORGE. Well, I'm a man. Whaddya want? I'm only human, you know.

IVY. You're too human, that's your trouble.

GEORGE. You wouldn't like me if I wasn't so human.

IVY. Well, pardon me! Honest, George Baker, sometimes I don't know why I have anything to do with you.

GEORGE. First because I'm rich and handsome and second because I'm so madly in love with you that if you don't go out with me on Saturday I'll either shoot myself or ask somebody else.

IVY. (In spite of herself) You got some line, I must say.

GEORGE. Thousands of girls have told me they can't resist me.

IVY. Hmph!

GEORGE. So?

IVY. What, so?

GEORGE. So, you wanna go out Saturday?

IVY. Since I don't want your blood on my hands, I'll go.

GEORGE. Great! I'll pick you up around eight, O.K.?

IVY. Fine.

GEORGE. Well, back to the salt mine. I'll see you. Keep your powder dry. (As he exits, Ivy smiles.)

Blackout

SCENE 5

Ivy enters the restaurant, looks around, sees Susie, who is reading and eating at a table by herself, and walks over to the table.

IVY. Hi, Susie.

SUSIE. (Looking up) Hi.

IVY. Mind if I sit down? Place is kinda mobbed today.

SUSIE. Sure. Be my guest.

IVY. (Sits down opposite Susie) Thanks. Watcha reading?

SUSIE. Thomas Wolfe. *Look Homeward, Angel.*

IVY. Any good?

SUSIE. Oh, it's beautiful. He's got so much deep feeling. You oughta read it.

IVY. It looks thick.

SUSIE. It's kinda hard to read, but it's so good.

IVY. You read a lot, huh?

SUSIE. I think you could find out a lot from books.

IVY. Maybe, but what I always say is you can't actually learn about life from books.

SUSIE. Well, I wonder if--

IVY. Oh, you know what I mean, I mean, real life isn't in books. It's a whole other world--

SUSIE. But, Ivy, a book can be like a magic ship that carries you into uncharted seas.

IVY. Gee, that sounds nice.

SUSIE. I think I read it in a book once.

13

IVY. Oh, I didn't mean to say that a person couldn't get a lot out of a book.

SUSIE. Because a person really could..

IVY. Sure. But you know what I mean. I mean there are people that, like, bury themselves in books.

SUSIE. Oh, I couldn't agree with you more. Life is here to be lived, is what I say.

IVY. Uh-huh.

SUSIE. Because the saddest thing is to sit on the sidelines and let life pass you by.

IVY. Mm.

SUSIE. I read in the *Reader's Digest* where some doctor said that even hating everything wasn't as bad as if you just don't care. I really believe that.

IVY. Yeah. (Picks up menu.) Yeah. So what's good today?

Blackout

SCENE 6

Ivy is at her desk sorting papers. Ray stands at the desk.

IVY. How much longer you got?

RAY. Two weeks. Then back to good old Michigan State.

IVY. Glad to be going?

RAY. Beats working anytime.

IVY. No, come on. Really, you glad to be leaving?

RAY. I had a good time this summer. But I'll really have a ball when I get back.

IVY. I guess college is pretty rough, huh?

RAY. Yeah, it's rough.

IVY. You must hafta study a lot.

RAY. You know it.

14

IVY. What're you gonna be taking up this year?

RAY. Oh. principles of marketing., techniques of promotion, stuff like that.

IVY. Gee, they sound like real brain work.

RAY. Well, between you and I those profs really work your-- work you hard, But don't get me wrong. I love it. That's a great school. We got a terrific football team. Best in the U.S.A.

IVY. Mm. Seems to me George said something about them.

RAY. You better believe it. We're going to have one of the best teams we ever had this year.

IVY. Those games must be something!

RAY. They're the greatest! There's the game and a cocktail party at the house and a dance. Then Sunday we got bombed out of our minds all over again!

IVY. Boy, what a life, huh?

RAY. Yeah, it's wild! But I wanta finish up and get a job.

IVY. Yeah. I suppose that studying gets kinda boring after a while.

RAY. It's dullsville, all right,

IVY. We'll sort of miss you, you know.

RAY. (Wanting to hear more) Yeah?

IVY. Oh, everybody in the office says you could come back to work anytime.

RAY. That's great!

IVY. Because you're not like most of the college guys that they take on in the summer.

RAY. What do you mean?

IVY. Well, most of them act kinda -- not exactly stuck up, but like they're better than other people.

RAY. That's cruddy. Just because you go to college doesn't mean you're something special.

IVY. You're right. People are people.

RAY. Besides it's, like, against the American way of life.

IVY. Yeah. All men are created equal, is what I say.

15

RAY. We read a great poem in college about "You got to walk with kings, nor lose the common touch."

IVY. That's good. When certain people start thinking they're better than other people, that's communism.

RAY. Check.

IVY. Because that's what made this country great. I mean people in every walk of life oughta be the same.

RAY. Right.

IVY. You start getting all those ideas like rich people are better than poor people and you haven't got America any more, you know?

RAY. You tell 'em, baby. (Pause)

IVY. Ray, you wouldn't mind a suggestion, would you?

RAY. No, what?

IVY. If I was in your shoes, know what I'd do? I'd see Mr. Choate about next year. I mean, since he's so enthused about your work, and all.

RAY. Hey, good idea. (Musing) Yeah, I'll line him up and then if something better comes along later on--yeah. (To Ivy) Great. Thanks a lot, Ivy. I'll go see him right now. Hey, I'll have to get you a job as my agent. (Exits.)

Blackout

SCENE 7

Ivy and Betty are seated side by side, typing.

IVY. Only ten more pages to go and I'll be through with this report.

BETTY. You're lucky. Mine looks like a two-day job.

IVY. I hate those sixty-page ones.

16

BETTY. Me, too. (Stops typing.) Going to church Sunday? I'll stop by for you.

IVY. I don't think so. I'm going out with George Saturday night. (Stops typing.)

BETTY. Gee, Ivy, it isn't any of my business, I know, but didn't you miss last Sunday, too?

IVY. (Somewhat defensively) Yeah.

BETTY. But, Ivy--

IVY. Oh, Betty, I don't think it makes that much difference if I go or don't go.

BETTY. I know what you mean, but still--

IVY. I think religion is, like, in your mind.

BETTY. (With a faint note of shock) You--you aren't losing your faith, are you, Ivy?

IVY. Oh, no! I mean, you just gotta believe in God, right?

BETTY. Gee, yes!

IVY. Because we all gotta have faith in a higher power.

BETTY. I don't know how a person could live without faith.

IVY. Me neither. But I don't think you have to go to church to have faith, is what I'm saying.

BETTY. No, but--

IVY. Look at all the people that go every Sunday and then cheat and lie all the other days of the week! You can't call them Christians!

BETTY. Oh, I agree, but--

IVY. And some people that don't go to church are very good Christians.

BETTY. True.

IVY. Because religion is really in your heart.

BETTY. I wouldn't deny that a--

IVY. Besides I won't get home until two or three. So I guess I'll skip this Sunday.

BETTY. (Back at her typing, she speaks resignedly) Whatever you say, Ivy.

Blackout

SCENE 8

Ivy is at her desk when Mr. Choate enters.

CHOATE. (Somewhat embarrassed) Uh--Ivy.

IVY. Yes, Mr. Choate.

CHOATE. Er-uh, Ivy, I've got a little matter to take up with you that's a bit difficult--

IVY. (Somewhat uneasy) Of course, Mr. Choate.

CHOATE. Well, it's -- it's (He gets hold of himself.) Some of the girls in Mrs. Barnes' department have complained that you won't let them use our coffee-maker. They have to send out during their coffee breaks.

IVY. It's true, Mr. Choate, but there's a good reason for it. They burned out a unit in it, and besides they never wash it. We always get it back dirty.

CHOATE. I certainly sympathize with you, Ivy. I know you wouldn't do something like that without a reason. But still, it does seem to be making for friction in the office. And we don't want that, do we?

IVY. No., Mr. Choate, but there's no reason they can't chip in the way we did and buy one of their own.

CHOATE. Of course there isn't, but until they do, I think it would be nice of you and the other girls in the pool--

IVY. It isn't that we've got anything against them, you know. It's only that they're so inconsiderate.

CHOATE. It certainly sounds as if they are, but still--

IVY. I mean, like, they don't ever think about anybody else. After

18

all, when they do that somebody's got to wash up after them.

CHOATE. Ivy, I'm on your side one hundred percent, but unfortunately we just have to get along with Mrs. Barnes' staff, too.

IVY. Oh, I know you're right, Mr. Choate. I didn't mean that we wouldn't go along with you. It's just that we get so mad at them.

CHOATE. I understand perfectly, Ivy. But all this arguing does upset our routine. And, since it does make for difficulties, I'm afraid I'll have to insist--

IVY. Oh, gee, Mr. Choate, I didn't mean to cause trouble with other people, because if there's one thing about me, I do like people.

CHOATE. Yes, I know that, Ivy.

IVY. I always say that people are the most important thing there is, right?

CHOATE. Right .

IVY. Because if you don't like people, who can you like?

CHOATE. (Anxious now to break off the conversation) Who indeed?

IVY. I mean, I never trust a person who doesn't like people. We've all got to try to get along together, right?

CHOATE. Right, Ivy. So you'll straighten this out, will you?

IVY. Oh, sure, Mr. Choate. Don't worry. I'll take care of it.

CHOATE. Good. I'll leave it up to you, then. Thanks, Ivy.

IVY. Oh, that's all right, Mr. Choate. Like you always say, we're all playing on the same team here. And we have to try to get along with other people.

CHOATE. (Retreating) Right, Ivy. (Exits)

Blackout

SCENE 9

Ivy and Peggy are back on the subway, straphanging as before. Peggy is still chewing gum.

IVY. So I says to him, "You're too human, that's your trouble." And he says, "You wouldn't like me if I wasn't so human." And then I says, "I don't know why I have anything to do with you anyway." And he says, "Because I'm so madly in love with you that if you don't go out with me on Saturday night I'll shoot myself."

PEGGY. (Depressed, but trying to enter into the spirit of things) Say, he's got some line.

IVY. Yeah. (Pause) Talk to Bill today?

PEGGY. (Stiff and embarrassed) No. I didn't.

IVY. Oh. (Hurrying on to the next topic in an effort to cover her embarrassment) So guess what. I hadda have lunch with that dope Susie. You know, I toldja about her-- the one that's always reading?

PEGGY. Yeah.

IVY. Well, she's sitting there with some great big thick book, but there wasn't any other seat. So what could I do? So I sit down and she gives me something about a book is a ship that takes you on trips, or something.

PEGGY. Hmph.

IVY. If you ask me, I bet she doesn't even read them.

PEGGY. Mm.

IVY. So I didn't even pay attention to what I was doing, and you know what I went and did?

PEGGY. No, what?

IVY. I ordered a chicken salad sandwich. And ma's making chicken salad for tonight! How about that for stupid? I should have had tuna fish. I need the brain food.

PEGGY. Gee, too bad,

IVY. After lunch I had a nice talk with Ray, though.

PEGGY. Ray?

IVY. That kid from Michigan State that's working in the office for the summer.

PEGGY. Oh.

IVY. Yeah. We were talking about college kids that think they're better than other people.

PEGGY. That makes me sick when they're like that.

IVY. That's just what I said to him. "All men are created equal," I said.

PEGGY. Good for you. I hate stuck-up people.

IVY. But the big thing today was about the coffee-maker. Remember, I told you that the girls in mailing were always taking it and bringing it back dirty, so I told them they couldn't borrow it anymore.

PEGGY. Uh-huh, I remember.

IVY. That old bat Barnes went and complained to Mr. Choate about it.

PEGGY. He bawl you out?

IVY. Are you kidding? He's too smooth for that. Nah, he was real nice. He just asked me to straighten it out for him.

PEGGY. Nice.

IVY. Yeah. He's just great.

PEGGY. Mm.

IVY. So I walked into mailing and I said to Barnes, "Mr. Choate told me I'm supposed to let you use our coffee-maker whenever you want to. Well, please feel free. And if you have the chance to wash it out after you're through, we'd try to get over the shock." And then I walked right out before she had a chance to make some snotty remark.

PEGGY. Good.

IVY. Well, the last time-- Hey, look! We're at Roosevelt. (In haste)

Listen, I'll call you Sunday night. Have a nice weekend, Peg, (She rushes out,)

Blackout

SCENE 10

Ivy is sitting at the table. Her mother is offstage.

IVY. And then I says to her, "You can't learn about real life from books." (Pause) You listening, ma?

MOTHER. (Offstage) Yes, dear.

IVY. "And you shouldn't just bury yourself in a book."

MOTHER. Yes, dear.

IVY. So I says, "Don't let life pass you by while you got your nose in a book."

MOTHER. Uh-huh.

IVY. "Because," I says, "It's real sad for a person to just sit on the sidelines."

MOTHER. (Enters carrying a platter) You couldn't be more right. That's just what I've always said.

IVY. Salad looks good, Ma.

MOTHER. Thank you, dear, I always like a salad on a hot night. It even looks cool, you know? (She serves.)

IVY. (Eating) And the coffee -maker thing came to a head today.

MOTHER. You didn't get into any trouble over it, I hope.

IVY. Oh, no. You know how nice Mr. Choate is. He just asked me to smooth it all over.

MOTHER. He's right, dear. It was making entirely too much hard feeling. You've all got to try and got along together in the office.

IVY. That's exactly what I said.

22

MOTHER. Show me a person who doesn't like people and I'll show you an unhappy person and a troublemaker.

IVY. Anyhow, I got it all straightened out. And I didn't kowtow to Barnes either. That sour old witch!

MOTHER. Now, Ivy, what have I always told you? "The greatest of these is charity." But I'm glad that you got it fixed up without losing your self-respect. You gotta be true to thy own self.

IVY. Funny you should say that. I was thinking the same thing this afternoon. Can you imagine, that nosy Betty started in on me about going to church.

MOTHER. I'm sure she was only thinking of your good, dear.

IVY. Maybe she was and maybe she wasn't. But the nerve! After all, it's none of her business. She only wants somebody to go with.

MOTHER. Of course, you're right, Ivy. She is taking a lot on herself.

IVY. She should mind her own business.

MOTHER. We all have enough to do taking care of our own affairs, I say.

IVY. That buttinski!

MOTHER. Just don't let her get under your skin, dear. She'll see soon enough that she'd better let the subject alone. Although I must say I wish you went more regularly.

IVY. (After a pause, during which both eat) George asked me out tomorrow.

MOTHER. (Not chilly, but not enthusiastic) That' s nice.

IVY. (Deciding that it is better to turn to another subject) So how was your day?

MOTHER. Oh, the usual, I cleaned a little, washed out a few things, then I went to the A & P with Mrs. Newman and came home and watched T.V. Gee, *The Quest for Happiness* was good today. Remember what I was telling you how this mysterious stranger from the city was hanging around the mother's sister and the mother was always saying to the sister that she shouldn't trust the stranger? Well, today she found out that the stranger was really an embezzler and there was this big scene where she had to break the news to her sister. That actress took a real good part.

IVY. Sounds good.

MOTHER. (After a pause) Did you see the paper today?

IVY. Nah. I read a headline-- something about some guy that killed a woman up in the Bronx.

MOTHER. Just imagine-- she was sixty-seven! He forced his way into her apartment and attacked her. Oh, this city's a jungle. I don't know where it's all going to end.

IVY. It's terrible, all right.

MOTHER. And there was another good story about some blind girl who's supporting her crippled mother. I mean, she goes out to work in a factory. And she won't take a penny from welfare.

IVY. Isn't that something!

MOTHER. A story like that restores your faith in human beings, you know?

IVY. Yeah.

MOTHER. Oh. Ivy, by the way, did you get a chance to pick up that cotton print for me today?

IVY. Gee, I'm sorry! Really, I'll get it Monday,

MOTHER. No, Ivy, If it's too much trouble--

IVY. It's not too much trouble, Ma. I'll go for sure on Monday.

MOTHER. I don't want you to put yourself out, but it does seem that, since you're right around the corner.

IVY. Please, Ma! I said I was sorry, didn't I? So I'm sorry. Please drop it, Ma.

MOTHER. All right, Ivy. (Pause) Say, how about a movie tonight?

IVY. Anything good playing?

MOTHER. *Hellcat Unchained* and *Hope for Tomorrow*. Sounds good.

IVY. O.K., Ma.

MOTHER. It starts at seven. Let's just leave the dishes. I'll clean up when we get back.

IVY. Whatever you say.

MOTHER. I'll go put on something more respectable. (Gets up.)

IVY. You look fine, Ma.

MOTHER. (She stands in the doorway and turns to Ivy.) So you had a good day, Ivy.

IVY. (Without any great enthusiasm, but with sincerity) Yeah, Ma, it was a nice day.

Blackout.

CURTAIN GOING UP

COUNT THAT DAY LOST

CAST OF CHARACTERS

Barry, an actor
Carol
Brian Eastman, a drama critic
Lynn Berger
Tom, a writer*
Ted, a painter*
Tim, an actor*
A bartender

* played by the same actor

The time is a day in autumn.

The play proper can, but need not, be preceded by a film, the background music for which should be "Autumn in New York," played in a rock arrangement.

As the first scene of the film fades in, Barry is getting out of a large double bed in the sumptuous bedroom of Carol's apartment. He wears a pair of expensive pyjamas on which a large B is embroidered. As he gets up, Carol stirs, comes half-awake and holds out her arms. He slides across the bed, kisses her and then stands up. She smiles, turns over and goes back to sleep. Fade out.

Fade in on Barry coming back into the bedroom, shaved, showered and dressed in rather extreme clothes, up-to-the-minute and obviously very expensive. He walks over to Carol's side of the bed, sits down and kisses her. She half-wakes again. He reaches over to her bedside table, takes her purse lying on it and opens the purse. He slides out three fifty-dollar bills, then looks at her questioningly. She smiles. He removes the bills, takes out his billfold and slides the three bills into it, while the camera moves in for a closeup and we see the identification card, on which his name, Barry Geismar, appears. He kisses her and exits. Fade out.

Fade in on a series of brief shots of Barry in a gym working out., in a barber shop, making a purchase in an exclusive haberdashery, in a steam bath, with a masseur, and returning to Carol's apartment. Fade out.

Fade in on Carol and Barry leaving for a party. They enter a cab, the camera follows the cab, and we see them stepping out of it. They cross the lobby of an apartment house and enter the elevator. As they exit from the elevator, the camera pans ahead of them and stops on the figures who are downstage when the action of the play begins. The screen rises.

The scene is a lavishly and tastefully furnished Manhattan house. Background music plays throughout the action: it is Muzak-style, sweet, trivial and unobtrusive. Upstage are as many mannequins, male and female, as are required to suggest a crowded cocktail party; they are in groups of three or four. Upstage right is a bar, behind which stands a bartender, who occasionally passes drinks among the guests. Downstage a man of about 40, dressed well but in a style better suited to one of 25, stands talking to a woman of about 35, very chic, with a superficial charm but a predatory hardness right beneath the surface, The man, who seems slightly effeminate, has the habit of looking around the room rather than at the person he is talking to.

BRIAN. —absolutely the worst bomb of the year. The worst.

LYNN. As if you didn't know your review was the talk of the town!

BRIAN. I must admit I rather liked it myself.

LYNN. Perry was saying he bets it's the shortest review ever written. And the meanest.

BRIAN. Well, honestly, Lynn. So many of these playwrights just lead with their chins. If some clod is stupid enough to write some cheap, tasteless sex comedy and call it "Try Me", the only logical thing to say is, "Tried and found wanton."

LYNN. Darlings, it was inspired. I adored it,

BRIAN. You're sweet. Oh, but I haven't told you the latest. The next day Hank and Maggie and I were having lunch at Sardi's — I don't know what there is about Sardi's that brings out the best in me—and we invented a marvelous new game. You see, we were talking about censorship--

LYNN. I just loathe censorship.

BRIAN. Yes. So Hank was telling us that there's a highschool principal in Iowa or Idaho or one of those places who said he'd let all the English teachers teach modern drama if they took out all the dirty words.

LYNN. Oh?

BRIAN. And then it occurred to me that we should be ruthlessly consistent about it. Why take just the dirty words out of the language? Why not take out the dirty syllables, too? If we substituted for the dirty syllables, we'd have a 100% antiseptic language and every puritan in the country would be happy.

LYNN. I don't see--

BRIAN. What you do is come up with a word that has a syllable like "damn" in it and you substitute "darn." Or "heck" for "hell." So we sat around for hours thinking up words like "darnage" and "heckiport" and things like that.

LYNN. (After a pause) Oh, like "That's the most darnable statement I ever heard."

BRIAN. Yes. Sort of. The best one of all, though, was one that Maggie came up with a couple of days later. I ran into her at the *Capricorn* opening and she said, "I'm getting so old the first thing I turn to in the paper is the oshrewuary page." Isn't that delightful?

LYNN. (After a second or two) Oh, yes. Fabulous! (She laughs somewhat insincerely.) And she's right, you know. She is getting old.

BRIAN. Maggie? She's just too much. I can't stand her as a person, but she is clever.

LYNN. She simply breaks me up.

BRIAN. You can't imagine who was with her at the opening. Ready for a shock? Greg Brewer.

LYNN. Not really!? But I thought he and Carol---

BRIAN. No. Not for ages. Well, months anyway. That's what you get for burying yourself in Dubrovnik. It'll take you weeks to catch up on everything. (Pause) But how long ago was it that you and Greg—

LYNN. Oh, eons. Right after the divorce. Let's see-- that would be six, no seven years ago. My God! Was it that long ago?

BRIAN. He's really made the rounds, hasn't he?

LYNN. He and Carol were the perfect pair. A worn-out chorus girl who struck oil and a hustling chorus boy.

BRIAN. Now, now, dear. You don't want them to bring you Gainesburgers instead of canapés, do you?

LYNN. (Looking around) Where's Sheila?

BRIAN. She's in the other room, I think. (Tom enters from right.) Oh, hi, Tom.

TOM. (Comes over, shakes Brian's hand lackadaisically.) Hello, Brian. Do you know Lynn Berger? Tom Reynolds. Tom's a writer.

TOM. .Hello.

LYNN. Hi. Tom. Look. I hate to meet and run, as Brian always says, but I haven't even seen our hostess yet. I'll be back soon. (She exits right,)

BRIAN. How goes it?

TOM. Still plugging away at the new opus.

BRIAN. Making progress?

TOM. Oh, slowly, slowly. Writing is such hard work.

BRIAN. I know.

TOM. Of course, you're reviewing. But have you ever written fiction?

BRIAN. Not since I was a political reporter.

TOM. No, honestly, Brian, writing fiction is unquestionably the worst. It's like — like pulling teeth.

BRIAN. M-hm.

TOM. And it's such lonely work. That's what I hate about it.

BRIAN. Mm.

TOM.There you are and there's a blank piece of paper. And you have to make something out of nothing.

BRIAN. Yes.

TOM. And the self-discipline, too! Every morning when you wake up, there's that same old temptation to take the day off, or at least the morning. And you just go ahead and force yourself to sit down and start grinding out the words.

BRIAN. If it's really such a chore--

TOM. Oh, come on, now. Don't pretend to be naive, Brian. You know I'm a writer because I have to be. There are certain things that have to be said and I think they have to be said the way I want to say them.

BRIAN. Of course.

TOM. Besides, who is there today who's handling the really big themes? Love, race, the alienation of the individual, the loss of identity?

BRIAN. Well---

TOM. Oh, I'll admit there are people who're playing around with them, but nobody's actually coming to grips, if you know what I mean.

BRIAN. M-hm. (Pause) Are you doing short stories or a novel now?

TOM. I've given up on short stories. I must've written a dozen and the powers that be just weren't interested.

BRIAN. Any nibbles?

TOM. Not a one. I had high hopes for one I called "Conversion Factor." It was about an anti-social research scientist who met a very good-looking girl with a lot of social consciousness. She made him see that human problems are more important than test-tubes, so they got married and he went back to college to study sociology. But I couldn't peddle it. Too caviar-for-the-general, I guess.

BRIAN. I see .

TOM.You know what the slicks are like.

BRIAN. The editors are all Ivy-League types and if you don't give 'em the same old tried-and-true garbage you can't get to first base.

BRIAN. Maybe you'll hit the jackpot with the novel.

TOM. I just might, you know, It's about a young guy from Indianapolis who's trying—well, I suppose you could say he's sort of trying to find himself. His father's a hardware dealer, very big in the Rotary Club and Kiwanis, and his mother's in the Red Cross et cetera and his sister's engaged to marry a mortician. So he quits college and comes to New York. Right now I've got him at the point where he meets this colored girl who goes to N.Y.U.

BRIAN. I'm afraid—

TOM. Oh, I know what you're going to say. It's been tried before, right? I'll admit the theme isn't exactly original, but I've got a whole new approach. And after all it's the freshness of viewpoint that really counts, isn't it? (Pause) But, say, I'd better circulate a little. I'll talk to you later. (He moves upstage, pantomimes talking to various groups of mannequins and eventually exits left.)

BRIAN. (goes to the bar upstage, gets a drink; in the meantime Lynn has returned and is looking around for him.)

LYNN. D'I miss anything earth-shaking?

BRIAN. Only the chance to talk with one of the Titans of American literature, that's all.

LYNN. Really?

BRIAN. That's one of the things I like most about you, dear. Your sensitivity to my irony,

LYNN. I loathe irony. I can never tell when people are being ironic.

BRIAN. Nonsense, darling, Why, if you--

LYNN. (As Carol and Barry enter left, move upstage and start talking to a group of mannequins.) Oh, no! But this is too funny! I simply can't believe it!

BRIAN. (Looks over his shoulder.) Is that Barry with Carol? But I thought you and he—

LYNN. Oh, where have you been, Brian. Barry and I haven't seen one another for months. Why do you think I went to Europe? I agreed to disagree.

BRIAN. Frankly, I must say I approve. You know, of course, that he's hopeless as an actor?

LYNN. So they say. But if you want the truth, I didn't have him around because he was a good actor.

BRIAN. Oh— (Laughs softly.) Lynn, I adore you. If you're not the world's most honest woman, I don't know who is.

LYNN. Why not? I always assume we fool fewer people than we think.

BRIAN. Now that it's over between you two, may I ask you a question?

LYNN. Ask away.

BRIAN. Did you back *Heavenly High* and *File Three Copies*?

LYNN. I was one of the backers.

BRIAN. You lost a bundle, then.

LYNN. Yes. That was one of the reasons I broke it off. It's fun to have a hobby, but that one was getting too expensive. But that won't have to bother Carol. She's got enough to make the Rockefellers look like paupers.

BRIAN. (Again looking at Carol and Barry) But this is not to be believed! Barry with Carol! It's almost obscene. What does she do? Specialize in your exes? (Pause) It's almost as if she were running some kind of an amatory thrift shop. If you want to go, Lynn, I'll be glad to take you. At a party like this, partir c'est vivre un peu.

LYNN. Are you serious? This is too delicious. I wouldn't miss it for the world!

TED. (Moving downstage from the bar, he looks around, then approaches Lynn and Brian) Hello. I don't know if you remember me. We met at Sheila's last party. I'm Ted Lundberg.

BRIAN. (Searching his memory) Oh, yes. You paint, if memory serves.

TED. That's right.

BRIAN. Have you met Lynn Berger?

TED. She was at the last party, too, but I'm afraid I'm not as memorable as she is.

LYNN. Oh, Brian, get this man a commission for several million dollars. Right away. Do I know your work, Mr. Lundberg?

TED. Ted, please. I'm afraid I'm about the only one who knows my work.

LYNN. Too bad.

TED. Actually I'm not surprised. Any artist who's not running with the pack has to expect to be anonymous. At least until after he's dead.

LYNN. What a grisly thought!

TED. It's the truth, though. I could switch and do the Norman Rockwell kind of stuff and probably make a mint, but I'll be damned if I'll do it.

LYNN. Good for you!

TED. After all, painting is work, and if I'm going to put in all that time and effort, I'm damned well not going to pour it down the drain by selling out.

LYNN. I know what you mean. I took painting classes myself for years.

TED. Then you know what it's like. I mean, what you put down on that canvas is you. There's no compromise and no excuses.

LYNN. Oh, you're so right!

TED. But even so it does get discouraging every once in a while. I can just ignore the ones who say, "If that's supposed to be a street, where are the sidewalks?"

LYNN. They're just philistines, anyway.

TED. The people that really bother me are the ones who know a little about art, but not enough. The kind that say something like, "I love the structure and the colors are simply great and 'The Metamorphosis of Ambiance' is a fabulous title. But what is it saying?"

LYNN. You—

TED. Of course it means one thing to you and another to him and something else to somebody else, What's in it is what each person finds in it, you know?

LYNN. That's true of all great art.

TED. Sure.

BRIAN. Are you showing at all, Ted?

TED. No, I haven't had a show for a couple of years now. But you know what it is.

BRIAN. No, what?

TED. Oh, unless you give these gallery-owners the usual commercial, romantic stuff they aren't interested. The French are the only ones who can get away with anything really original.

LYNN. The French are soo — oh, I don't know.

TED. I have got one ace up my sleeve, though. What you have to have to make it in art these days is some kind of gimmick. So I'm working on a new technique that might just set the art world on its ear.

LYNN. What is it?

TED. It's called "mop art." What I do is dip each strand of a mop in a different color and then draw it over the canvas. I've been getting some really striking effects.

BRIAN. Interesting.

TED. Yes, when I get it perfected, it could start a whole new movement.

LYNN. I hope it works out.

TED. Thanks. We'll just have to see. You never can tell about art in the good old U.S.A. It might catch on and it might not. But what can you expect from a country where a baseball player makes a hundred thousand and a painter doesn't even dare ask five hundred for a good oil? (After an embarrassed pause) Uh, I guess I'll — Nice seeing you again. (He moves upstage, talks to some of the mannequins and eventually exits left.)

BRIAN. (As Ted walks away) So long.

LYNN. Is he any good, Brian?

BRIAN. Are you kidding? Let's say he's one of New York's best-known anonymous celebrities.

LYNN. Too bad.

BRIAN. Is it?

LYNN. Yes. He's cute. And very serious-minded. He's got a lot to say.

BRIAN. He certainly does. (During the last few lines, Carol and Barry have been moving downstage. She is 30-35, expensively dressed, looking younger than her years, with the same sort of predatory hardness beneath a surface charm that characterizes Lynn. He is about 26 - 28, handsome in a very masculine way, but with a certain boyishness in his manner. They catch sight of Lynn and Brian, then cross to them.)

CAROL. Hello, Lynn. Brian.

LYNN. Hello, Carol. Hello, Barry. Barry, do you know Brian Eastman?

BARRY. (Says something inaudible to her, smiling wanly.)

BRIAN. How are you, Barry. We've met. (Holds out his hand, which Barry shakes without enthusiasm.) Carol, hi, darling. (He kisses her cheek.)

CAROL. Why don't you get us a drink, Barry? Same way for me. (Barry goes upstage to the bar and is busy there for a few minutes.)

LYNN. How've you been, Carol?

CAROL. Just blooming, darling. And you?

LYNN. Never better. I was telling Brian. I'm taking a course in set design at the New School.

CAROL. Since losing interest in actors?

LYNN. Why, yes, dear. I find a certain superficiality in actors.

CAROL. In some cases, it's a godsend not to be able to see below the surface, isn't it? But I really don't agree. I think actors are simply fascinating.

LYNN. Evidently. (With a sidelong half-glance upstage) What've you been doing?

CAROL. I'm surprised you asked. Sure the answer wouldn't be too humiliating?

LYNN. On the contrary. I think I'd find it very amusing.

CAROL. I don't know whether it's amusing or refreshing to run across somebody honest enough to admit he's made a mistake.

LYNN. And who can't wait to top it.

CAROL. Or who's discovered how to avoid making it again. *Some* people are able to learn from experience. (Barry returns carrying his own drink and another which he hands to Carol. There is an embarrassed silence. Barry senses it and looks as if he wished he were elsewhere.) Barry, why don't you be a dear and circulate a little? (Barry moves back upstage.) Where was I?

LYNN. You were talking about high IQ's, or something.

CAROL. Or good taste.

LYNN. Oh, let's stick to subjects we can *all* talk about.

CAROL. (A stage sigh.) I suppose when you get the brass ring you have to expect the losers will be envious.

LYNN. Not the ones who got it first and realized that brass has a very limited appeal.

CAROL. Don't you think Freud is a godsend, Brian? Where would people be without rationalization?

LYNN. Thinking they won the brass ring when it was handed to them, I suppose.

CAROL. Yes my shrink is right: there are just no limits to self-delusion, are there, Brian? (Turning) But we must go say hello to Sheila. See you later, darlings. (Moves upstage to Barry, exits.)

LYNN. She's got an analyst? That should set psychiatry back a good fifty years. What she really needs is a head transplant.

BRIAN. Whew!

LYNN. God, I simply can't stand her. Did you ever hear such vicious, catty—

BRIAN. I must say, Lynn, you didn't do so badly yourself. I may have to reassess Ilse Koch.

LYNN. Ilsa who?

BRIAN. Never mind, dear girl. All I'm saying is, your instinct for the jugular vein makes Count Dracula look like a vegetarian.

LYNN. (Preening) Do you really think so?

BRIAN. My dear, if you can't--

TIM. (In an artificial, stagy voice with a half-British accent) Lynn, how are you! And Brian! Why, you old so-and-so--

LYNN. How are you, Tim?

BRIAN. Hello, Tim.

TIM. But where have you two been keeping yourselves? I haven't seen you in ages. (He kisses Lynn on the cheek.). Mm-mh! (He takes Brian's right hand in both of his,) Brian! Everybody went wild about your review of *Try Me*. God, I loved it! You know, at Joe Allen's they all call you "The Astronomer," because you're the man who knows all about shooting stars.

BRIAN. How clever they are at Joe Allen's.

TIM. Now, Brian, don't be that way. Lynn, I haven't seen you since *File Three Copies* folded its reviews like the Arabs. Where have you been? I'm just so delighted to see you both again. (And he thinks he means it.) Are you and Barry still— (He sees that he has struck a sour note.) Oh, too bad. Well, I always said he was never for you. If you ask me, he—

BRIAN. What've you done since *File Three Copies*, Tim?

TIM. (During this speech Carol and Barry re-enter, go up to the bar, get more drinks and then move off to talk to some of the mannequins.) Oh, I've been all over the landscape. I spent six weeks in L.A. in some total fiasco. You know, the usual thing — a Hollywood type who thought he was another Budd Schulberg wrote something about an AC-DC designer and an AC-DC actress — it was appalling! But I must say I learned an awful lot doing it. And then I went up to Frisco for a while and — you won't believe it — they're so grim and serious about art up there — I was with a group that did *Everyman* and three mystery plays in repertory. It was really awfully good for me, you know, technically.

BRIAN. But, how the hell could they--

TIM. Need I add they had a grant?

BRIAN. And what are you doing now?

TIM. Wait a minute! I haven't finished. I went out to a barn over the summer. I was asked to be in a "Carousel" package, but I didn't see how it could help me as an artist, so I turned it down. So, can you imagine what I did?

LYNN. No, what?

TIM. I spent the entire goddam summer in Ishpeming, Michigan. And what did I do? You won't believe it! You honestly won't believe it! (Eyes skyward, he counts on his fingers.) *Oliver, Lear, Student Prince, Streetcar, Bye-Bye Birdie, Sound of Music* and *Mother Courage.* How's that for a season?

BRIAN. Quite a test of your versatility.

TIM. You probably won't believe it, Brian, but I got absolute raves in everything. Look, I know it's only the straw hats, but the critics were ecstatic.

LYNN. Excuse me. I'll get us another drink. (To Brian) Same way?

BRIAN. Please.

TIM. Thanks, love, Some kind of low-cal, no-cal for me.

LYNN. Right. (She moves upstage.)

BRIAN. Are you doing anything now?

TIM. I certainly am. I'm in an Off-Off-Broadway show in the Village and I've got a couple of TV commercials.

BRIAN. They'll pay the rent, anyway,

TIM. More than. I've got a deodorant spot where they just show my armpit and a cold-tablet commercial —

BRIAN. Where they just show your mucous.

TIM. Oh, really, Brian. Honestly, you're too much! No, they just show me in Bloomingdale's.

BRIAN. What's this OOB thing?

TIM. If I may say so, Brian, that's the trouble with you Broadway critics. You never come downtown to see what's going on. I do believe this is one of those productions that's setting the pace. It's easily ten years ahead of its time.

BRIAN. (Faintly interested.) What's the name of it, anyway?

TIM. It's called *Trials of Torquemada*. I play Torquemada. It's all about the way sadism is tied in with sex. See, there are three girls named Honoria, Verity and Fräulein Schönheit, and they're led in one by one, by these two executioners, a man and a woman. Then they're found guilty and they're all tortured to death. And the interesting thing is they never know what they're guilty of.

BRIAN. Mm.

TIM. And then the executioners turn on Torquemada and torture him to death, you see. In the end they start to take off their clothes and you don't know whether they're going to make it with each other, or what.

BRIAN. I see.

TIM. But the most unusual thing about the play is that there's no dialogue at all. All there is are grunts and screams and moans and Torquemada's laughter. See, they're all done sort of like counterpoint and the rhythm is supposed to suggest the rhythm of the sex act. And in the background there's a chorus that chants poetry by Rosetti and Swinburne and all those old Romantic poets to show the other side of sex.

BRIAN. It sounds positively cosmic. (Pause) But you're right, Tim. I should be looking over some of the experimental stuff.

TIM. So you'll be down to see it?

BRIAN. I'll see. Maybe next week or the week after.

TIM. I really think you owe it to yourself. I'm having an absolutely great time. It's so different from anything I've ever done. And it's so good for me. I have such a sense of freedom. And Tony — Tony Madison directed it-- Tony's so good about letting us do what we feel in—

LYNN. (Returns with drinks.) Low-cal, no-cal, Scotch. Don't tell me you two are still working out the future of American drama.

TIM. (Not ironically) Oh, Brian's always so interesting to listen to.

BRIAN. Any chance of a shot at Broadway?

TIM. I keep making the rounds, but it's terribly discouraging. You know, Brian, that all the casting directors are either faggots or nymphos, and if I can't get a part on the basis of my talent, I just don't want one.

BRIAN. I see.

LYNN. Oh, for Christ's sake, look who's coming back — the Dragon Lady and Little Boy Blue. (Barry and Carol move downstage.)

CAROL. We're taking off now and I wanted to say "So long" to Brian. (To Tim) We have to keep on the good side of Brian, don't we? Barry's going to be doing something soon and we'll want all the good will we can get from the critics, right?

BRIAN. (Quite stiffly) Really, Carol, I--

CAROL. Brian, you're much too sharp and sensitive for me to try buttering you up and expect to slip it by you.

BRIAN. What can I say?

LYNN. Say something sharp and sensitive. That's what the script calls for. (Carol gives her a hate-filled look.)

BRIAN. What are you going to be doing?

CAROL. We've optioned a simply magnificent musical. It's based on *The Magic Mountain* and Barry's going to star, aren't you, dear?

BRIAN. Sounds, uh-- interesting.

CAROL. We're sure it'll turn out to be very big, Yes, indeed, Brian, Barry's finally on his way. (Barry nods assent.)

Curtain

41

CURTAIN GOING UP

JUDGMENT DAY

CAST OF CHARACTERS

Frank
Steve
A waiter

The time is an afternoon in spring.

The scene is a bar in a bus terminal. Frank is seated alone at a table. Steve approaches carrying a half-filled pilsner glass in one hand and a beer bottle in the other. From time to time in the course of the play a juke box plays a currently popular tune ; each time the music begins, Frank looks momentarily annoyed and, as each record plays, Steve keeps time with his foot or his hand.

STEVE. Mind if I sit down, pal?

FRANK. Uh-- no, go ahead.

STEVE. Thanks. I hate standing up at a bar when you can't get within three feet of it, you know?

FRANK. Yes, it's irritating.

STEVE. This place is always crowded, though. I can't figure out. why. It's a shitty bar.

FRANK. Probably because it's so convenient.

STEVE. Yeah, I guess. You waiting for a bus?

FRANK. So I am.

STEVE. Me too. I'm waiting till the rush hour's over. I don't feel like standing up on some goddam bus for a half an hour.

FRANK. That's exactly why I'm waiting, too.

STEVE. Yeah, I had some day today. I don't mind telling you I want to ride home, you know what I mean?

FRANK. Yes.

STEVE. What do you do for a living, pal?

FRANK. I 'm a high-school teacher.

STEVE. Yeah? Don't tell me. Let me guess. I bet you're an English teacher.

FRANK. Right the first time.

STEVE. I could tell.

FRANK. Oh?

STEVE. You got that English teacher way of talking.

FRANK. What's that-- the English teacher way of talking?

STEVE. I don't know but-- I don't know. All English teachers sound the same when they talk. I wouldn't say -- It isn't phony, but it's different from the way people talk.

FRANK. (Tolerantly amused) I see.

STEVE. I'll tell you one thing. You're lucky you never had me in none a your classes. Jesus! Did I do lousy in English!

FRANK. Really?

STEVE. Yeah. Me and English - I mean I and English just didn't get along. That's one a the reasons I quit school.

FRANK. It's too bad you're not in school now. A lot of us think that what people have to say is more important than how they say it.

STEVE. You mean they threw out grammar and participles and all that?

FRANK. No, they didn't exactly throw them out, but they don't think they're so important any more.

STEVE. Well, I don't mind telling you I think that stinks. You gotta have rules or the whole thing could turn into a mess. I mean, how are you going to tell Shakespeare's writings from Joe Doakes's?

FRANK. Maybe so. (Pause. He sips his drink.) What kind of work do you do?

STEVE. I'm a salesman. I mean, I used to be a salesman. As of today I'm a district sales manager. That's where I was today. They were giving me all the dope on how to be a manager.

FRANK. Congratulations.

STEVE. Thanks.

FRANK. What do you sell?

STEVE. Oh, different things. I sold brushes, magazine subscriptions, wall plaques, encyclopedias. But what I been selling the last two years, what they made me manager for, is knives.

FRANK. What, as in switchblade knives?

STEVE. No, knives like you use in the kitchen. Carving knives, breadknives, all that kind of thing.

FRANK. You must have to sell millions of knives to make any money.

STEVE. Nah, not if the price is right. Now, this company I work for, they sell a set of knives for $350.

FRANK. $350!? What's in the set? Two hundred knives?

STEVE. No. Ten knives.

FRANK. Are they made of gold?

STEVE. No. Sheffield steel. Best there is.

FRANK. But who-- How on earth do you get anybody to shell out $350 for a set of knives?

STEVE. It's easy. I'll tell you how the pitch works. See, first of all you gotta keep in mind that a married woman ain't -- uh, isn't a good bet, because half the time you get her signed up and get the deposit and then the old man comes home and he takes a fit and makes her try to get her money back. Then you get all kinds a scenes in the office and these old broads are crying and screaming, and all that shit. So you figure most of the time it isn't worth it, you know? (Pause) So what you do to get the best leads is you read the engagement columns in the paper, see? Now, the first thing is how to get into the house to make your pitch. And what you do is give 'em something. You tell 'em there was a contest and they won a prize and you got the prize in your case. But, see, you never open the case unless they let you into the house. So then you start working your way in the door. So you're in the living room, right? Then you give her the prize -- it's them cheap steak knives with the plastic handles -- and nine times out a ten she says something about how lucky she is because she just got engaged and they'll come in real handy.

FRANK. What about the tenth one?

STEVE. You look at her ring. What else? But you gotta get around to the subject some way. Then you say, "So you're engaged? Well, I got something here that'll really interest you."

Then you know what you try to do? You try to get 'em out in the kitchen. It's a funny thing about broads, you know? They really feel safe in the kitchen. It's like you could con 'em in the living room or con 'em in the bedroom-- and you could-- but you couldn't con 'em in the kitchen because that's where they're the boss, see? Oh, and another thing-- most a the time the broad's old lady is home, so you drag her in to help you make the pitch. So you get 'em both out in the kitchen and you take out the knives and you don't talk about Sheffield steel and naturally you don't talk about the price, because it'd be off right away. You start in with stuff like, "You know you can't run a kitchen without you got good knives, right, mom?" And the old lady is sitting over there and she starts to nod and she says, "That's right," and you got her hooked. Then you really turn on the steam. What you say is, "Now picture like after you and your hubby have been married a month. You spend all day cleaning the apartment and maybe you wash the curtains and the whole place looks just right. And you put a roast in the oven and you put a good linen tablecloth that you got for a wedding present on the kitchen table, and the new silverware, and it really looks great, right, mom?" And old mom's over there nodding her ass off. And then you say, "So then you put on a nice dress and he comes home and he kisses you and he puts his arm around you and you put your arm around him and you walk out to the kitchen and he tells you how great it looks. Then he sits down and you get him a beer and he tells you what a rough day he had. And he finishes the beer and you take the roast out and it's cooked just the way he likes and it looks terrific. So he stands up and he grabs the old carving knife you got and he tries to cut the roast and the knife is dull and he saws away harder and harder and the table starts to rock back and forth and the juice slops out a the platter and the ketchup bottle falls over and the tablecloth is all massy and he gets madder and madder and the whole day is spoiled. Right, mom?" And this time she says, "He's right. That's just the way it is." And then you quick pull out the contract and the pen and talk fast, about Sheffield steel and how she'll still be using it on her golden wedding day and then you grab the deposit, and you made a sale.

FRANK. Amazing!

STEVE. I done-- did damn' good at it. One week I sold ten sets. (Confidentially) And there's one big fringe benefit -- you wouldn't believe how much ass 1 got. Not so much from the engaged ones, although, I swear it, even some a them were hot to trot. But them married broads -- Christ! You married, pal?

FRANK. Yes, I am.

STEVE. Well, even if you're married, if you want a line on some live ones — (He takes a little black book out of his pocket.)

FRANK. No, thanks.

STEVE. OK. (Pause. He puts the book back.) I musta scored at least twice a week. And some real high-class chicks, you know? Man, there's sure a hell of a lot of broads that ain't getting enough.

FRANK. Sounds that way.

STEVE. Don't get me wrong. I'm not knocking it. But a helluva lota guys are married to hoors. (Pause) A helluva lot! Poor dumb bastards.

FRANK. (Finishes his drink, looks at his watch and then turns in his chair and cranes his neck.) Still too much of a mob. Looks as if I'll have to force down another martini. Listen: in honor of your promotion, let me get us a round.

STEVE. That's damn' nice, pal. But I got an idea what school-teachers make. No I'm buying. (He signals a waiter.) Some waiters in this place, huh? Can't tell the live ones from the dead ones without a scorecard. (A waiter comes over to the table and stands, mute.) Give us a dry martini-- right, pal?-- and a bottle a Bud. (The waiter leaves.)

FRANK. So you had a hard day.

STEVE. Yeah. They spent the, day showing me how to run a sales crew. Hey you should a seen the guy that runs the operation. I thought I was good, but, Christ!, he makes me look than an amacher! Talk about a salesman! Listen to this: He started out with a plastics company, see, and he gets to be the sales manager in six months. So this company is selling parts to the government -- parts for rockets and satellites and like that. So one day down in Florida they launch one a them and it's a dud. The thing goes up in the air about 20 feet and then it flops over on its side and it just lays there, ten million bucks shot in the ass, right? So they put out the fire and they start this big investigation. All these generals and scientists get together and they take that goddam rocket apart piece by piece to find the trouble. So you know what the trouble is? Some little plastic part this guy's company made — cost about two bucks. So they send a telegram to the company and tell them they gotta send somebody to a board that's meeting in Washington to explain the foulup. And the president of the company is too chicken to go, so he sends this guy. So he goes down there and they take him to some building and they make him wait in this fancy waiting room for about an hour. So then some guy comes out and takes him into this big room with a big table at the other end — and here's all the big brass and VIP's and scientists, and they're all looking at him very sour. (The waiter returns and sets down the drinks, mixing up the order. He leaves and Steve switches the drinks.) Slob! (Pause) So the guy in charge says, "Your firm has had our report on the failure of the part you supplied. What do you have to say?" And, like I said, this part went for about two-three dollars. So this guy looks at the guy in charge and he says, "What I have to say, sir, is that my com-

pany stands four-square behind its money-back guarantee."
How's that for balls, huh? Well, one of the generals gasps and
then one of the scientists starts in laughing and pretty soon
they're all laughing like crazy, including the guy in charge, and
finally he waves his hand and says, "Get the hell out a here,"
so the guy leaves and that's the end a that. They never heard
another word. And they didn't even lose the contract.

FRANK. (Amused) That's quite a story, all right.

STEVE. You got to admire a good con man, but a guy that can con
you and make you laugh because he conned you, that's an
artist, pal. An artist.

FRANK. I suppose that's true.

STEVE. You're goddam right it's true. I'm telling you, the guy's an
Einstein!

FRANK. And now you're a district manager.

STEVE. Yeah. Mostly that means I train the new salesmen.

FRANK. I imagine you'll be very good at it.

STEVE. All you gotta do is spot who's gonna be good and who
ain't. See, in this racket, you never turn a guy away if he says
he wantsa be a salesman. So, you start 'em off with a training
program and you have a long talk with each guy so' s you can
size him up, What you gotta do is spot the guys that are really
hungry, you know what I mean? You can send them guys out
right away with some good leads and they'll deliver. Then what
you do with the clunks is give 'em this long pep-talk about
what great prospects they are and how you can tell they're
gonna make it big as salesmen. Then you give 'em a sample
case and tell 'em you'll set up some good leads and they should
come back in a week. See, what they do then is, they want to
prove they're as good as you said, so they sell a set to their sister or maybe their mother-in-law. Then when they come back
you give ' em a whole lot a tough leads, and most a the time
they don't sell a goddam thing, so you kick 'em the hell out.

FRANK. Isn't that-- well, a little-- unfair?

STEVE. It ain't exactly the buddy system, but what the hell. If they're so dumb —

FRANK. I don't know —

STEVE. That's what it's all about, pal. You're not in no finishing school when you're in this business.

FRANK. I certainly couldn't do it, I know that.

STEVE. You could if you wanted to be a district sales manager for my company.

FRANK. (Musing) Yes, I suppose you're right,

STEVE. (After a pause) So, what do you think? About time to leave this dump?

FRANK. You really ought to let me buy a round.

STEVE. Nah, I'm fine. It looks like the crowd's thinning out now. Besides, I got a little something on the line for tonight — one a my "customers," you know?

FRANK. Ah, I see.

STEVE. Yeah. Christ, you should see the lungs on 'er! (Pause) Hey, (He rises and reaches for his wallet.) how does that old song go: "The end of a perfect day"?

Curtain.

DANCE OF LIFE

CAST OF CHARACTERS

Young White
Young Girl
First Black
Second Black
Male Voice

The play takes place in Greenwich Village.

The time is a warm summer evening,

CURTAIN GOING UP

The scene is a street in Greenwich Village. Upstage a Young White stands talking on the steps of a brownstone with a Young Girl (white) both dressed in the most contemporary style. Down the left aisle come two blacks in their early twenties; both are high on marijuana, but the First Black is noticeably more so,

FIRST BLACK. Man, that's what I call a blast!

SECOND BLACK. Yeah! Talk about good weed!

FIRST BLACK. That George is one good shit! When he got it, he sure lay it on you.

SECOND BLACK. Mm-hm. (Pause) Wheweee! Am I zonked!

FIRST BLACK. Bro, you don't know what zonked is! This cat is flyin' higher than a fuckin' astronaut! I may even take a moon shot without no space ship!

SECOND BLACK. (Dimly realizing how high his companion is) Hey, you really in orbit, ain'tcha?

FIRST BLACK. (Smiling a silly, "high" grin) Just call me Apollo 69, man. (He laughs uproariously.) Oh, man, do I feel good! (Pause) I feel like all the different pieces of me was all put together.

SECOND BLACK. Yeah, I know what you mean.

FIRST BLACK. Know what I'd like to do? I'd like to climb me a mountain and then win a good fight and then ball about twenty chicks! (By this time the two blacks are up on the stage apron.)

SECOND BLACK. Man, you find a mountain in Greenwich Village, you higher than I thought!

FIRST BLACK. All right, then, I just win me a fight and ball me them chicks.

SECOND BLACK. You wanna have you a fight, you go ahead, bro. I'm gonna go ball my old lady.

FIRST BLACK. You always runnin' up there. Shit, man, you might's well be married!

SECOND BLACK. Certain cats that their old lady tole 'em to split

52

seems to me to be talkin' mighty sour grapes, like.

FIRST BLACK. Certain cats better find out who told who to split or they goan end up with they catty ratty asses in a sling! (He laughs.)

SECOND BLACK. Bro, you zonked outa your motherfuckin' mind! You comin' uptown? (No response) All right, man. You on your own. (He turns and exits up the aisle.)

(The First Black moves around the stage in a big circle, his step clearly showing that he is high, his eyes surveying his surroundings constantly. As he walks past the whites, they notice him, turn and smile with a sort of tolerant understanding, since they recognize the symptoms. The First Black starts on another circuit of the stage and as he arrives upstage, deliberately bumps into the Young White's shoulder.)

YOUNG WHITE. Hey, man, who you bumpin'?

FIRST BLACK. I bumpin' you, man.

YOUNG WHITE. You better watch your bumpin', man.

FIRST BLACK. I bump anybody I feel like, man.

YOUNG WHITE. You don't bump me, man.

FIRST BLACK. I bump you if I wanna bump you, man. (So saying, he bumps him again.)

YOUNG WHITE. (He jumps back, fists balled ready to fight. Seeing this, the First Black does the same. They begin what is almost a dance, crouched over, every muscle tense, arms out slightly, describing the circumference of a circle as they move slowly. Throughout, however, the Young White seems to understand that the First Black is more interested in going through the motions of engaging in a charade than in actual fighting. Nevertheless, he takes no chances; he is tense and wary.) OK, man. You asked for it.

FIRST BLACK. And you gonna get it, man.

YOUNG WHITE. You just take a swing and you'll see who's gonna get it, man.

FIRST BLACK. Oh, you gonna be one sorry dude.

YOUNG WHITE. Yeah? They's gonna be one sorrier dude, man. (Both fall mute as they continue to circle. Both are sweating profusely. The First Black reaches for his back pocket. As he does so, the Young White reaches into his back pocket with a lightning-like motion and pulls out a switchblade knife, which he holds in one fist. The First Black's hand returns from his pocket and he is holding a handkerchief, with which he makes a quick sweep over his forehead before replacing it. The Young White looks at the knife quickly and appears almost embarrassed that he has drawn it. The dance continues.)

FIRST BLACK. Hey, what you up to, man?

YOUNG WHITE. (Somewhat defensively) You still lookin' for trouble, man? (As they continue to circle, the First Black seems to realize that the Young White is not going to attack him with the knife and so looks less worried, but still keeps every muscle tense. Again they become mute.)

YOUNG WHITE. (After a pause) C'mon, man, make your move. (From an upper-story window of the brownstone upstage comes a raucous, strident male voice.)

MALE VOICE. That's it, kid! Kill that fuckin' nigger! (The First Black stops, straightens up and looks up toward the place where he thinks the voice came from. The Young White stops and looks at him. Slowly the First Black's shoulders sag, his high ends and he seems to crumple. Dejectedly he walks to the curb downstage, sits down on it, doubled over, and cries silently. The Young White starts to reach out a hand to him, realizes he cannot help, turns to the brownstone and yells up.)

YOUNG WHITE. You bastard! You dirty, rotten son of a bitch! Whadju have to do that for? (He turns back to the First Black, his every muscle showing compassion, again makes a tentative gesture toward him and lets his hand fall hopelessly.)

Quick curtain.

GONE TO THE DOGS

CAST OF CHARACTERS

Underwood

Mrs. Forsythe

The scene is the rather posh office of a veterinarian. The only furnishing necessary, apart from a desk and two chairs, is a diploma on which the letters DVM appear larger than life. Dr. Underwood, the veterinarian, is indeterminately middle-aged and there is a good deal of the unctuous manner of the successful specialist in his make-up. Mrs. Forsythe is young middle-aged, dressed in excellent taste, and is obviously the type who, under different circumstances, would be almost slick and brittle. She enters and sits down during his first line; he of course rises.

UNDERWOOD. (Cheerily) Good afternoon,, Mrs. Forsythe.

FORSYTHE. (Dispirited) Hello, Dr.Underwood.

UNDERWOOD. How are you? And how's Mr. Forsythe? Haven't seen George since last summer at the club.

FORSYTHE. He's working on his-- problem, Tapered off quite a lot. He's down to a fifth a day. His broken arm healed just perfectly, and the pelvis--

UNDERWOOD. Pelvis?

FORSYTHE. Yes. He had a little fall down the cellar stairs.

UNDERWOOD. Oh, sorry.

FORSYTHE. It's coming along nicely, though.

UNDERWOOD. (Falsely jovial) Goood! Glad to hear it. But now to really important things. How is Bowser?

FORSYTHE. (Her face falls.) He's- - he's-- (Stiff upper lip) Not good.

UNDERWOOD. What's the matter? Why didn't you bring him with you?

FORSYTHE. It's-- well, honestly, doctor, I don't know whether I want to be seen in public with him. I wonder if I ought to put him through analysis.

UNDERWOOD. If you want a list of canine analysts in the area, I can give you the names of several reliable men. What's your guess, offhand, Mrs. Forsythe? After all, you re no tyro in psychology and I certainly respect your opinion. What would you say? Schizophrenic? Manic-depressive? Paranoiac?

FORSYTHE. (Deep sigh) Oh, I don't know, doctor. Sometimes I'm about ready to give up.

UNDERWOOD. (Cajoling) Come on now, Mrs. Forsythe. You can trust me. If I'm not Bowser's friend, who is?

FORSYTHE. It's- it's-- (Losing her composure) Just too humiliating.

UNDERWOOD. It's not enuresis?

FORSYTHE. Oh, no, Doctor, I'd get down on my knees and thank God if it were as simple as that,

UNDERWOOD. (In hushed tones) It's not-- homosexuality?

FORSYTHE. No.

UNDERWOOD. It isn't--

FORSYTHE. All right. Sooner or later I know you'll worm it out of me. (Pause. She gathers her resources.) Bowser is becoming an alcoholic!

UNDERWOOD. (Genuinely sympathetic) Oh, I am sorry. The journals are all full of articles about its becoming an increasing problem among dogs.

FORSYTHE. It's certainly becoming an increasing problem among Bowser. He can't leave the stuff alone.

UNDERWOOD. Tell me about it, Mrs. Forsythe.

FORSYTHE. It began at a party. We gave Bowser a little beer in a saucer. Just a few sips. Just as a joke. He took to it like- - like a quadruped W. C. Fields.

UNDERWOOD. Hmmm.

FORSYTHE. Then George tried him on light wines. He liked them, too. He's even developed into a connoisseur. His favorite is 1951 Chateauneuf du Pape, and he can't stand Pouilly Fuissé 1954.

UNDERWOOD. Can't say I disagree. A bad year for Pouilly.

FORSYTHE. But his trouble really started with a few sips of martini.

He went mad over it. Finished his first and then looked up at me-you know how expressive his face is-- he can't keep anything from me-- as if to say, "Where the hell has this been all my life?"

UNDERWOOD. Tsk, tsk.

FORSYTHE. He's gotten so that he can't leave them alone. Other families are softening their kibble with water-- but not us. We have to use martinis. And (Momentarily losing her composure), doctor, they have to be eight to one!

UNDERWOOD. Well, I must say that's the way I like them.

FORSYTHE. Doctor! I hope this doesn't imply your approval. I'm afraid it has other ramifications. Since he's been on cocktails, Bowser's been going around with a completely different class of friends.

UNDERWOOD. Oh?

FORSYTHE. Yes. You remember how proud I used to be of his friends-- Jean-Paul, that lovely poodle from next door, and Heinrich, the Lawtons' Weimaraner. Now he picks his companions indiscriminately. And, doctor,--

UNDERWOOD. Yes?

FORSYTHE. They're all in that gang that hangs out at the Haute Cuisine Tavern. A low crowd!. And what's worse they egg each other on. It's reached the point where Bowser won't even give me his paw for less than a saucer of Schenley's!

UNDERWOOD. That does sound bad.

FORSYTHE. It's awful. We can't give a cocktail party any more. Bowser turned the last one into a shambles! Why, when Mrs. Lawton reached for her martini, Bowser actually bared his fangs so that she was afraid to touch it.

UNDERWOOD. Shocking.

FORSYTHE. And drank it himself! What a comment on his qualities as a host!

UNDERWOOD. What a comment indeed.

FORSYTHE. But what's even worse is that, after he gets-- well, let's call a spade a spade--

UNDERWOOD. (Playfully) A bad phrase to use when you're talking to a veterinarian, Mrs. Forsythe. (Chuckles,)

FORSYTHE. (Not amused) Please, doctor! After he gets-- drunk, he howls until we put on his favorite record and keep playing it.

UNDERWOOD. Peculiar.

FORSYTHE. Yes, we think so, too. You remember, doctor, we got a German shepherd because we had such a high regard for the Germans. You know, math and science and Schopenhauer and all that. But you know how disgusting the Teutonic type gets when they've had too many. All that Gemütlichkeit!

UNDERWOOD. And Bowser--

FORSYTHE. Insists on "Fritz Mueller and His Gesellschaft Sing Old Düsseldorf Favorites." It's a whole long LP.

UNDERWOOD. Has he any favorites?

FORSYTHE. (Weary sigh) Yes, the ones they all like, "The Lorelei," "Ach, du lieber Augustin.," "Eins, zwei, sufa," and things like that. But above all "Schnitzelbank." We have to play that endlessly.

UNDERWOOD. God, that sounds tedious!

FORSYTHE. (Stiffly) That's not the worst! (More stiffly) I assume your professional confidence here, doctor. The last time we put Bowser out to stud, he wouldn't-- uh, perform-- without a drink. He just stood there eying the prospective bride and-- doing nothing. It was as if he were asking, "What am I offered?"

UNDERWOOD. And then?

FORSYTHE. We gave him two jiggers of Cutty Sark. He stood up and shook himself- then he seemed to be saying, "Boy, I needed that!" Then he-- uh, performed, He was almost like George since he reached sixty.

UNDERWOOD. (Slightly embarrassed) I--

FORSYTHE. (Losing control) What are we going to do, doctor?

UNDERWOOD. Frankly, Mrs. Forsythe, the prognosis is not good.

FORSYTHE. (Horrified) Oh?!

UNDERWOOD. I consider my honor as a Doctor of Veterinary Medicine to be at stake. Now, frankly, some of us have been thinking about the possibility of setting up a kind of Canine AA chapter here in Darien, but I frankly wonder in his case, He-- he may be too far gone.

FORSYTHE. My God, no!

UNDERWOOD. Please, Mrs. Forsythe, we must be strong. I know these things are hard to face, but—

FORSYTHE. It's easy enough for you to talk, doctor. It isn't as if he were one of your own--

UNDERWOOD. Now, Mrs. Forsythe, it isn't completely hopeless. With efficient professional help--

FORSYTHE. (Wild by now) He'll never recover! That's what you're saying! There's no hope!

UNDERWOOD. (Oozing sympathy) Do try to get hold of yourself. We mustn't give up the ship, must we?

FORSYTHE. Oh, I can see him lurching down the Bowery, maybe leading some blind alcoholic--

UNDERWOOD. You must calm yourself, Mrs.-- (The phone on his desk rings and he answers.) Underwood here. Yes, she is. Just a moment. (He holds out the phone to her.)

FORSYTHE. (Rising, she steps nearer the desk to take the phone.) Yes? Yes, Cynthia. No! The other arm?! (Putting her hand over the speaker, she speaks to Underwood.) It's George. He just had a little fall. Broke his other arm. (Resuming the phone conversation) Yes, Cynthia, right away. (Hangs up.)

UNDERWOOD. (He has risen during her conversation on the phone and stays on his feet after she hangs up, assuming that she will be exiting immediately. His face registers surprise when she walks back over to her chair and sits down again.) But, George's arm--

FORSYTHE. (Lighting a cigarette) Can wait. He's tough. Our thoughts have to be on Bowser now; he's so easily hurt. (Brief pause) Doctor, where is your sense of perspective?

Blackout

BAD GUY

CAST OF CHARACTERS

Bill, age 9
Johnny, age 8
Eddie, age 8
Joe, age 7

All roles must be played by adults.

The time is the day after Christmas, The scene is a boys' clubhouse in Orange, New Jersey.

The scene is the interior of a boys' clubhouse, no larger than fifteen by twenty feet. It has a solid door right and a single window left; the window is small, high up and rather precariously installed. The roof consists of plywood and masonite sheets, pieces of rug and other odds and ends. The room has been furnished with junk, including some torn rug fragments on the floor; right are a kitchen stool whose enamel has been badly chipped and a table with a braced leg; on the table is a sleazy dresser scarf and atop the dresser scarf a saucer in which there is a candle partly burned down. Upstage center is a battered dresser on which are a roll of masking tape and a five-foot length of rope. Left are a massive old sofa with the cushion upholstery torn and the springs showing beneath and, upstage of the sofa, two arm-exercisers bolted to the wall. From the ceiling downstage left hangs a trapeze. The walls are covered with posters and photographs of rock stars and sports figures.

At rise, the stage is dark and remains so as we hear two or three verses of "God Rest Ye Merry, Gentleman." Then, outside the door a chain rattles and the sound of a padlock being unlocked is heard. Bill opens the door, steps in, shivers, slaps himself to get warm and lights the candle; he then goes over and closes the door, putting a two-by-four across it. Very ostentatiously he looks at his wristwatch and his boots. He sits down on the kitchen stool and, taking the current issue of *Playboy* from under his jacket, spreads it out on the table and removes the centerfold. Taking it to the dresser, he puts masking tape on it and, after surveying the walls, finds a blank spot and puts it up. He turns away and then, half-surreptitiously, reaches back, and touches one of the model's breasts. Smiling, he goes over to the arm-exercisers and starts to work out. There is a sound as of someone trying the door, at which Bill rushes over to the centerfold picture, evidently prepared to take it down; then comes a knock: once--pause-- twice--pause--thrice. No longer uneasy, Bill moves to the door.

BILL. Who's there?

JOHNNY. Number Seven.

BILL. Who?

JOHNNY. Oh, come on, Bill. It's me.

BILL. (Taking the two-by-four from. the door, which Johnny pushes open) Come in, Number Seven.

JOHNNY. (Enters wearing a policeman's hat and badge, with a holster hanging from the belt; in the belt is a club and over it hangs a pair of handcuffs.) Hey, dju get the bike?

BILL. Yeah. Pretty cool, huh?

JOHNNY. Yeah. Is it a real racing bike?

BILL. Yup. And I got a watch. (He pulls up, his sleeve to the elbow.) And a camera and a Louisville Slugger and my aunt in Ohio sent me ten bucks. (Pause) And look! (He sits on the sofa and pulls up his pants legs, revealing a pair of boots.)

JOHNNY. (Slightly awed) Man! Real cowboy boots! (Brightening) I got this cop outfit and a transistor radio and a Chinese checker game and a real nice German sled.

BILL. I got a whole turkey leg!

JOHNNY. Me too. And two pieces of pumpkin pie!

EDDIE. (Who, meanwhile, has come to the clubhouse door, wearing a cop outfit just like Johnny's. Finding the door open, he enters.) Hi.

BILL. Hey, you can't come in just like that. (He rushes over to him and propels him toward the door.)

EDDIE. Why not? I'm a member, aren't I?

BILL. C'mon. You gotta give the signal. (He pushes the unprotesting Eddie outside and shuts the door.) Go ahead. (Eddie knocks: once-pause-twice-pause-thrice.) Who's there?

EDDIE. Number Eleven.

BILL. Who?

EDDIE. (Louder, slightly exasperated) Number Eleven.

BILL. (Reopening the door) Enter, Number Eleven.

EDDIE. Hey, who got the racing bike? You, Bill?

BILL. Yeah. And look! (He shows the boots.) And I got a watch and a real camera.

JOHNNY. You got a cop outfit just like mine!

EDDIE. Yeah. And I got a chemistry set and a pair of skis and a magic magnetic game.

JOHNNY. I got a terrific German sled and--

BILL. And I got a Louisville Slugger and ten bucks, too.

(During this, Joe has come up to the door. He is physically smaller than the others. He sees the door partly open, but gives the official knock anyway.)

BILL. Who's there?

JOE. Number Thirteen.

BILL. Enter, Number Thirteen.

JOE. (Entering) Hi. Is that your bike, Bill? Wow, what a bike!

JOHNNY. Whadja get?

JOE. I got a baseball glove and some games and a lot of clothes. (He looks at Johnny and Eddie.) Hey, you guys both got the same cop outfits!

EDDIE. Yeah. How about that!

BILL. They're real nice. (Pause. Bill, Eddie and Joe sit; Johnny wanders aimlessly over to the wall, catches sight of the *Playboy* centerfold and surreptitiously touches one of the breasts. He too then sits.) Hey, let's do something. Let's don't just sit around.

JOHNNY. What'll we do?

EDDIE. Let's play cops and robbers!

JOHNNY. Yeah? C'mon! (He draws his gun and aims it at Bill, while Eddie draws his and aims, it at Joe.) Khew! Khew!

EDDIE. Khew! Khew! (Joe pretends to be hit and falls. Bill does not.)

BILL. How can we play cops and robbers? I haven't got a gun.

JOE. Me neither.

EDDIE. It's too cold for a baseball game. And there's no snow for the sleds.

BILL. Hey, let's have a secret meeting. We can make up a new code.

JOHNNY. Aw, we had a secret meeting last week. All you want to do is have secret meetings.

EDDIE. I know! Let's play good guys and bad guys. Bill, you be the judge and Johnny and I'll be the cops and Joe can be the bad guy.

JOE. Why do I have to be the bad guy?

BILL. What a jerk you are! You can't be a cop because you didn't get a cop outfit. They have to be the cops. And I got to be the judge because I'm the president of the club. OK, let's go. (He moves the stool behind the table and sits on it, pulls the dresser scarf from the table and drapes it over his shoulders.) The court will come to order! Bring in the prisoner. (Johnny and Eddie each grab one of Joe's arms and propel him toward the desk.) Prisoner at the bar, how do you plead: guilty or not guilty?

JOE. What's the charge, your honor?

BILL. Uh, let's see--

JOE. How about robbing the First National Bank?

BILL. Nah, we know you didn't do that.

JOE. How about killing Mr. Jansen?

BILL. Nah. If you did that, everybody in the whole school 'ud give you some kind of a prize or something.

EDDIE. It should be something you really did,

JOHNNY. Yeah, c'mon. What did you do that was bad?

BILL. OK, officers, refresh the prisoner's memory! (At this, Eddie and Johnny draw their clubs and pretend to club Joe over the head, meanwhile shouting. "Bam," "Wham," "Take that, you

66

rat," etc. Going along with the game, Joe plays at being bloody and bowed.)

JOE. I'll talk, your honor,

BILL. Go ahead, prisoner at the bar.

JOE. I stole a pack of spearmint when Mr. Farber wasn't looking.

EDDIE. Big deal! We all did that!

JOHNNY. Yeah!

JOE. I-- uh, I copied off Carol in the arithmetic test last week.

BILL. Who doesn't copy off Carol when they sit next to her?

JOHNNY. Yeah! Gee, some bad guy!

EDDIE. Public Enemy number eight thousand three hundred and thirty-two.

JOE. I--

BILL. C'mon, spit it out.

JOE. (Half boastful) Last Saturday I took two bucks out of' my old lady's pocketbook so I could go to the movies.

JOHNNY. Two bucks!

EDDIE. Didn't she find out?

JOE. Naw, she never remembers how much money she's got.

BILL. That's good enough, Prisoner at the bar, you are charged with grand larceny. How do you plead?

JOE. Grand larceny? How come?

BILL. Grand larceny. One buck is petit larceny, two bucks is grand larceny.

JOE. Who decided that?

BILL. I did. Now, how do you plead?

JOE. Don't they always plead "not guilty" on TV?

BILL. So you plead "not guilty," prisoner?

JOE. Uh-huh.

BILL. Officers, you'll have to help him change his mind. (Again Eddie and Johnny pretend to belabor him with their clubs.) Well, what do you say now, prisoner?

JOE. Uh, I changed my mind, your honor.

BILL. OK. The judge finds you guilty of grand larceny. You are sentenced to ten years in jail.

JOE. I protest, your honor. Ten years is too much.

BILL. No, it's not. You crooks have got to be put away. We have to make an example of you. Ten years isn't even enough. (He looks at Eddie and Johnny.) You cops better handcuff him so he won't escape before you take him to the pen.

JOHNNY. Right, your honor. (He lets go of Joe's arm In order to work the handcuffs out of his belt. Seeing this, Eddie does the same.)

JOE. (Both arms free, he runs out the door.) You gotta catch me first!

BILL. The prisoner's escaped! After 'im, men! (Eddie and Johnny also run out the door. There is much offstage shouting of "He went that way," "Where'd he go?" "He's over here" and "Get 'im!") Get 'im! ! He's over there!

JOHNNY. (Offstage) Ja get 'im? Good!

EDDIE. (Leading Joe in) Here he is, your honor. He sure gave us a lot of trouble. (Johnny trails him in.)

BILL. He's a tough customer, all right. Better get the cuffs on him. And watch him. (Eddie gets behind Joe and pinions him. Joe, cooperative and still playing the game, holds out his hands. Johnny takes out his handcuffs and puts them on Joe's wrists.)

JOHNNY. There we are, your honor,

EDDIE. I don't think we should take any chances with 'im. I think we should handcuff his legs, too.

JOHNNY. Right. Let's do it. (He grabs Joe around the waist and wrestles him to the ground. Eddie takes his handcuffs out of his belt and, while Johnny lies across Joe's chest, Eddie tries to fasten a handcuff on Joe's right leg, although it will not fit.)

JOE. Hey, you guys, that hurts! C'mon, you're making it too tight! Honest! I mean it. It's pinching my skin! (Eddie keeps trying.)

EDDIE. (To Bill, who is watching the developments closely) Hey, these things won't fit. Throw me that rope, Bill. (Bill reaches over to the dresser, grabs the length of rope on top of it and hands the rope to Eddie, who ties it very tight around Joe's right leg.)

JOE. Cut it out! Oww! Take it off or you'll be sorry. I'm warning you! (Eddie, having tied the rope around Joe's right leg, reaches for his left leg.) OK, you asked for it! (He draws back his left leg and kicks Eddie hard, knocking him back several feet. As Johnny turns to look, Joe pulls his hands from beneath Johnny and hits Johnny beside the head knocking him over. Joe then struggles to his feet.)

EDDIE. Ohh, my shoulder!

JOHNNY. You little rat! (He rubs his neck.)

EDDIE. (Getting up as far as a crouch, he tackles Joe and lies across his legs.) Hey, let's really fix him!

JOHNNY. Yeah! He's got it coming to him!

JOE. (A bit apprehensive) You're the ones who had it coming to you. That thing (He gestures toward his right ankle.) really pinches! C'mon, take it off! (He sits up and reaches for his ankle.)

EDDIE. No you don' t! C' mon, guys, let' s show him he can' t get away with kickin' us!

JOHNNY. Right! (He throws himself back on Joe, who struggles wildly.) C'mon, Bill, help us! Are you for the good guys or what?

BILL. (Throws himself into the struggle, helping Eddie put the rope on Joe's left ankle.) Sure I am. This guy's dangerous.

JOE. C'mon, don't do that! It's too tight! You're gonna cripple me!

BILL. Keep quiet, you!

EDDIE. Hey, I know what we should do so he won't escape! Let's handcuff 'im to the trapeze!

JOHNNY. Yeah! (Quickly they stand Joe up, half drag and half carry him to the trapeze, take the handcuff from his right wrist, hold one hand on either side of the trapeze bar and put the handcuff back on his right wrist. This is accompanied by much squirming and grunting.) There!

JOE. Hey, what're you doing? C'mon, let me go!

BILL. That'll teach you to meddle with officers of the law!

JOHNNY. (Rubbing his neck) What a dirty rat! Boy, I oughta kill you! (He walks over to Joe and hits him hard on the arm.) That's for hitting me in the neck!

JOE. That's rotten! Three against one and then you hit me when I can't even fight back! (Seriously) Wait'll I get free, Johnny, and will I get you!

JOHNNY. You had it coming to you, you little stinker!

EDDIE. That's right! What a louse!

BILL. C'mon, now that we've got 'im behind bars, let's go do something.

JOHNNY. Hey, come over and take a look at my new sled.

BILL. Yeah. I want to see what it's like!

JOHNNY. It's really terrific! It's got, like, a gear shift, so you can slow down if you get going too fast.

BILL. I didn't know they made them like that. (They move toward the door.)

JOE. C'mon, you guys! You can't leave me here shut up alone!

BILL. After what you did to Johnny and Eddie, solitary is too good for you! Let's go, gang!

JOHNNY. Right!

EDDIE. (Rubbing his chest) Just a minute. I'm gonna give him something to remember me by, (Slowly he walks over behind Joe and gooses him hard with his club. Joe yells.) Kick me, will ya? That'll teach ya! (He moves to the door.)

JOE. Ooo, you really hurt me, Eddie. I mean it! (He sees them starting to exit and gets slightly panicky.) I thought this was supposed to be a game. You guys acted like it was a game!

(Bill blows out the candle, the lights fade except for a spot on Joe, and the others exit. We hear the chain rattle and the padlock being shut.) You can't do this! (Pause) C'mon back in! (Pause) I know you guys are out there! (Pause) Let me out of here! (He rattles the trapeze, trying to break loose.) Let me go! (Pause) All right, if that's the way you want to be! (The trapeze rattles again.) When I get loose, I'm going to kill you, you stinking rats! You yellow-bellied cowards! You-- bastards! (More rattling of the trapeze. Pause) You're not going to get away with this! I'll get you all! (Pause) C'mon. Let me go! (Loud) Help! Help! (Long and drawn out) Help! (Pause) I'm telling you guys, I'll kill you! (More rattling) If I ever get loose-- (Pause) YOU SHITS! (Pause, after which Joe cries hopelessly. Gradually his crying subsides, he wipes his nose on his arm and raises his head. His expression is now set and sullen. Silence.)

(After about ten seconds, Bill, Johnny and Eddie are heard talking and laughing outside the door.)

BILL. That's some sled, all right. I'm going to start bugging my old man to get me one.

EDDIE. It sure is. Wish I had one.

BILL. (Rattling the chain and unlocking the padlock) We'll have to see how our prisoner is doing.

JOHNNY. That fink! Boy, when he hit me, he almost broke my neck!

(The three enter the clubhouse. Johnny lights the candle and the lights go up. Joe stands silently, feigning unconcern, but inwardly seething and ready to jump into action.)

BILL. Well, prisoner, how'd you like that? (No response) I hope you learned your lesson. Don't mess with the law. (No response) Boy, what a rotten sport you turned out to be. (To Johnny and Eddie) Let 'im go, men, (Johnny takes the handcuffs from Joe's wrists; Joe rubs his wrists. With considerably more difficulty Eddie removes the rope from Joe's ankles. Joe walks around a little, stamping his feet to restore the circulation. From the corner of his eye he watches Eddie, who is putting his handcuffs into his bolt. Suddenly Joe rushes wildly at Eddie, fists flailing, and knocks him onto the table, whose braced leg collapses so that Joe, Eddie, and the table fall together.)

JOE. I'll kill you! I'll kill you! (Like one possessed, he flails away at Eddie, who is underneath him.)

EDDIE. Hey, he's goin' crazy! Help me, you guys! (Bill and Johnny approach Joe warily, each thinking to grab one arm. They do not exert enough strength, however, and Joe lashes out at them, hitting each hard, Sensing that he is going to be overwhelmed, Joe decides to wreak as much havoc as he can before he is overpowered. He runs behind the collapsed table, picks up the stool, pretends he is going to throw it at the other three, who recoil, and hurls it through the window. He then runs upstage and throws the dresser over onto the floor.)

BILL. Geez, he's wrecking the place. Let's get him. (By this times Joe is behind the couch, which he has pushed out from the wall. He picks up a cushion that is slightly torn and rips the upholstery off it completely.) Now we've got 'im cornered! Let's go! (The three approach him from three sides. He flails at them with the cushion, but after considerable struggle, punctuated by grunts, groans and shouts, he is subdued. Johnny and Eddie lead him out from behind the couch, each holding an arm behind his back. The chests of all four are heaving from exertion, and the clothing of all four has been scuffed up. There are tears on Joe's cheek.)

JOE. That's not fair! Ganging up on a guy like that!

BILL. Shut up! Look what you did to our clubhouse! You practically wrecked it! Boy, wait'll we show you! C'mon, guys, let's put 'im back where he was. We're not safe as long as he's loose.

(Amid much wild swinging of arms, the three manage to get Joe handcuffed to the trapeze again. Then they combine to tie his ankles as well.)

JOE. You're not going to put me there again! You can't do it!! (As the rope is finally tied) Let me go! (Pause) Help!

BILL. Shut up! (He surveys the room.) Look at our clubhouse! (To Johnny and Eddie) Boy, he deserves whatever he gets!

JOHNNY. Let 'im rot!

JOE. (Yells.) You're not going to leave me here again! (He rattles the trapeze, trying to break loose.) You finks! You dirty shits!

BILL. (Walking over and hitting him in the ribs) You shut up or we'll really give you something to yell about. Look at who's calling who dirty shits! (Pause) We'll leave you here if we feel like it and we'll come back when we're good and ready.

JOE. I'm gonna tell my father on you guys!

BILL. Yeah? So you're a squealer, too? (Mimics him, using a falsetto) "I'm gonna tell my father on you guys!" Little fairy! (Menacingly) Listen, you tell him and we'll tell everybody all about you -- how you steal from the candy store and cheat in school and about the money you take from your old lady's pocketbook and about wrecking our clubhouse and kicking your buddies. So, you better keep your trap shut, wiseguy! (Pause) 'Cause maybe we'll just keep all that in mind and maybe we can even think up a few things if you ever get wise with us again.

JOE. LET ME LOOSE!

BILL. Fat chance! (He walks over to Johnny and Eddie.) Let's leave for a while and teach this rat a lesson. (He walks back to Joe, who winces, expecting another blow.) You know, I never knew it before, but you really are rotten. You're not fit to associate with decent people. You better start shaping up, 'cause right now you're a real bad guy. (He walks over to the candle, preparatory to blowing it out.) A real bad guy. (He blows the candle out and all the lights fade except for a spot on Joe. Joe stands sullenly, silently immobile, as the other three exit and are heard padlocking the door. We hear "It Came upon a Midnight Clear." After the phrase "Peace on the earth, good will to men," the spotlight, which has been fading, fades out completely.)

Slow curtain

OUT OF THE FRYING PAN...

Justin

Laura

Barbara

SCENE I

The scene is the Williams' living room.

AT RISE: Laura is seated, reading, when Justin enters.

JUSTIN. Hello, Laura.

LAURA. Hello.

JUSTIN. How was your day?

LAURA. Well, I'm still having the twinges in my kneecap. I hope I'm not getting arthritis. And I had a sharp pain in one of my molars. I'm probably going to have an abscess. And then this afternoon I developed a kind of dull ache in my stomach. For all I know, it could be the start of an ulcer.

JUSTIN. I'm sure you'll be just fine. You'll be batting .400.

LAURA. Since it's nine o'clock, I imagine you won't want dinner.

JUSTIN. No, I had something sent in to the office.

LAURA. It's just as well. I tried making chicken Kiev, but I didn't seal the meat well enough so all the butter ran out and got all over the pan.

JUSTIN. Too bad. (Pause) Any mail?

LAURA. A couple of bills. I don't know when we're going to finish paying off that big-screen TV. It just goes on and on.

JUSTIN. Anything else?

LAURA. A letter from Mother.

JUSTIN. (Flatly, dreading the answer) How is she?

LAURA. Oh, she's been having heart palpitations again. The doctor says it's just tachycardia, but she's convinced it's the warning sign of a heart attack.

JUSTIN. I think I'll get a drink. (He exits to the kitchen, speaking from offstage.) Anything else new?

LAURA. (Louder, since he is still offstage) UPS delivered the shirts you ordered from Betterman's. They sent the wrong size.

JUSTIN. (Returning with his drink) You call them?

LAURA. Uh-huh.

JUSTIN. Want a drink?

LAURA. I don't think so.

JUSTIN. You may want to have one.

LAURA. What do you mean?

JUSTIN. I want to have a talk. (Pause) A serious talk.

LAURA. Oh?

JUSTIN. I mean a very serious talk. This is going to be an extra-innings conversation.

LAURA. (Pause) Well?

JUSTIN. Let's kick off by saying--

LAURA. There's somebody else.

JUSTIN. There's--what?

LAURA. You've got somebody else.

JUSTIN. That's right. But how did you guess?

LAURA. I didn't guess. I've known since you started your--your affair.

JUSTIN. It's more than an affair. It's the Super Bowl of my life! It's a grand slam in the bottom of the ninth! It's a three-pointer with four seconds left on the clock! It's—

LAURA. I'm not surprised. I always knew it would happen.

JUSTIN. What do you mean?

LAURA. The day we were married, I knew it wouldn't last. I just had a feeling.

JUSTIN. But that was 11 years ago! I mean, this hasn't been a sprint. It's been a marathon.

LAURA. God knows, I always try to look on the bright side, but no one knows better than I do that every silver lining has a cloud.

JUSTIN. But you don't look on the bright side. With you it's always fourth down and 30 to go with the goal line 80 yards away.

LAURA. What do you expect? My life hasn't been exactly a bed of roses, you know. I mean, there was that time in third grade when Marie O'Connell said I was a fat little snot, and-

JUSTIN. (Striking his forehead) My God, you mean--?

LAURA. And there was a day in eighth grade when I woke up late and got dressed in a hurry and went to school with two different socks on and all the other girls made fun of me.

JUSTIN. For the love of--

LAURA. And in tenth grade I was madly in love with Gary Butler and he wouldn't even look at me. I mean, I was devastated!

JUSTIN. But that all happened -- Jesus Christ!

LAURA. And in twelfth grade I got nominated for secretary of my homeroom and I lost. It wasn't even for anything important, like secretary of the student council. It was just my homeroom.

JUSTIN. Forget the ancient history, for God's sake. You're talking about a time when they still played basketball in cages.

LAURA. I just wanted to make the point that my life hasn't been a series of summits. I've had some valleys, too. A lot of them. And this is just one more.

JUSTIN. Is that all you have to say?

LAURA. What do you want me to say? And what can I say that's going to make any difference? Like I told you, I saw this coming a year ago when you started your "overtime."

JUSTIN. Why didn't you say something then?

LAURA. What good would it have done? Things always get worse before they get worse.

JUSTIN. (Shaking his head) It's like giving up the fight before the first punch is thrown.

LAURA. You can make all the comparisons you want, but I just felt it in my bones that sooner or later it was going to happen.

JUSTIN. Since our wedding day.

LAURA. That's right. (Pause) But at least I have my memories. (Pause) Remember the time when the boiler blew up and we had two feet of water in the basement? Or the time when we were driving back from the shore and the car threw a rod and we had to be towed 15 miles? Or when-

JUSTIN. I remember. (Pause) Look, so we don't have to go into overtime on this, I want a divorce..

LAURA. Yes, I figured that's where all this was heading.

JUSTIN. And that's all you have to say?

LAURA. Like I said, what good would it do? I mean, look at Samantha.

JUSTIN. Samantha? Samantha who?

LAURA. Samantha Merrill on *A Brighter Yesterday*. When Geoffrey told her he wanted a divorce, she yelled and screamed and cried up a storm, but it didn't do her any good. They still got divorced.

JUSTIN. My plan is that we'll split everything down the middle-the house, the furniture, the car, whatever. I don't want to end this match on a bad line call. I figure if we sell everything, we'll get about $250,000, so your cut will be $125,000.

LAURA. Sell the house?

JUSTIN. Unless you want to buy out my share.

LAURA. I won't have enough to do that.

JUSTIN. There are times when you just have to punt.

LAURA. I'm not going to be able to afford a decent place to live. I'm probably going to have to move to some tenement with rats and roaches and people I won't have anything in common with--

JUSTIN. Now, don't count your losses before--

LAURA. --in a rundown part of town with gangsters and drug addicts so I won't dare to go out of my railroad flat after it gets dark out.

JUSTIN. C'mon, Laura.

LAURA. And I won't be able to buy respectable furniture. I'll probably have to shop for deck chairs to sit in and get orange crates for tables and dressers and put linoleum on all the floors.

JUSTIN. It won't be like that at all, I'm sure.

LAURA. I'll certainly have to go back to work! I don't see how I can avoid it.

JUSTIN. I suppose you will. But you'll enjoy getting back into the lineup.

LAURA. I don't know. Since I've been out of the job market for so long, I probably won't be able to get a job that pays anything. I'll have to get one that's only minimum wage, like slaving for McDonald's or Burger King or Wendy's or some place like that.

JUSTIN. Well, you gotta play in the minors before you make it to the bigtime.

LAURA. What about alimony?

JUSTIN. I was hoping you wouldn't want alimony. I mean, what with splitting everything down the middle, like I suggested.

LAURA. Oh, I think I'd have to have at least a little alimony. Enough to buy a crust of day-old bread and some watery tea made from used tea-bags. I mean, I wouldn't ask for much.

JUSTIN. I think the best thing for you would be to get a lawyer. I expect to talk to Bob about handling it for me.

LAURA. I don't know. I don't trust lawyers. Most of them are so sleazy and dishonest. They just don't have any principles.

JUSTIN. What about Ed Parker? I'm sure you can trust him. He's as honest as an NFL referee.

LAURA. I guess he's the best of a bad lot. He'll cheat me, but maybe not as much as the others. He'll probably take all I get from the settlement, but what the hell.

JUSTIN. Oh, I think he'll be fair. (Finishing his drink) It's about time for me to turn in. (Pause) The way things are, I'll sleep in the guest room. I'll move out this weekend.

LAURA. Whatever you say. The bed's all made up, although it's kind of lumpy.

JUSTIN. I'll be all right.

LAURA. I'm going to stay up. I want to watch the late news. There were a couple of stories on at six o'clock that'll probably have follow-ups at ten or eleven.

JUSTIN. Oh?

LAURA. Some little boy fell into his family's swimming pool. He was under water for ten minutes and they finally revived him. He's in the hospital on the critical list. He'll probably die, but I want to check on it anyway.

JUSTIN. (Turning to go) Well,--

LAURA. And there was another one about some old couple that have lived in their house for forty years and they're trying to evict them. It looks like they haven't got a prayer.

JUSTIN. Yes. I'll be turning in now. (He exits.)

Blackout

SCENE 2

The scene is Barbara Johnson's living room.

AT RISE: Barbara is seated, plucking her eyebrows, when Justin enters.

JUSTIN. (Crossing and kissing her lightly) Hi, honey.

BARBARA. Hi, Justin. How are you, love?

JUSTIN. Fit as a fiddle and ready for--anything. (Pause) How was work?

BARBARA. Oh, I had a great day at the office! Evelyn got back from her vacation and she had some wonderful stories to tell about the Club Med. We'll have to go there sometime. And I had lunch with Sonia. I had a really terrific tuna salad on rye--I couldn't have made better myself. But I don't want to ramble on about tuna fish. You have some really big news for me, right? (Justin nods assent.) Well?

JUSTIN. I spoke to Laura last night about the divorce. She'll go along with it, although she may want some alimony.

BARBARA. Good! I knew it would turn out all right. And she probably won't want too much alimony.

JUSTIN. I dunno. You know how people get when the contest is up in the air.

BARBARA. I know. But I'm sure she's a good person and she'll be more than reasonable.

JUSTIN. Geez, you act like you've got a 42-to-nothing lead at the two-minute warning.

BARBARA. I'm just certain that everything will turn out for the best.

JUSTIN. So, apart from the tuna fish, how was the rest of your day?

BARBARA. First sit down and let me mix you a drink. Martini?

JUSTIN. Great! (He sits as she gets up to make the drink.) Going to join me?

BARBARA. I don't need one. As the old saying goes, I'm high on life.

JUSTIN. As high as a World Series winner, right?

BARBARA. Whatever you say, dear. (She takes him the drink.) Like I said, my day was absolutely great! I thought it was going to start out badly because I missed the 8:30 bus, but I was standing there waiting for the 8:50 when who should drive up but Bill Phillips from accounting and he gave me a lift right to the office! (She returns to her chair.)

JUSTIN. Nice.

BARBARA. And when I got to the office I had a run in my panty hose, but then I remembered I'd hidden a pair in my desk for emergencies.

JUSTIN. Good.

BARBARA. And then I had that terrific lunch and the afternoon just seemed to fly by! But enough about me. Tell me about your plans.

JUSTIN. I thought I'd move in this weekend, if that's OK with you.

BARBARA. Fabulous!

JUSTIN. And we can start looking for a bigger apartment then.

BARBARA. This apartment's very nice, but a bigger one would be even better.

JUSTIN. I'll just bring my clothes and shoes and things. The other stuff I can pick up later.

BARBARA. Whatever you say. It sounds good to me.

JUSTIN. And then we can settle down and live happily ever after. (Pause) My God, I feel like a guy coming in for a penalty shot with a blindfold on the goalie!

BARBARA. I've never been happier! I'm even happier than I was when you said you wanted to marry me! (She crosses and kisses him.) Mmm. I love you!

JUSTIN. And I love you.

BARBARA. I'll never forget that night. Dinner at Ernesto's-- everything perfect--dancing at the Green Parrot--the drive out to the lake--sitting in the car with the moonlight on the water. I thought it was heaven, but every day is heaven when you're around! (She kisses him again, then crosses to her chair.)

JUSTIN. I know we're going to have a wonderful life together-- like two battery mates collaborating on a no-hitter.

BARBARA. You know what I see for us eventually? The two of us settled in a vine-covered cottage far away from the city-- maybe in Upper Saddle River.

JUSTIN. I don't know whether they have any vine-covered cottages in Upper Saddle River.

BARBARA. All right, then, Scarsdale or Bronxville. With a perfect lawn in front and a big flower garden in back, maybe with a brook running through it.

JUSTIN. Hold on a minute, baby! Don't put on your Super Bowl ring before the game is over! We're going to have to see what happens with this alimony thing! If Laura gets a big chunk of my salary--

BARBARA. I'm sure it will work itself out and we'll be just fine. Nothing but the best for us!

JUSTIN. I hope so.

BARBARA. It just has to be! So it will be!

JUSTIN. You're a wonder. Do you know that? Just a wonder.

BARBARA. I've always been very lucky. Everything has always gone my way. My folks were so good and kind and understanding. And then I won the Beautiful Toddler contest when I was three—

JUSTIN. You may not be a toddler any more, but you're still beautiful, in case you didn't know it.

BARBARA. Oh, I know it. I'd be lying if I said I didn't. Sometimes I think it's a curse, but then I think of the alternative and I'm happy again.

JUSTIN. I should hope so.

BARBARA. I guess the first time I really realized it was when I was the junior prom queen in high school--but I've already told you about that.

JUSTIN. Mm-hm.

BARBARA. And then I got into the state Miss Adolescent contest--even though I only got the Miss Congeniality award. Being in the middle of all those beauties made me feel that I must be pretty good myself--I mean, good to look at.

JUSTIN. And so you are.

BARBARA. Oh, Justin! (Pause) You know, I love flattery.

JUSTIN. That's what I was counting on.

BARBARA. You're so manipulative! That's one of the things I like best about you, because I don't at all mind being manipulated-by you, that is.

JUSTIN. And I like being the coach, provided there's a star player to manage.

BARBARA. And, not so incidentally, I'd better start thinking about manipulating some food so we can have dinner. I bought a couple of beautiful steaks today or I can rustle up a tuna casserole if you feel fishy.

JUSTIN. Listen, why don't we eat out? Save the steaks for tomorrow and let's have something exotic. I'm as hungry as a kid from the slums in his first at-bat in pro ball!

BARBARA Wonderful! (Pause) But where should we go?

JUSTIN. Why don't you decide? What about Ernesto's?

BARBARA. Oh, I just love Ernesto's! They have absolutely the best saltimbocca in the world! And the fettucini alfredo is marvelous!

JUSTIN. Or how about Calcutta Corners?

BARBARA. You know I'm simply mad for curry--and they have the best! Just spicy enough to be exciting but not enough to send you to the bicarb.

JUSTIN. Or Chez François?

BARBARA. François' pate is fabulous and his chicken cordon bleu is one of my favorite foods! (Pause) Oh, I don't know--why don't you decide?

JUSTIN. It's like trying to decide between baseball and football and basketball. Oh, I don't know. Let's try Ernesto's.

BARBARA. Terrific! But I want to go and change before we go.

JUSTIN. Why? You look great!

BARBARA. No, I don't like to go out in my work clothes. I won't be but a minute. (She stands.) I wonder if I should wear my yellow pants suit.

JUSTIN. That looks nice.

BARBARA. Or maybe that slinky red dress.

JUSTIN. That's a sexy number.

BARBARA. Yes, I guess I'll wear that--with the matching shoes with the high, high heels.

JUSTIN. You'll look like a million bucks!

BARBARA. (Crosses to him, bends over and kisses him.) Oh, Justin, I just couldn't be happier! But I already said that.

JUSTIN. Me, too. I feel like I'm coming down the home stretch with a 20-length lead!

Blackout

SCENe 3

The scene is Barbara Johnson's living room.

AT RISE: Barbara is sitting, staring into space and smiling. There is a knock at the door and Barbara goes to answer it.

BARBARA. Yes?

LAURA. You're Barbara.

BARBARA. That's right. What did you want?

LAURA. I'm Laura.

BARBARA. (Taken aback) Oh! (Pause) Uh, won't you come in?

LAURA. (Flatly) Thanks. (She enters and stands inside the door.)

BARBARA. (There is still a note of apprehension in her voice) Won't you sit down?

LAURA. Thanks. (She sits, as does Barbara.)

BARBARA. Well, here we are.

LAURA. Here we are. (Pause. She toys with her wedding ring.) I should explain why I'm here. It's not to make a scene or cause any trouble. I just wanted to meet you. I came tonight because I know it's Justin's Rangers night.

BARBARA. So it is. (Trying to be upbeat) It's very nice to meet you.

LAURA. And it's nice of you to be so hospitable. I mean, not everybody would be willing to see another person--I mean, under the circumstances.

BARBARA. I suppose we can't do anything about the circumstances, can we? It's pretty much up to Justin.

LAURA. I suppose it is.

BARBARA. Yes. (There is a long pause) Did you have anything specific in mind that you wanted to talk about?

LAURA. No, I'm not very good at introducing topics. Generally, I'm not very successful as a talker.

BARBARA. Oh, I'm sure that's not true!

LAURA. No, it's true. I realized it in high school when I got an F in public speaking.

BARBARA. Oh, public speaking isn't the same as--uh, private speaking. I don't think you ought to feel that you're inarticulate just because you fl--you had difficulties in your public speaking class.

LAURA. You're very kind to make excuses for me, but most of the time I'm just sort of tongue-tied. It doesn't really bother me-I'm sort of resigned to it.

BARBARA. Oh, I'm sure you're being overly harsh with yourself. I'm sure it's not as bad as you think.

LAURA. It's pretty bad, but I don't mind. It's OK.

BARBARA. I see. (Long pause) How are you otherwise?

LAURA. Oh, I'm all right. I'm getting ready to readjust my life.

BARBARA. (Sympathetically) Of course.

LAURA. Justin's decision didn't really come as any surprise to me, but I hadn't thought about all the changes I'd have to make.

BARBARA. I can understand that.

LAURA. I mean, there's so much.

BARBARA. I'm sure.

LAURA. It isn't just getting rid of the house, although that's not easy. It isn't only the memories, but it's selling the furniture and deciding what to take with me when I get an apartment.

BARBARA. It must be difficult.

LAURA. It's depressing, but I'm used to that. But I'll manage to carry on. "Stiff upper lip" is my motto.

BARBARA. That's a good philosophy to have.

LAURA. It's the little things that upset me the most. Like the waffle iron. We got it as a wedding present and I never did learn how to use it right. My waffles always stuck to the iron.

BARBARA. Too bad.

LAURA. But even so, it has a kind of sentimental value.

BARBARA. Uh-huh.

LAURA. And the blender. The first time I used it, I didn't realize that you had to have the top on. What a mess! It was days before I found all the glop around the kitchen!

BARBARA. Quite an ordeal.

LAURA. And I have to say Justin hasn't helped me very much with sorting stuff out.

BARBARA. Well, he's been awfully busy at work and then he's had to pack his clothes and all. I'm certain that, when it comes to deciding about the big things, he'll be only too glad to help.

LAURA. I hope so. Maybe he'll be able to give me a hand next weekend.

BARBARA. I think he's planning to go to a basketball game on Saturday afternoon.

LAURA. Are you interested in sports?

BARBARA. Who, me? No, I don't know the first thing about any sport. I do a lot of walking and a little jogging, but, when it comes to baseball and football and basketball, as I say, I'm a complete ignoramus.

LAURA. Justin's very interested in sports.

BARBARA. I know.

LAURA. I thought maybe one of the reasons Justin--left was that I wasn't interested in sports and you were.

BARBARA. I don't think so.

LAURA. When we were first married, he took me to a lot of games, particularly baseball games, but I was just bored. He tried to explain the rules to me, but I wasn't really interested, so I couldn't remember them.

BARBARA. I think a husband and wife can have different interests that the other one doesn't care about. I don't think they have to do everything together.

LAURA. Oh, I agree. But Justin isn't just interested in sports. He's very interested.

BARBARA. Even so--

LAURA. I mean, do you know how many sports there are on TV? I mean, not just the major sports, but water-skiing and arm wrestling and stuff like that--and Justin is fascinated by them all.

BARBARA. If he enjoys them--

LAURA. But in the fall, when the football season is on, he used to be glued to the set all day Saturday and all day Sunday. It wasn't that I couldn't get him to help around the house. I expected to do all the chores myself, because a woman's work is never done.

BARBARA. Well,--

LAURA. But we couldn't even have people in, so we stopped getting invitations to parties because we never entertained ourselves. Not that I'm fond of parties--I'm pretty much of a wallflower at parties. I just can't seem to get into the spirit of things.

BARBARA. (Without much conviction) Oh, I imagine you're an asset to any social event.

LAURA. Not really. For some reason people don't seem to enjoy my company. I guess maybe I'm too serious.

BARBARA. (Again without conviction) Oh, I think you're exaggerating. (Pause) Can I get you a drink?

LAURA. No, thanks. I don't drink. If I drink I get depressed and gloomy.

BARBARA. (Brightly) How about coffee or tea?

LAURA. Thanks, but the caffeine would keep me awake all night, tossing and turning, turning and tossing, tossing and turning--

BARBARA. How about Coke or 7-Up?

LAURA. No, carbonated drinks upset my stomach.

BARBARA. (Beginning to get depressed) If you don't mind, I think I'll have a drink. (She crosses to the bar and pours herself a drink.)

LAURA. So, as I was saying, Justin and I got pretty isolated socially.

BARBARA. Mm-hm.

LAURA. And then, on account of the sports, we sort of got isolated from each other.

BARBARA. Mm-hm.

LAURA. It's not that I'm not used to being alone. I was an only child and, when I was little, I didn't play with the other kids much. And then, after I quit college, the first job I got was as a receptionist.

BARBARA. (Trying hard) Oh, that must have been nice.

LAURA. Not really. I had to sit at a desk all by myself, with nobody to talk to--I couldn't even read books or magazines. I just had to sit and smile. It was hard.

BARBARA. I'm sure it was.

LAURA. So, as I say, I'm used to being alone. I don't really mind.

BARBARA. (Flatly) That's a good attitude to have.

LAURA. But you've probably never had to deal with it.

BARBARA. No, that's not true. When I didn't go back for my fourth year of college, my parents wouldn't speak to me for six months.

LAURA. Oh, that must have been terrible.

BARBARA. It was. I was very upset. Very upset. And then, when my first marriage broke up, I felt very much alone. Lee and I hadn't been married that long--just three years--when we both realized it had been a mistake. But, even so, it wasn't easy.

LAURA. I know.

BARBARA. But I think the time I felt most isolated was when I got fired. It was the only time that ever happened to me. See, my company was taken over by another company and the new boss cut back on staff. I was the low gal on the totem pole in my department, so I got the axe.

LAURA. Oh, I'm sure it wasn't anything but a question of seniori-ty.

BARBARA. I know that now, but at the time all kinds of thoughts went through my head--about how I didn't have what it took and not working hard enough and things like that. I just shut myself up in my apartment for about six weeks. I didn't want to see anybody or talk to anybody.

LAURA. Mmm.

BARBARA. So, you see, my life hasn't been only floating from Cloud 9 to Cloud 9. There've been some low spots, too...

LAURA. I see.

BARBARA. But I always try to put the best face on things and come up smiling--not that it's always easy.

LAURA. No, it certainly isn't.

BARBARA. But I felt--I feel I've turned a corner with Justin com-ing into my life. I mean, he's so kind and loving and affection-ate.

LAURA. (Dubiously) Well, yes, but-- Maybe I shouldn't be telling tales out of school, but Justin probably told you we lived together for almost a year before we were married.

BARBARA. Yes. He did.

LAURA. (Musing) It was very strange. I mean, before we got

married, he was so romantic and--how can I put it?--so ardent and virile. And, as soon as we got back from the honeymoon, he just seemed to lose interest in--that side of marriage. I don't know if I should even say this, but ever since then I've been lucky if we made love once a month.

BARBARA. (Taken aback) Oh!

LAURA. I've thought about it a lot. At first I figured it was me, but then I remembered how it had been before we got married and I realized that Justin likes--uh, intimacy--when it's sort of illicit and sinful, but he doesn't enjoy it at all when it's all, like, legal and moral.

BARBARA. Well, we'll see.

LAURA. Sure.

BARBARA. I see us spending the rest of our lives together in a little cottage with a white picket fence around it and a lovely green lawn.

LAURA. I bet you'll have to mow the lawn and paint the fence, with Justin watching TV all the time.

BARBARA. (With a crooked smile) Oh, we'll manage to work something out.

LAURA. Of course. (Pause) But there'll be one consolation having Justin in front of the TV set all the time. He won't be out gallivanting around.

BARBARA. Gallivanting?

LAURA. Well, you know. There's always a chance that a married man who had one--uh, friend outside his marriage will do it again.

BARBARA. Oh, no, not Justin!

LAURA. I don't think so either, but there's always a possibility, isn't there?

BARBARA. (Now quite depressed) Oh, I don't think so. If I thought so-

LAURA. But let's not talk about that. Let's talk about happier things. When's the wedding?

BARBARA. Oh, we're not going to have a wedding--I mean, a big wedding. We're just going to a justice of the peace or a judge or something. In March.

LAURA. That's nice. (There is a long pause.) I guess I ought to be running along. (She rises.) It was nice meeting you.

BARBARA. (Insincerely) Likewise.

LAURA. And I wish you and Justin all the happiness you can have.

BARBARA. (Glumly) Thank you. (She rises and escorts Laura to the door.)

LAURA. G'bye. (She exits.)

BARBARA. G'bye. (She closes the door, returns to her chair and sits, looking totally glum.)

Blackout

SCENE 4

The scene is Barbara's living room.

AT RISE: Barbara and Justin are talking.

JUSTIN. Oh, I'm sure it can't be as bad as that, honey.

BARBARA. If anything, it's worse. The way the soufflé collapsed before I even got it to the table and then I knocked over my wine glass-

JUSTIN. Don't worry about it, Barb. I mean, even a top quarterback has an occasional interception.

BARBARA. It just hasn't been a good day for me.

JUSTIN. Well, you can't clinch the pennant every day.

BARBARA. I know, but-- (The doorbell rings and she crosses to open the door.) Oh! Laura! Come in. (Laura enters.) Uh--how are you?

LAURA. (Smiling and, for her, rather bouncy) Hi, Barbara. Hello, Justin.

JUSTIN. (A bit apprehensively) What brings you over?

LAURA. I was going to phone, but it's such a nice, clear night I thought I'd walk over. I've got some good news. (Beat)

JUSTIN. Well?

LAURA. We've got a buyer for the house. And they don't even want to haggle. They'll pay the 175 thousand.

JUSTIN. Great!

(BARBARA. Rather flatly) That's nice.

LAURA. And they may even want to buy some of the furniture. They like the idea of the bookcases in the long hall and the conversation pit around the redwood slab.

JUSTIN. Very good! What does Wally say?

LAURA. He says, "Grab it!" He says we'll never get a better offer.

JUSTIN. OK. I'll call him in the morning. (To no one in particular) Gee, I feel like a guy who just holed a 60-foot putt for an eagle! (To Laura) Is it all right with you to go ahead?

LAURA. Of course. Go. (Beat) How are you, Barbara?

BARBARA. (Without much conviction) Oh, I'm fine, thanks.

LAURA. You sound kind of down.

BARBARA. Somebody dented my fender yesterday in the company parking lot.

JUSTIN. It isn't that bad, Barb.

BARBARA. Three hundred dollars worth of bad. That's bad enough. But what I really don't like is that it must have been somebody else who works at Evertrue. I mean, if you can't even trust your fellow-workers--

LAURA. Maybe it was a delivery truck.

BARBARA. Maybe. But I doubt it. Oh, well, what the hay!

JUSTIN. That's the spirit.

BARBARA. (Not especially spirited) How are you, Laura? I mean, besides the house.

LAURA. Things are sort of looking up. I called this girl I went to school with and she knows of a job in her company that I might be able to get. It only pays 13 thousand, but--

BARBARA. That's not very much.

LAURA. I know.

BARBARA. It's hardly enough to make ends meet.

LAURA. I'll just have to make do, that's all. But I think I'll be able to manage.

BARBARA. Rents are terribly high right now. I'm paying 800 for this place and everybody tells me it's a bargain.

LAURA. I haven't had time to go apartment-hunting what with showing the house and packing stuff and discarding stuff. But I'll be able to start looking now.

BARBARA. Justin and I have been out searching. We've been looking in the suburbs and actually it's kind of discouraging.

LAURA. Really?

JUSTIN. We feel like Little Leaguers trying to play in Busch Stadium.

BARBARA. Even the smaller houses with just a tiny bit of land are terribly expensive.

LAURA. I'm sure you'll find something good.

BARBARA. We'd better. I've had it with living in the city.

LAURA. Really? I kind of like it.

BARBARA. I mean, with all the crime. You could get raped.

LAURA. I was never raped.

BARBARA. Or mugged.

LAURA. I was never mugged either.

BARBARA. I wasn't either. But it could happen.

LAURA. I guess I don't think about it that much. I'm glad I'm not as worried about it as you are.

JUSTIN. That's right, Barb. Why that's like thinking the horse you're betting across the board is going to break a leg coming down the home stretch.

BARBARA. Well, I was only saying it could happen. (Beat) But I've got another reason for wanting to get out of the city. I didn't tell you, Justin, but the garage raised the rent for my space again. It's going up to 300 a month.

JUSTIN. That's too bad.

BARBARA. I always thought I was so smart, living in the city with the job in Yonkers. You know, I was always going the wrong way at the right time. I mean, heading out of the city when everybody else was heading in, and vice versa. But if I have to give up the car--

LAURA. Oh, I'm sure something will work itself out. You'll find a nice place in the suburbs.

JUSTIN. Sure we will. It'll be like hitting a lob to the baseline when the other guy's in at the net.

BARBARA. (Gloomily) That remains to be seen. Right now I feel as if things will get worse before they get worse. (Long pause)

LAURA. (Looking at her watch) It's getting late. I'd better be getting home. It's almost time for the Kendall Komedy Klub. I just love that show!

BARBARA. We don't watch TV that much. (Flatly) Except for sports.

LAURA. I know. (Rising and speaking to Justin) I just wanted to give you the good news about the house. (Bubbling) I thought you'd be as pleased as I was!

JUSTIN. I am! Like I said, I'll call Wally tomorrow and get the details and then I'll be in touch with you.

LAURA. Great!

JUSTIN. A hundred and seventy-five thou! Boy! It's like running the mile in three minutes!

BARBARA. Mmm.

LAURA. So long. (She exits.)

JUSTIN. It's almost time for the Ranger game. It's going to be on cable from Chicago.

BARBARA. Maybe I'll turn in early.

JUSTIN. At nine o'clock?

BARBARA. Why not?

JUSTIN. Don't want to watch the game? It'll be a good one.

BARBARA. (Dispiritedly) No, I'll pass.

JUSTIN. Gosh, your fanny is really dragging.

BARBARA. No, I'm all right.

JUSTIN. Remember, even a 20-game losing streak has got to come to an end.

BARBARA. Uh-huh.

JUSTIN. (Putting his arm around her shoulder) You'll feel better in the morning.

BARBARA. (With no conviction) Yeah.

Blackout

CURTAIN GOING UP

DEAD CENTER

CAST OF CHARACTERS

John Middleton, middle-aged
Roger Ransom
Rose Ransom, his wife
Leslie Lawson
Laurel Lawson, his wife

The Ransoms and the Lawsons are all in their twenties. All wear wigs of gray hair, but they do not try to act middle-aged in voice, gesture or body motion. The wigs are essential to the production, because they establish the fact that this is not a realistic play.

The scene is the living-room of John Middleton's home in Rolling Hills, New York, an exclusive Westchester County suburb. It is evening of a last spring day in the present year.

Throughout, stage left and stage right refer to the audience's left and right.

The scene represents an upper middle-class home. Stage left and stage right are sofas, a cocktail table in front of each and an end table with a lamp on the upstage of each. Upstage center is a single overstuffed chair with a floor lamp behind it. On the walls are expensive prints of French impressionist paintings. The entrance to the house and to the living room is stage right. The door to the kitchen is stage left.

AT RISE: John Middleton is seated in the chair upstage center, smoking a pipe and reading. The doorbell rings. He gets up, goes to the door and admits the Ransoms. Roger wears a small over-the-shoulder bag and Rose carries a purse.

MIDDLETON. Hello there, Ransoms! How are you? C'mon in!

ROSE and ROGER. (Simultaneously) Hello John, Hi John.

MIDDLETON. (Closing the door) Sit down. (He gestures toward the sofa stage right. He puts his book down on the cocktail table in front of the sofa right.)

ROGER. (Looking at it) Whatcha reading? (He picks it up.) Oh! "The Decline of the West." As the kids say today, "Heavy!" (Pause) How is it?

MIDDLETON. Well, it's food for thought.

ROSE. "The Decline of the West." Is that that Evelyn Waugh book?

ROGER. No, Mrs. Intellect. That's "Decline and Fall."

ROSE. (Sarcastically) Pardon me. I bow to your superior literary background.

ROGER. Literature is just not your forte, my sweet. You go on thinking Sidney Sheldon will win the next Nobel Prize and you'll be OK.

ROSE. And of course the dealer in cabbages and cauliflowers has a Ph. D. in literature.

MIDDLETON. How is the produce business, Roger?

ROGER. As wholesalers, we're doing pretty well. For a while, when prices were going through the roof, I was worried about a big drop in sales, but the fact of the matter is everybody can afford to pay more for food.

MIDDLETON. A comforting thought.

ROGER. You bet your posterior! After all, I've got to keep the little lady here in diamonds and sables and champagne and caviar and--you name it, she needs it.

ROSE. Don't knock it, Rog. Behind every great man, et cetera, et cetera.

ROGER. Behind every great man is a nag.

ROSE. My, aren't we in a lovely mood today. Forgive him, John, he knows not what he does.

MIDDLETON. Can I get anybody a drink? Rose? Rog?

ROSE. Sure. I'll take that new Polish sensation -- Perrier and water. (She laughs and the men smile.) No, seriously, just some Perrier with a twist.

ROGER. Scotch and water on the rocks, please, John.

MIDDLETON. Coming up. (He exits to the kitchen.)

ROSE. So I can count on a continuation of the charm you've shown here once we get to the Cortlands'?

ROGER. Why do you ask?

ROSE. Because if I can I'll make it a particular point to stay away from you all evening.

ROGER. I'll be good. Stick with me. We've got to collect as many signatures on the petition as we can at the party. Why, they may have thirty or forty people there.

ROSE. If you're going to combine business with pleasure, I guess I can go along.

ROGER. Wrong. I'm going to combine pleasure with business. The Cortlands' parties are always dull as hell, but they usually have a slew of influential people.

MIDDLETON. (Entering from the kitchen) Perrier. Scotch. Perrier.

ROGER. Not drinking, John?

MIDDLETON. I'm trying to cut down. I find as I get older I can't bounce back as well the morning after.

ROGER. True, but what the heck! (Raising his glass) Here's to middle age, the golden years without the pains of youth or the aches of senility!

ROSE. I'll drink to that.

ROGER. You'll drink to anything.

ROSE. (Warningly)   Roger!

MIDDLETON. Say, what's new with you two?

ROGER. I'm glad you asked that, John. Rose and I stopped by --
(The doorbell rings.) Damnation!

MIDDLETON. Excuse me. (He goes to the door and admits the
Lawsons. Leslie is wearing an over-the-shoulder bag and
Laurel is carrying a purse.) Come in, Laurel, Les.

ROGER. (Rising, he is clearly less than enthusiastic about seeing
the Lawsons. He and Les shake hands.) Laurel, Les, how are
you?

ROSE. (Flatly) Hello.

LAUREL. Hi, Rog. Hi, Rose. How are you? (The Lawsons are not
overjoyed to see the Ransoms, either.)

MIDDLETON. Sit down, folks. (He gestures toward the sofa left.)

LES. Why not? (He and Laurel cross left and sit down.)

MIDDLETON. Drink?

LES. Why not? Laurel?

LAUREL. I'll have that new Polish drink -- Perrier and water. (She
and Les laugh, as the others smile politely.) No, just Perrier,
thanks.

LES. And I'll have Scotch-rocks, please, John.

MIDDLETON. (Exiting to the kitchen) Be back in a flash. (After
he leaves, there is a long, awkward pause.)

LES. Beautiful day.

ROGER. It's pleasant. (Another pause) You through for the semes-
ter?

LES. That's right. Three months of vacation looming ahead of me.

ROSE. Nice work if you can get it.

LES. I need the three months to recuperate from the nine months
of work I don't do during the year. (He and Laurel laugh.)

ROGER. (Flatly) Many a true word is spoken in jest.

LES. It really isn't that easy. You should try teaching a section of remedial freshman English. It's harder than coal-mining or hod-carrying.

ROGER. No, thank you. I'll leave it up to you to elevate the offspring of the toiling masses. I assume these intellectually underprivileged youths you work with aren't the children of Ivy League grads.

LES. They're good, hard-working kids and they give lots of time and effort to making up their deficiencies.

ROSE. (Sarcastically) Bully for them! (Laurel gives her an icy glance.)

LES. And they're a hell of a lot nicer to work with than spoiled-brat rich kids.

MIDDLETON. (Returning from the kitchen) One Perrier, one Scotch. (He gives the drinks to the Lawsons and sits down upstage center.) How are things?

LES. Our committee is still working very hard to pressure our congressman to get a bill setting up a system of wage and price controls.

ROGER. Just what we need--another bunch of bureaucrats sticking their noses into our business!

LES. Something has to be done to keep food prices from going up and up.

ROGER. Why?

LES. Because poor people are simply being squeezed to death by the price of everything. Business won't do anything about it, so it's up to the government.

ROGER. You people still haven't changed your tune, have you? The government can solve everything. Only it can't.

LES. It can do a hell of a lot better than the businessman. They're part of the problem. All you have to do is look at American history. The founder of every great fortune was nothing more than a high-level white-collar crook.

ROGER. That's one man's opinion--and not a very well thought-out one, if I may say so. What if food prices do rise? Let poor people eat potatoes instead of asparagus tips.

LES. And cake instead of bread, right?

ROSE. If we left the running of the country to you people, the government would control everything.

LAUREL. And why not? The free-market system doesn't work at all.

ROGER. And our country would go down the drain. It wouldn't be any different from China.

LES. It's very possible to have political democracy and economic controls. Any dunce knows that.

ROGER. Hogwash!

MIDDLETON. (Hastily) How's the solar energy campaign coming along, Laurel?

LAUREL. Mostly we're concentrating on stopping the nuclear industry. I was in that demonstration at Exeter Plant Number Four last weekend and --

ROGER. I saw that on television. You mean to say you were with all those wild-eyed, screaming nuts with --

LAUREL. Those "nuts," as you call them, were deeply concerned people who care about the future of this country! They don't want the next generation to be a bunch of mutants!

ROSE. They looked to me like a bunch of mutants themselves!

LAUREL. Anyhow, even if the police did keep us from the plant, we destroyed hundreds of yards of fencing. It'll cost them a pretty penny to replace that!

ROGER. Laurel, the last poll I saw showed a majority of the public in favor of nuclear power. Don't you care about that?

LAUREL. Sometimes people don't know what's best for them. They have to be told.

ROGER. And you're the one to tell them, right?

LES. I think Laurel meant they have to be shown what's best for them.

ROSE. And you'll show them, right?

LES. Rose, I think you're choosing to misunderstand us.

ROGER. (Coldly) I think she understands you all too well.

MIDDLETON. (Hastily) Well, what's new around town?

ROSE. That's what brings us here, John. It seems the new element in town wants to put up street signs and we've got a petition to stop them.

LAUREL. What a coincidence. We're circulating a petition to get the signs put up.

ROGER. That figures.

LES. What's that supposed to mean?

ROGER. It's supposed to mean that you people are just the types who take particular delight in destroying traditions.

LES. Look, it's almost impossible for delivery men to find anybody's house.

LAUREL. Last week the UPS man drove around town for half an hour and finally called me from the post office because he couldn't deliver a package.

ROSE. Rolling Hills is over 90 years old. It has never had street signs and there's no need to have them now. That's part of the charm and uniqueness of the town.

LES. It may be unique, but it's hardly charming when nobody can find their way around.

ROGER. The residents can, and, as for the outsiders, let them work at it. They'll get where they want to go if they really care about getting there.

LAUREL. The whole system is a remnant of a time when people had all the leisure time in the world to waste. Life is different now.

ROGER. There's no reason not to hold onto things from the past that are gracious. But you people wouldn't understand about that.

LAUREL. Stop calling us "you people!"

LES. There's also no reason for holding onto something simply because it's part of the past.

ROGER. History is a kind of distillation process. What was no good in the past gets filtered out and what was good is left over and gets passed on to the present.

LES. What a taste for metaphor you have, Rog. (He turns to Middleton.) John, we need your signature on our petition and I know that, as a forward-looking person, you'll want to sign it. Do you have two minutes? (Middleton nods assent.) You just can't deny the inevitability of change! Right from the start philosophers were aware of that. Look at the ancient Greeks. (Looking resigned, Rose reaches into her purse and pulls out a jar of soap bubble mix and wand, while Roger reaches into his bag and pulls out three balls. Rose starts to blow bubbles and Roger starts to juggle the balls. They continue all the time Les is talking.) It all started with Thales. He said that water is the single elemental reality. But since earth and air and fire are obviously not water, the change of water into these other elements is implied.

MIDDLETON. Of course.

LES. But the most important early philosopher is Anaximander, because he was the first to ask how we can account for change. He said there was no single elemental reality and so we have to account for opposites. And that idea was expanded on by Anaximenes, who theorized that the world is constantly changing.

MIDDLETON. Right.

LAUREL. And then there was Heraclitus. He taught that the only unchanging thing in the world is change. What he said was, "You can't put your foot in the same river twice." He saw the world as the warring of opposites, which eventually combine to produce harmony. So the unity in the world results from a reconciliation of diversities. And, if that's the case, harmonies are constantly being created, so change has to be constant.

MIDDLETON. Obviously. (His chair starts to move slowly and imperceptibly toward the left.)

LES. And Plato said there are absolutes, like Absolute Truth and Absolute Justice, and that each developing thing starts from the original absolute and loses its perfection to the degree in which it changes and in which its similarity to the original decreases. You can see that the implication here is that change occurs steadily, with everything consistently moving away from the absolutes.

MIDDLETON. I see. (His chair continues to move left.)

LAUREL. Aristotle also taught that change is constant. He believed the final cause is the end toward which any movement aims. And this movement involves the actualization of some of the potentialities inherent in the essence of a thing. Thus the soul or nature of that thing is inherent in its principle of motion. So he also saw change as an inevitable part of existence.

MIDDLETON. M-hm. (His chair moves closer to the left.)

LES. But come closer to the present and consider the philosophy of Hegel. His theory of thesis, antithesis and synthesis implies constant motion and change. You start with the original situation, which he called the thesis, and the thesis turns into its opposite, which he called the antithesis, and then there evolves a sort of blending of the two, which he called the synthesis. For example, take the changes in France in the period from 1780 to 1810. First you have an absolute monarchy, then you have its antithesis, which is rule by the people, and then you have Napoleon, the synthesis, the man of the people who becomes an absolute monarch. And of course synthesis doesn't represent the end of a process, a final coming to rest, so to speak, because each synthesis in turn becomes a thesis, and the process begins all over again.

106

MIDDLETON. Yes, that's clear. (His chair continues to move to the left.)

LES. And, if you look at Eastern thought, change is basic to the thinking of Buddha. The central idea of Buddhism is that everything is constantly becoming. Nothing on earth has absolute unchanging reality. Buddha said, "Whatever is subject to origination is also subject to destruction." Everything that is born must die. A few things may last for many years and others for only a short time, but they are inexorably headed for their death. And there is never a time that is static, when becoming ends and being begins, for, at the very moment we develop a conception of something, it is changing to something else. At one and the same time everything is simultaneously being and becoming. So, for Buddha, change is the ultimate reality.

MIDDLETON. I see that.

LES. I could go on with yang and yin and with zen, but I think you get the picture. You see, even if the question of adding street signs seems trivial, it's a symptom of a bigger picture. You can't fight change, and that's that! (Roger stops juggling and Rose stops blowing bubbles. They put their equipment back into their bags.)

ROGER. Look, you'd have to be some kind of an imbecile to deny that there's such a thing as change. Of course I'm not trying to say that there is no change. What I'm talking about is the reason for change and the rate of change. The fact of the matter is that you can fight change, if only to slow it down--and it should be slowed down. John, there are lots of reckless people who want change just for the sake of change (He gives a significant look toward the Lawsons.)--I mention no names-- but that's a great danger, because change should come only after long and careful deliberation. (Les reaches into his bag and pulls out a paddle-ball set; he starts to bounce the ball. Laurel reaches into her bag and pulls out a yo-yo; she starts to play with it. Both continue with these activities while Roger and Rose are talking. John's chair starts to move slowly to the right.)

MIDDLETON. You have a point.

ROGER. You see, John, a lot of it boils down to how much faith you have in the common man's intelligence. I've got to say my faith in John Q. Public's brains is limited. And, since that's so, you've got to question his desire for change. I mean, isn't it better to stick with what all of society has evolved over generations of trial and error than to grab at something just because it's a novelty? After all, the cumulative wisdom of the past has to count for something, doesn't it?

MIDDLETON. It certainly does. (His chair continues to move to the right, slowly and imperceptibly.)

ROGER. So what we have to do is preserve and reform at the same time. We have to keep the useful parts of what precedent has established, then we have to compare the suggested change with what we already have and to consider all the possible expedients. On the one hand we want to avoid the kind of stubbornness that rejects anything new or improved, but on the other we can't let ourselves fall victim to the kind of frivolousness that would do away with everything as it now exists. And that means each change should take a long time. The operation of change has to be slow because we stand to lose so much by it, if we happen to be moving in the wrong direction. It's really our duty to be circumspect and cautious, since patience always achieves more than a sudden, forceful wrenching away of something, right?

MIDDLETON. Right. (His chair continues to move to the right.)

ROSE. If we take the time to examine every proposed change, we can see any possible evils in it and take care of them as they arise. We can reconcile, we can balance, we can compromise.

And that way we end up with a much better change, a change that is complex, because it combines the best of what is old with the best of what is new. That's why it's even better to have a change take place over a long period of time, so we can get the benefit of the wisdom of several generations.

MIDDLETON. M-hm.

ROGER. Listen, so often the people who advocate change do it because all they can see around them is vices and faults -- not that vices and faults don't exist -- I'd be the last one to deny that -- but there's an awful lot more to the world than that. And, because all they see is what's wrong with the world, they simply assume that anything would be an improvement over what we have. I mean, we don't have to be Pollyannas and go around saying, "God's in His heaven, all's right with the world," but we have to concede that plenty of what we have is good and is worth holding onto.

MIDDLETON. I'll agree with that. (His chair keeps moving.)

ROSE. And, even if things aren't perfect, sometimes it's better to accept them as they are than to bring about some change that only makes matters worse. So often people offer solutions that are no solutions at all because they insist on change and ignore reform. A change alters everything, but a reform is a sort of grafting on, so that the thing we are reforming isn't changed fundamentally. Every time we pick change over reform, we run the risk of disposing permanently of something good. Innovation and novelty are always dangerous, but reform is always safe. And basically that's why I'm against this adding of road signs to Rolling Hills. We have to do a great deal more thinking about it than we've done, because I'm not convinced that the so-called cure is better than the so-called disease. It's a radical change and I honestly don't think we need it! (She turns from John. Les and Laurel put the equipment they have been playing with back into their bags. Les reaches into his pocket and pulls out a piece of paper and a pen.)

LES. Well, John, you've heard the voice of reaction. Now you can sign the petition to put up street signs in good conscience. (John's chair moves slowly toward the center.)

ROGER. (Also pulls a piece of paper and a pen from his pocket.) And you've gotten all the arguments from the radicals, so you'll be glad to sign my petition to leave things the way they are. (John's chair continues to move toward the center.)

LAUREL. (She and Les walk toward John.) Don't join the fascists, please, John.

ROSE. (She and Roger walk toward John.) That's right, John. Join the communists instead.

LAUREL. Sure. March forward bravely into the past -- say, the 14th century.

ROSE. Be one of the wreckers and help pull down everything we've built up in the past.

MIDDLETON. (Amiably, holding his hand up, palm out) Look, folks, don't press me. On the one hand, I think there's a lot to be said for putting up street signs, but, on the other hand, there's just as much to be said for not having them.

LAUREL. The only reason not to have them is that people are in love with the past and afraid of the future!

ROSE. And the only reason to have them is that some kooks want change just for the sake of change.

LES. Don't call us "kooks," you wacko!

ROGER. Watch your step, Les. Don't call my wife a "wacko!"

LES. (With exaggerated politeness) Oh, I am sorry. I meant the term to include you, too.

MIDDLETON. Just a minute, gang. Let's don't get bitter about this thing. Les and Laurel, your arguments are very convincing and, Rose and Roger, what you have to say is just as persuasive.

LAUREL. But you can't agree with us and with them, too. John, you certainly don't want to be tarred with the brush of the radical right.

ROSE. Or with the brush of the nut left either!

(The next four speeches are delivered simultaneously.

LES. John, you can't hold back progress. Look, if we hadn't fought for our independence, we'd still be a British colony today. And, if the French hadn't had their revolution, they'd still be bowing down to some successor to Louis XIV. And, if the British hadn't beheaded Charles I, they'd still have a rubber-stamp parliament and be taking their orders from the throne. And if Luther hadn't challenged the power of the papacy, we'd still all be under the thumb of the clergy. So, you see, we simply can't stand still!

LAUREL. You can't turn back the clock, John. If there hadn't been change) we might still be living in the trees or hiding out in caves and eating our meat raw. Or we might all be in mud huts in the Tigris--Euphrates Valley. And we'd be wearing bearskins and getting our wheat by throwing it up in the air and letting the chaff blow away. Or we might not even have bread. We might be moving things by sliding them along the ground because we didn't have the wheel. Change is progress, John!

ROGER. John, abrupt changes are simply no good. Look at what happened in France. Oh, I'll admit that the masses didn't have much of a look-in under the kings. But, when the radicals took over, you had the Terror and Robespierre and you had the gutters running red with blood. And then along came Napoleon and millions more Frenchmen died fighting for some empty dream. All because people didn't have the patience to wait and work out some kind of a compromise and maybe end up with a constitutional monarchy that would have given them democracy anyway.

ROSE. You have to be careful with change, John. Take Russia, for instance. The communists took over with all sorts of talk about ending tyranny and then they established a tyranny ten times worse. They put millions of people in labor camps to work themselves to death and, when they decided to start the collective farms, they forced millions of peasants to starve because they wouldn't cooperate. So obviously the country would have been better off without change. And so would the world, since we wouldn't be facing the threat of an invasion by Godless hordes of Reds!

LAUREL. "Godless hordes of Reds!" Jesus!

MIDDLETON. Look, everybody, you're all right. (To the Ransoms) What you say is credible and (To the Lawsons) what you say is plausible, too. And, when it comes down to the specific issue, I can't really make up my mind.

LES. (Angrily) John, you have to decide!

ROGER. (Also angrily) That's right! You must take a stand!

MIDDLETON. But --

LES. Either you sign our petition or you sign theirs.

ROGER. Yeah! Pick one side or the other!

MIDDLETON. No, I honestly don't want to. (At this, Les, Laurel, Roger and Rose all run to their bags. Each pulls out a revolver and they all shoot John, who slumps over dead in his chair. They then put their guns back into their bags, pick up the bags and head for the door.)

LES. Wishy-washy S.O.B.!

ROGER. Absolutely gutless.

LAUREL. If there's one thing I hate it's somebody without principles.

ROSE. And somebody who refuses to stand up and be counted.

LES AND ROGER. (As they reach the door, they are the last to exit.) There's no doubt about it. The world's a better place without people like that. (They exit.)

Curtain

GIFT OF TONGUES

Being a cursory examination
of the contemporary condition of
the language which produced
Shakespearean dramaturgy
Miltonic versification
and Keatsean lyricism

CURTAIN GOING UP

CAST OF CHARACTERS

Bartender

Chuck

Buck

The scene is a barroom on West 23rd Street in Manhattan, near the waterfront.

The time is the present.

AT RISE: The bar runs from upstage left to downstage right. The bartender stands behind the bar upstage of the two men seated at the bar. Chuck sits upstage left of Buck. There is a door stage right.

CHUCK. So I says, "Don't fuck me around, 'cause you fuck wit' me, you're fuckin' well gonna get fucked!"

BARTENDER. Fuckin' aye!

CHUCK. Yeah! "Fuck around wit' me, an' I'll fix your fuckin' wagon!"

BARTENDER. I guess you fuckin' told 'im!

CHUCK. You bet your fuckin' ass I did! "You fuck wit' me an' I'll wipe up the fuckin' floor witchez," I says.

BARTENDER. Fuckin' right!

CHUCK. "So, fuck off, you little fucker!" I says.

BARTENDER. An' he fuckin' split?

CHUCK. He took off from that fuckin' bar like a fuckin' shot!

BUCK. (Rousing himself from his stupor) Hey, gimme a fuckin' beer, will ya?

BARTENDER. Mm. (He pulls out a bottle of beer, uncaps it and slams it onto the bar.)

BUCK. Hey, man, watch the fuckin' bottle! Fuckin' beer's gonna have a fuckin' head a mile high!

BARTENDER. OK, OK. Don't getcher fuckin' balls in a fuckin' uproar!

BUCK. It's just I don't want no fuckin' head on my fuckin' beer, man! I can drink fuckin' beer all fuckin' night, but, I got a fuckin' head on it, I'm all fucked up the next day, ya know?

BARTENDER. Yeah. Fuckin' head'll do it to ya every fuckin' time.

BUCK. Yeah.

CHUCK. Ah, that's fuckin' bullshit!

BUCK. Whadju say, pal?

CHUCK. I said, "That's fuckin' bullshit!" It's all fuckin' beer!

BUCK. It's all fuckin' beer, butcha get that fuckin' air in it, it'll fuck ya up every time!

CHUCK. Fuckin' head on a fuckin' beer don' t fuck me up.

BUCK. It sure as shit fucks me up.

CHUCK. I'd rather drink fuckin' whiskey anyway.

BUCK. Not me. Fuckin' stuff gives me a fuckin' hangover like you wouldn't fuckin' believe!

BARTENDER. It's crazy, ya know. Fuckin' whiskey fucks some guys up and it don't fuck other guys up. Fuckin' crazy.

CHUCK. It's a fuckin' crazy world, pal. Like that fuckin' guy I'ze tellin' him. (He gestures toward the bartender with his thumb and keeps talking to Buck.) See, I'm sittin' in a fuckin' bar down on fuckin' 12th an' I'm watchin' the fuckin' ballgame an' after them fuckin' Mets lose, we start talkin' and this fucker says to me, "You know you smoked ten fuckin' cigarettes in two fuckin' hours?" "So, what the fuck?" I says. "You're gonna fuckin' roon your fuckin' lungs," he says. "So? They're my fuckin' lungs," I says. "Ya know," he says, "I c'n fuckin' hypmatize you so you'll never fuckin' smoke again." "Fuck off!" I says. "Whyncha give it a fuckin' try?" he says. Then he picks up his fuckin' glass an' he starts, like, movin' it around in a fuckin' circle an he says, "Now, look in the middle of the fuckin' glass," an' I look an' the fuckin' beer is goin' around an' I'm gettin' fuckin' dizzy an' all of a sudden I fuckin' snap out of it an' I look at this fucker an' I says, "What the fuck kinda bullshit is this? What the fuck you tryna do anyhow?" So he says, "You're all fucked up wit' smokin' an' I'm gonna fuckin' help ya." So I says, "Go peddle ya fuckin' papers, bub. Go fuck wit' somebody else!"

BARTENDER. Sounsa me like he was the one was all fucked up.

CHUCK. Fuckin' aye! "You're the one's all fucked up," I says, "so don't go fuckin' tellin' me I'm all fucked up!"

BARTENDER. Fuckin' queer!

BUCK. Fuckin' faggot!

CHUCK. "Ain't no fuckin' nut gonna fuck me around," I says. "Fuck around wit' me and I'll fuckin' fix your fuckin' wagon!" That's what I fuckin' told 'im!

BUCK. (Shaking his head) World's full a fuckin' crackpots!

CHUCK. You c'n fuckin' say that again! (To the bartender) Gimme a fuckin' drink. (The bartender does so, pouring a shot with a water chaser.)

BUCK. I dunno. Fuckin' kids goin' crazy, fuckin' broads goin' crazy--

CHUCK. My fuckin' kids and my fuckin' old lady ain't goin' fuckin' crazy! They better fuckin' shape up or fuckin' ship out! That's what I fuckin' tell 'em! "Don't fuck wit' me," I tell 'em. "Shape up or ship out!"

BUCK. 'Atsa way to run a fuckin' family! Start lettin' 'em fuck around witchez an' all they do is fuck around witchez.

CHUCK. (Abstractedly) Yeah. (He drains his drink.) Reminds me, I gotta fuckin' get goin'. (He slides off his barstool.) Told my old lady I'd put in a fuckin' washer. (He picks up his change.) An' if I don't fix the fuckin' thing all I'll get is fuckin' pissin' an' moanin' all fuckin' week! (He heads for the door.) If it ain't one fuckin' thing it's somepn else! (As he exits) Some fuckin' world!

BUCK. (To the bartender) Yeah. I better fuckin' take off, too. (He slides off his barstool.) Gotta keep peace in the fuckin' family, right?

BARTENDER. (He picks up a glass and polishes it with his rather dirty on.) Take it easy!

BUCK. (Moving to the door) I'll take it any fuckin' way I can get it! (He exits.)

BARTENDER. (He takes the beer and the glass from the bars looks at his watch, rinses glasses, puts them down to drain and looks at his watch again.) What the fuck! (He goes over to the door, turns the lock in it, turns off the main lighting and heads back toward the bar.) Fuck it!

Curtain.

DOWN HOME

CAST OF CHARACTERS

A woman

A man

The scene is the front porch of a house in a small Middle Western town.

(A middle-aged woman and a middle-aged man sit in rocking chairs on a front porch. The actors wear pepper and salt wigs to indicate middle age.)

WOMAN. Quite a wind tonight.

MAN. But not too cold.

WOMAN. The sun's very red.

MAN. Good, "Red sky in the morning is a sailor' s warning, Red sky at night is a sailor's delight."

WOMAN. Right. Radio says it'll get up to about 70 tomorrow.

MAN. Yeah. That's what the paper says, too.

WOMAN. So we should have a good day.

MAN. M-hm.

WOMAN. Yessir, a good day. (Waving to someone passing by.) Hi, Lucy!

MAN. (Saluting the passing woman) Lucy.

WOMAN. What a nice girl.

MAN. Hmph.

WOMAN. What do you mean by that?

MAN. By what?

WOMAN. By "hmph."

MAN. Just what I said.

WOMAN. You don' t think Lucy's a nice girl?

MAN. Oh, she's nice all right, but not the way you mean.

WOMAN. Oh, you men! You're all the same.

MAN. Boys down at the Rendezvous say she's no better'n she should be.

WOMAN. I don't believe it!

MAN. She did go out with Tony Crawford, you know,

WOMAN. I know.

MAN. Well?

WOMAN. Well what?

MAN. You know his reputation. He wouldn't go out with a girl five minutes if he didn't get what he wanted from her.

WOMAN. That's what they say. But I don't believe it. He's always nice as pie whenever he meets me.

MAN. Maybe he's got his eye on you.

WOMAN. Oh, Duane, really!

MAN. Yup, that must be it.

WOMAN. (Smiling) Honestly!

MAN. Anyhow, he's quite a feller with the ladies.

WOMAN. So I've heard.

MAN. And that means he didn't go out with Lucy Sherman because he likes her smile. No, siree.

WOMAN. I think she's the exception that proves the rule.

MAN. Some exception!

WOMAN. Huh?

MAN. Remember how she went away for a week after her 'n' Tony broke up? I always thought she went to get an abortion.

WOMAN. Duane! What a thing to say!

MAN. That's what I think, anyway.

WOMAN. A nice girl like that? She wouldn't do that!

MAN. You mean she'd have the illegitimate kid?

WOMAN. No. I mean she'd never get in trouble in the first place.

MAN. Hmph.

WOMAN. Well, I don't think she would. She's a nice, kind, sweet girl.

MAN. M-hm.

WOMAN. And her parents are goods decent, God-fearing people.

MAN. M-hm.

WOMAN. Why, I'll bet they haven't missed a Sunday in church in twenty years.

MAN. M-hm.

WOMAN. Why, they're as regular as the minister.

MAN. M-hm.

WOMAN. Duane, you're just terrible! I mean it.

(The lights go out for seven seconds. The couple continue to rock. When the lights come back on, the couple are minus their pepper-and-salt wigs. They now appear to be in their late twenties or early thirties.)

MAN. Nip in the air.
WOMAN. Sure is. Winter'll be here before we know it.
MAN. Not too many out today.
WOMAN. No. It's a bit chilly for taking a walk.
MAN. Want to go inside?
WOMAN. Let's stay out for a while. I'm not cold.
MAN. OK.
WOMAN. Besides, I'm thinking of all those dishes I've got waiting in the kitchen.
MAN. And I'm thinking of all those storm windows down cellar that've got to be washed.
WOMAN. You cold?
MAN. Nope. I'm fine.
WOMAN. (After a pause) There's Billy Barton. Hello, Billy!
MAN. (waves.)
WOMAN. What a cute little feller.
MAN. How old's he now?
WOMAN. He must be about eight. (Musing) Wish we had one like him.
MAN. Well, it's not for want of trying. (Pause) Matter of fact, if you want to try again right now--
WOMAN. Duane!
MAN. I don't know why you always got so huffy about--
WOMAN. If I've told you once, I've told you a thousand times: I like to do it, but I don't like to talk about it. It's indecent!

MAN. If I live to be a million I'll never understand women. I swear, I--

WOMAN. Oh, look at that! He almost rode his bike right through my petunias! (Raising her voice) Billy, don't ride through my garden, all right?

MAN. Hey, did you see his arm? Those are some bruises!

WOMAN. Yes. They're really purple.

MAN. Seems as if that kid's always banged up.

WOMAN. Last month, when he had that black eye, I asked him about it. He said he fell off his bike. He said he's always doing that.

MAN. Look at him on that thing! He rides it like he was born on it. I can't believe he's always flopping off it all the time.

WOMAN. It is funny. I never thought of that.

MAN. You know what I think. I think Bill is beating on little Billy. He's got a vile temper, you know.

WOMAN. Oh, I just can't believe that about Bill!

MAN. He's pretty quick with his fists down at the Rendezvous. When he's got a few drinks in him, there's not many want to get into an argument with him.

WOMAN. No, he wouldn't hit little Billy. Why, that child is the most quiet, shy, nervous little boy. I don't imagine he ever gets into any real trouble.

MAN. Who says he has to get into trouble? If Bill's looking for someone to beat up on, he doesn't need an excuse.

WOMAN. I don't believe it, that's all. Bill's a hard-working man and a good provider and he's got a lovely family. He simply wouldn't do a thing like that!

MAN. Hm.

WOMAN. I don't know why you always seem to think the worst about everybody.

MAN. Hmph.

WOMAN. Well, it's true. You do, and I think it's too bad.

(The lights go out for seven seconds. The couple continue rocking. When the lights come up, the couple are wearing white wigs and granny glasses. Their rocking slows.)

WOMAN. There's Prince.

MAN. Uh-huh.

WOMAN. (Raising her voice) Hello, Prince! Here, Prince! Here, Prince!

MAN. What're you calling him over for? You're always yelling that he does his duty all over our front lawn.

WOMAN. Duane!

MAN. Well, you are!

WOMAN. Oh, he's such a cute little dog, and he's so friendly.

MAN. Ask little Barby Chalmers if he' s so friendly. He took quite a chomp out of her. She's scared to death of him.

WOMAN. Oh, she must've been teasing him or something. Those kids are always teasing that dog.

MAN. Sure.

WOMAN. They are! It just makes me sick. A few more years and they'll be just like those doctors in my vivisection magazine, torturing animals for no good reason.

MAN. I expect they're trying to find out something.

WOMAN. That's the excuse they give, but I think they do it because they like it.

MAN. Now, Geneva.

WOMAN. They must. What normal person could bring themselves to torture little dogs and cats and rabbits and guinea pigs? They're fiends, is what they are!

MAN. Don't you think they ever got anything out of it?

WOMAN. I don't care if they did! They're fiends! When I'm reading about what they do, all I can think about is Snoopy and Peter Rabbit. I think they're barbarians!

MAN. I bet some diseases 've been cured because of stuff they found out.

WOMAN. I don't believe it and, even if they have, it isn't worth it.

MAN. Well, that's all besides the point, anyhow. The important thing is keeping that damn Prince from leaving doggie-do all over our lawn.

WOMAN. I have to say I wish he went someplace else.

MAN. Lucy should have trained him better.

WOMAN. Lucy's had a hard life.

MAN. That's still no reason she can't train her dog.

WOMAN. I mean, with the illegitimate child and all-- not that I don't think little Phil's as cute as a bug's ear. He's just the sweetest boy you could ever want to meet!

MAN. Yeah. He's a nice kid.

WOMAN. Who ever would have thought Lucy would have a baby that way--and her so nice and all.

MAN. After God knows how many abortions, I'd've thought she knew how to get rid of it!

WOMAN. Duane! You're too much!

MAN. It's true. I counted three times she went out of town after she broke up with different fellers. Let's see-- there was Tony Crawford-- and Mario Cimaglia-- and, uh, Marty O'Sullivan. If not more.

WOMAN. And they say women are the gossips! Why, I'd forgotten all about Marty O'Sullivan.

MAN. Why, she had a regular UN going! (He chuckles.)

WOMAN. Honestly! Have a little charity!

MAN. I've got lots of charity. I'm only mad 'cause I didn't get in on it!

WOMAN. Hmph!

MAN. Course, I'm not even sure those three guys were responsible for the abortions. I always remember something I read in a book once. Feller says, "If you get chewed up by a buzz-saw, how you gonna tell which tooth did the cutting first?"

WOMAN. That's just being mean to poor Lucy.

MAN. I'm not being mean. Like I said, I'm just being envious.

WOMAN. I'd think you'd've outgrown that by now.

MAN. Geneva, there are some things a man never outgrows.

(The lights go out for seven seconds, As they come up, the couple are now wearing their pepper-and-salt wigs.)

WOMAN. Paper's not here yet.

MAN. Paper's never here on time.

WOMAN. It's just as well. Probably nothing but a bunch of murders and killings and fires and stuff like that.

MAN. Things like that go on.

WOMAN. I know, but I get tired of reading about them. I'd like to read about something good for a change,

MAN. Then you don't really care about not getting the paper.

WOMAN. Sure I do, I want to read some of the news.

MAN. (Snorting) Bake sales.

WOMAN. No, not bake sales. Engagements and weddings and obituaries. The important things.

MAN. If the paper doesn't get here you can forget about it all.

WOMAN. It'll get here sooner or later.

MAN. I don't know what's the matter with that Jackie.

WOMAN. I don't think his parents make him toe the line very much.

MAN. It's funny, After the bringing up Billy Barton got, you'd think he'd know how to make a kid behave.

WOMAN. Why, Duane, what an awful thing to say!

MAN. Oh, I was only joking, Geneva.

WOMAN. It's nothing to joke about. I'll never forget when Billy got his broken arm and Dr. Malcolm brought charges against Bill for child abuse! That poor little boy!

MAN. Well, you can't say I didn't tell you. (Smugly) I knew it all the time.

WOMAN. You just guessed right.

MAN. No, I knew it. (Pause)

WOMAN. There are the Travers girls. (She waves and raises her voice.) Hello, girls!

MAN. (Waving) Girls.

WOMAN. Nice girls.

MAN. If you ask me, they're real odd, You never see them with anybody else. Always just with each other.

WOMAN. It's nice for sisters to be close.

MAN. And I never see them with a boy. Do they ever date?

WOMAN. I'm sure I don't know.

MAN. It's funny. I mean, they're all pretty. You'd think the boys'd be around 'em like bees around honeysuckle.

WOMAN. Maybe they haven't got time for all that nonsense.

MAN. Most girls seem to have plenty of time for that nonsense. That whole family is odd. Joe Travers keeps himself to himself like nobody else I ever saw. Hardly get the time of day out of him.

WOMAN. Man's got a right to keep his private life private, if you ask me.

MAN. Not as private as Joe does. You got to do a little to get along with other people.

WOMAN. M-hm.

MAN. I'd hate to tell you what I think is going on between Joe and his girls.

WOMAN. (Genuinely shocked) Oh. Duane, that's a terrible thing to say! You mean you think-- Oh, that's too awful!

MAN. I wouldn't be surprised.

WOMAN. Well, I would! I can't imagine anything like that in this town. This is a nice town with nice people and nice people don't do things like that.

MAN. Who knows what goes on behind the scenes?

WOMAN. Certainly not stuff like that!

MAN. Hmph.
WOMAN. You'd never get me to believe it.
MAN. Don't believe it, then.
WOMAN. Don't worry. I won't.

(The lights go out for seven seconds. When they come on, the couple are in their late twenties again.)

MAN. Awful day!
WOMAN. It sure was hot.
MAN. Six days in a row over 90! 1 don't know how much longer we can take it!
WOMAN. As long as we have to.
MAN. Thank the Lord we have air conditioning in the store. Otherwise you couldn't stand it.
WOMAN. And thank the Lord we have the second-floor porch. At least a person can sleep at night.
MAN. Maybe the heat'll break soon.
WOMAN. I sure hope so.
MAN. It better. (Pause) I suppose it was because of the heat the garbage didn't get picked up.
W0MAN. I imagine so.
MAN. They've got their nerve! That's about the third time this month they've missed.
WOMAN. Second.
MAN. Whatever. The point is, with the taxes we pay, they shouldn't ever miss!
WOMAN. Uh-huh.
MAN. I mean it, Geneva.
WOMAN. Oh, of course, you're right. Probably they'll come and get it tomorrow,
MAN. They'd better. (Pause)

WOMAN. There's Millie and Mary. (Raising her voice, waving) Hi there!

MAN. (Waves perfunctorily to them.)

WOMAN. Nice women.

MAN. M-hm.

WOMAN. I've never forgotten how they took care of the Malcolms' kids after Doc and his wife got hurt in that car accident.

MAN. Why not? Millie's Dr. Malcolm's nurse.

WOMAN. Even so, she didn't have to do it. And Mary certainly had no reason to pitch in. I think it was very nice of them.

MAN. M-hm.

WOMAN. They're real good Samaritans.

MAN. M-hm.

WOMAN. And when old Mrs. Sutter broke her hip, they were over there every day taking her food. Why Mary even scrubbed the kitchen floor for her!

MAN. M-hm.

WOMAN. You don't seem to have much to say about them.

MAN. Nope.

WOMAN, I suppose you've got your usual evil thoughts about them.

MAN. What's that supposed to mean?

WOMAN. Just what I said.

MAN. Hmph.

WOMAN. So, what do you think?

MAN. About Millie and Mary?

WOMAN. Yes .

MAN. Well, if you want the truth, I think they're a pair of lezzies.

WOMAN. Oh. Duane!

MAN. You asked me what I think and that's what I think.

WOMAN. But why, Duane?

MAN. They've neither of them ever married and they've lived

together for years, Why, they moved in together when I was just a kid. I'll bet they've been together 20 years.

WOMAN. I don't know what that proves. Just because two women live in the same house doesn't mean anything. And they're so nice, like I said.

MAN. Where there's smoke, there's fire.

WOMAN. You're just impossible, that's what you are!

(The lights go out for seven seconds. When they come on, the couple are in their pepper-and-salt wigs.)

MAN. (Belches.)

WOMAN. Duane! Don't be vulgar.

MAN. It's that damned liver and onions we had for supper. You know I hate liver. I don't know why you're always giving it to me.

WOMAN. I'm not "always" giving it to you. Besides, it's got lots of iron in it. It's good for your blood.

MAN. I'd rather have lousy blood and do without the liver. (Belches again.)

WOMAN. Really!

MAN. I've been trying to tell you for years-- I'm a steak-and-potatoes man.

WOMAN. If you came down to the supermarket with me and saw what they're getting for steak, you wouldn't be a steak-and-potatoes man for long.

MAN. Then make it hamburger and potatoes, Just no more liver.

WOMAN. Look, there's Millie. (Raising her voice) Hi, Millie!

MAN. Millie.

WOMAN. Well, will you look at that! She didn't even wave!

MAN. Didn't even look up.

WOMAN. There's something the matter with her.

MAN. She hasn't been herself since Mary left town.

WOMAN. You're right.

MAN. Took the starch right out of her.

WOMAN. It's true. She just lost all her vim and vigor.

MAN. Bears out what I always said.

WOMAN. I don't like to admit it, but I think you may have been right.

MAN. Course I was. There was something between those two.

WOMAN. I wouldn't be surprised. If they'd only been friends, I can't see how Millie would've taken it so hard.

MAN. They weren't just friends.

WOMAN. Mmm.

MAN. And you thought I was full of beans when I told you what I thought about them.

WOMAN. I know I did, but--

MAN. No excuses. I was right and you were wrong.

WOMAN. I guess you were.

MAN. Let that be a lesson to you.

WOMAN. Hmph!

MAN. (After a pause) Beautiful evening.

WOMAN. Real nice.

MAN. We're s'posed to get rain tomorrow.

WOMAN. Doesn't look like it now.

MAN. That's what the paper said.

WOMAN. Must be right, then.

MAN. Oh, they're wrong sometimes.

WOMAN. Look, there's Earl Martin!

MAN. Imagine that! Him walking! Wonder where the Cadillac is.

WOMAN. Must be in the garage. I mean, getting repaired.

MAN. Must be. You just never see him walking.

WOMAN. I wonder where he gets the money. To own a Cadillac, I mean. His salary can't be all that much.

MAN. I wouldn't be at all surprised to hear he was dipping into the till.

WOMAN. Why, that's awful! The Martins are real pillars of the community. He wouldn't do anything like that!

MAN. Wouldn't he?

WOMAN. Of course not! Why, he's got his position as a community leader to think about! He's been the head of the United Fund Drive for years, and he's on the board of the Cancer Society and the Heart Fund and--

MAN. And that doesn't mean he couldn't dip into the till?

WOMAN. Of course it doesn't, but he works at the bank!

MAN. And that makes him something sacred?

WOMAN. No, but-- Bankers can't get away with that, can they? I mean, don't they have auditors coming around all the time to go over their books?

MAN. He's an accountant. He might know a few tricks.

WOMAN. I think it's just preposterous, that's what I think! Imagine—Mr. Martin!

MAN. Just wait and see, that's all I can say. Just wait and see.

(The lights go out for seven seconds. When they come up, the actors are wearing white wigs and granny glasses.)

WOMAN. I just can't believe she's gone.

MAN. She's gone, all right.

WOMAN. And the funeral's tomorrow?

MAN. That's right. Two o'clock.

WOMAN. She was a fine, Christian woman.

MAN. So she was.

'WOMAN. Practically a saint.

MAN. M-hm.

WOMAN. I don't know any woman had to put up with what she did.

MAN. She had a rough life, all right.

WOMAN. I'll never forget when Joe Travers shot himself. What a shock!

MAN. It sure was.

WOMAN. And that note he left, saying he'd been carrying on with his own daughters! It was awful.

MAN. It was awful, all right.

WOMAN. I remember like it was yesterday.

MAN. Mmm.

WOMAN. But Judith just went right on.

MAN. She was a strong woman, all right.

WOMAN. I don't know how she did it.

MAN. Pure guts, that's all.

WOMAN. I mean, with everybody in town talking, and all.

MAN. Yeah, there sure was a lot of talk.

WOMAN. And then the girls leaving town.

MAN. She had a lot of tragedy.

WOMAN. I wonder what ever happened to the girls.

MAN. Nobody ever heard a word from them after they left.

WOMAN. Maybe Judith did. But I never had the courage to ask her.

MAN. I don't blame you.

WOMAN. She had a terrible life

MAN. She sure did. (Pause) But you can't say I didn't warn you.

WOMAN. So you did.

MAN. I always thought there was something real odd about Joe and those girls,

W0MAN. I remember.

MAN. Yep. I told you so.

WOMAN. M-hm. (Pause) My, it's been quite a month for funerals. First old Mrs. Tregaskis and then Earl Martin and now Judith Travers.

MAN. I guess when you get to our age you notice them more. There's always been plenty of funerals.

WOMAN. Poor Earl Martin.

MAN. *Poor* Earl Martin?

WOMAN. Well, there was hardly anybody at his funeral.

MAN. That crook! No wonder there was nobody there to give him a sendoff.

WOMAN. Now, now, Duane. Say nothing but good of the dead.

MAN. The trouble is, there's nothing good to say about him.

WOMAN. Oh, Duane.

MAN. I always knew he was juggling the books and when they caught him it did my heart good. Imagine, $300,000!

WOMAN. But he spent five years in prison, Duane.

MAN. Not half long enough. They should have let him rot!

WOMAN. He paid his debt to society.

MAN. Hmph! I always know he was a crook. If I told you once, I told you a dozen times that he was dipping into the till.

WOMAN. Oh, Duane, sometimes you make me sick! You always think the worst about everybody!

MAN. And who's right all the time?

WOMAN. Oh, I'll admit you're right more often than not, but even so--

MAN. The important thing is that I'm right.

WOMAN. The important thing is that you have a horrible picture of human nature.

MAN. No matter where you live, you live in a world full of people.

WOMAN. Well, I don't like the way you see people.

MAN. That's your business. I'd rather see them my way, not through any rose-colored glasses.

WOMAN. Well, I think I'd just rather be wrong, thank you.

Blackout.

CURTAIN GOING UP

THE WILD WEST — A LIBERATED LOOK

CAST OF CHARACTERS

BIG MAMA MAYBERRY: A gunslinger known throughout the West, SHE is in her forties and no longer svelte. SHE wears a Western-style hat and shirt, Levi's, boots and two guns.

BLACK BARB: A cowhand, SHE is about twenty-five, lean and is a straightforward, candid person. SHE wears a Western-style hat and shirt, Levi's, boots and two guns.

SAL: bartender, anywhere between twenty and fifty. SHE wears a white apron, Levi's and boots.

RANDY: A male dancer, HE is about twenty-five and has no effeminate mannerisms. HE wears a white formal collar with a black bow tie, no shirt, black pants and black socks. HE is a male sex object and is handsome and well built.

ONE-GUN WANDA: About twenty-five or thirty years old, SHE is distant and dour. SHE wears a Western-.style hat and shirt, Levi's, boots and one gun.

BEV BARTON: A cattle rancher, SHE is between thirty-five and forty-five and is used to having power. SHE wears a Western-style hat and shirt, Levi's, boots and two guns.

HEATHER HARPER: A townswoman, soft-spoken but inwardly tough. SHE is about thirty to thirty-five. SHE wears a Western-style hat and shirt, Levi's, boots and two guns.

THE WILD WEST — A LIBERATED LOOK

SCENE

The Frisky Filly Saloon in Tumbleweed Flats, somewhere west of the Pecos.

Time: 1880.

SETTING: We are in the Frisky Filly Saloon in the Old West. Upstage right is the bar with three barstools in front of it; downstage left are a table and two chairs.

AT RISE: It is mid-afternoon. BIG MAMA is at the bar, sipping a Brandy Alexander. BLACK BARB is also at the bar, sipping a White Russian. SAL is behind the bar, cleaning glasses.

BIG MAMA. So I says to her, I says, "You may be the fastes' gun west a the Pecos, but you're up agin Big Mama Mayberry now." Yup, that's what I said: "You're up agin Big Mama now." (sips) Yeah, that's what I tole her: "Yore takin' on Big Mama."

BLACK BARB. (Who has evidently heard this anecdote dozens of times and is very bored) Right, Big Mama.

BIG MAMA. So then I says, "Yore gonna hafta slap leather if yore aimin' ta prove yore better 'n Big Mama." That's jes what I tole her: "Yore gonna hafta slap leather." Them was my exact words: "Slap leather." (Sips)So she went fer her guns an' afore her hands was even below her belt I plugged her twice. She was dead afore she hit the floor. Yup, she was dead. Dead as a doornail.

BLACK BARB. I shore don't envy you, Big Mama. In yore day you may have been the fastes' gun in Deadwood and Tombstone and Graveyard Gulch, but now every gal in the West is out to make a name for herself by gettin' you.

BIG MAMA. I know. (Sips) I know that better 'n anyone. An' I know someday some gal is a-gonna come along that can out-draw me, an' I'll end up on Boot Hill. Yup, that's where I'll fin-ish--on Boot Hill.

(RANDY enters and sits alone at the table downstage left)

BIG MAMA (Continued) Shore, I know some dirty sidewinder is gonna put me in Boot Hill.

BLACK BARB. Watch your tongue, Big Mama. Randy jes came in.

BIG MAMA. (Tipping her hat to Randy and looking apologetic) Sorry, Randy. Didn't realize there was a gentleman present.

RANDY. (Waving and shaking his head) That's OK, Big Mama. Don't worry about it. I hear plenty of rough talk here in the Frisky Filly.

BIG MAMA. (Downing her drink and slamming the glass on the bar) Gimme another, Sal!

SAL. Do you think you oughta have another, Big Mama? I mean four Brandy Alexanders is a lot a Brandy Alexanders.

BIG MAMA. Gol-ding it, I said, "Gimme another" an' I meant it! Now, gimme another!

SAL. (Frightened) Sure, Big Mama! Sure! Comin' right up.

BLACK BARB. And while you're at it, fix me up another White Russian and draw a beer for Randy here. (SHE walks over to the table and sits down)How ya doin', Randy?

RANDY. (Flatly) OK, I reckon.

BLACK BARB. Like workin' here at the Frisky Filly?

RANDY. It's a living.

BLACK BARB. Know whatcha mean. I s'pose it can't be too much fun havin' ta dance with every gal that buys you a drink.

RANDY. It's OK.

(SAL brings over their drinks. HE raises his stein to Black Barb.)

RANDY (Continued) Thanks, Black Barb. (Beat) After all, a man' s gotta do what a man' s gotta do.

BLACK BARB. (Sips her drink, then pauses, looking directly at him) It ain't none a my business, Randy, but how come a nice guy like you got into a business like this?

RANDY. Oh, it's a long story, Barb, and I'll bet you've heard it a dozen times before.

BLACK BARB. Go ahead. Try me.

RANDY. Well, it all started back East. I grew up in a little town in New Jersey called Minnewasa. My pop ran a hardware store-- Krumbein's Hardware. I went to high school and afterwards I went to Pine Barrens State College and I was studying to be a social worker. (He sips his beer) And then I met a girl-- Daphne. She was wonderful! Well, to make a long story short, she led me on. She made me think she wanted to get married, and then she left me--just like that! I finished college, but I wasn't much interested. She just took the heart right out of me.

BLACK BARB. I know.

RANDY. So, when I graduated, I figured I needed a change of scene. I moved to Dodge City, but there wasn't much call for social workers there. So I started hanging around the bars and then I met Diana--she was great! That's what I thought, any- way. See, I thought she liked me as a person. Then I started hinting around about getting married, and she just laughed in my face. Told me all she cared about (He casts his eyes down.) was the -- the physical side of our relationship. Then she took off.

BLACK BARB. You shore ain't lucky in love.

RANDY. So I came out here to Tumbleweed Flats.

BLACK BARB. They shore as shootin' don't need no social work- ers out here. Just cowhands.

RANDY. I know. But maybe society here will change and I can start helping people.

BLACK BARB. (Dubiously) Mebbe.

RANDY. See, I've got this dream, I want to find people with some impairment and help them find pairment.

BLACK BARB. Huh?

RANDY. (Carried away) I hope to see people who are running their lives ineptly and help them run their lives eptly.

BLACK BARB. Yeah.

(BEV BARTON enters left, greeting BIG MAMA and SAL and taking a seat at the bar)

RANDY. I dream of counseling people who are disgruntled and making them gruntled.

BLACK BARB. Uh-huh. (Very bored by now)

RANDY. I want to meet people whose ideas--

BLACK BARB. (Talking over him as SHE rises) I see Miz Barton just came in. I gotta talk ta her. (She goes to the bar and stands next to BEV's stool.)

RANDY. (Trailing off) --are inane and teach them to have ideas that are -- Oh, what's the use? (HE drinks his beer)

BLACK BARB. Howdy, Miz Barton. How are things at the 'Circle Bar Triangle Double B Flying W Reverse F Lazy S Ranch?

BEV. Howdy, Black Barb. We jes finished brandin' the dogies.

BLACK BARB. Big job.

BEV. Yup. Quite a lot of 'em's feelin' porely. Got second-degree burns and kinda draggin' around.

BLACK BARB. Mebbe if yore ranch didn't have such a long name--

BEV. Mebbe.

SAL. The usual, Miz Barton?

BEV. Right. (Waving) An' set 'em up fer the house.

SAL. Comin' up.

RANDY. (Rising) Thanks all the same, Miz Barton, but I'll skip this one. I'm gonna go upstairs and get some sleep. I got a long night ahead of me. (He exits right)

BLACK BARB. Pore Randy. I'z just havin' a talk with him. He's shore fallen in life. He went ta college, ya know. (SAL is serving drinks)

BEV. Well, the way I figger it, feller like that, he wanted ta slide downhill, he slud downhill. Like the gal says, he made his bed, so he's gotta lay in it, right? (SHE jabs BARB in the ribs with her elbow and both laugh heartily)

BLACK BARB. Still, Miz Barton-

BEV. What I alluz say is, it don't do no good ta git sentimental about fellers like that. They're only good fer one thing, an' I don't mean stirrin' chili. (Again both laugh uproariously)

BLACK BARB. I reckon yore right, as usual, Miz Barton. (Pause as SHE sips her drink) Uh, I hope ya don't mind me askin', but you signin' on any hands these days?

BEV. Tell ya, Black Barb. In about two weeks I'll be needin' a couple new cowpokes. Ef'n ya want, I'll hold a spot fer you.

BLACK BARB. That's right nice a you, Miz Barton. I can sure use the work.

BEV. Everybody tells me yore an A-number one wrangler, so I'll be glad ta have ya. (ONE-GUN enters, stands inside the door, arms akimbo, surveying the scene.)

SAL. Howdy, stranger. Come on in an' set.

ONE-GUN. (sourly) I'll set when I'm good 'n' ready ta set.

SAL. Suit yourself, stranger.

ONE-GUN. That's just what I aim to do. (SHE keeps looking around the room, then speaks to no one in particular) So this is Tumbleweed Flats! What a one-horse town! (Nobody reacts. SHE walks over and sits on the barstool next to BIG MAMA.) Gimme a Singapore Sling, bartender. And step on it! (SAL goes to work as One-Gun turns to Big Mama) My handle's One-Gun Wanda. They call me the Durango Destroyer an' I'm tougher 'n rawhide.

BIG MAMA. They call me Big Mama Mayberry an' I met my share a tough gals in my time. Yup, I've ran inta my share. Yes indeedy, I shore met a lot.

ONE-GUN. So you're Big Mama. I heard a you. I hear tell you got a lot a notches on your six-gun. (Takes a long pull at her drink)

BIG MAMA. I ain't figgered it up lately, but last time I counted I had 22. That's right. Twenty-two notches. That's how many notches I had — 22.

ONE-GUN. Well, you got one more 'n me. I got 21. But I only use one gun. (Drinks)

BIG MAMA. One or two--don't make no nevermind, No nevermind. Some use one, most use two--it don't matter so long 'z you get the job done.

ONE-GUN. (Finishing her drink, SHE slams the glass down on the bar, wiping her mouth with her sleeve) I needed that! (To SAL) Same way. (To BIG MAMA) Nothin' like a little red-eye to start the day off right. (Beat) Ya know, Big Mama, looks ta me like you're gettin' kinda heavy-set.

BIG MAMA. I ain't so heavy-set I still can't move fast. I can move when I have to. I still got plenty a speed when I need it.

ONE-GUN. A gal gets older, she kinda slows up, know what I mean? Why, you must be pushin' 60, Big Mama.

BIG MAMA. I'm 39 years old! That's what I am--39. Yes'm, 39 is my age.

ONE-GUN. My guess is you were 39 about the time Lee surrendered to Grant at Appomattox.

BIG MAMA. (Now very angry) Look, One-Gun, or whatever yore name is, yore jes' not very smart, goin' aroun' an' insultin' folks. You shouldn't be insultin' people. No, insultin' is not the thing ta do.

ONE-GUN. Look, ole Mama, you're not very smart, hangin' around the old West when every gal who totes a Colt is gunnin' fer ya.

BIG MAMA. You ornery varmint, I'm still the fastest gun in the West. The fastest gun! That's what I am--the fastest, an' don't you fergit it!

ONE-GUN. You're livin' in the past, ole Mama. Looks to me like your day is done.

BIG MAMA. Sounds ta me like yore lookin' fer trouble, an' I'll tell you right now, ef'n yore lookin' fer it, yore gonna find it right here. That's right--if yore lookin' fer trouble, you'll git it. Them as go searchin' fer trouble allus run into it.

ONE-GUN. Aaah, ole Mama, you're all talk. You're jes' livin' on your reputation.

BIG MAMA. (Starting to climb off her barstool) Oh, yeah? I'll show ya who's livin' off her-- (ONE-GUN shoots her before she is fully off the barstool and she slumps to the floor.) She got me. That gol-dinged little gal outa nowhere plugged Big Mama. She shot Big Mama Mayberry, the fastes' gun west a the Pecos. (ONE-GUN holds the gun barrel vertically, blows over the top of it, then leans on the bar and surveys the scene)

BLACK BARB. (Rushing over along with BEV) Big Mama, where'd she git you?

BIG MAMA. I dunno, but I'm goin' fast. That's right--fast. Big Mama's headin' fer the last roundup-- and soon.

RANDY. (Rushing in stage right) I heard shooting! (Beat, as he looks around) Oh, no, not Big Mama! (HE rushes over and kneels down beside her) Oh, Big Mama, speak to me! (HE starts to sob uncontrollably)

BLACK BARB. Git a-hold a yourself, Randy!

RANDY. (Wailing) But it's Big Mama!

BLACK BARB. (SHE reaches down and slaps RANDY's face) Sorry I had ta do that, Randy, but the last thing we need here is a lotta male hysteria.

RANDY. (Getting control of himself) Thanks, Black Barb. (HE sniffles, takes a handkerchief from his pocket and blows his nose)

BEV. (Kneeling down, she lifts BIG MAMA's head.) Take 'er easy, Big Mama.

BIG MAMA. I'm feelin' real porely. 'At's right, pardner, real pore ly. I reckon I'm feelin' so porely I won't--(SHE dies. BEV lowers her head to the floor)

BEV. (SHE rises, as does RANDY) She's gone. (RANDY weeps silently. SHE puts an arm around his shoulder and leads him stage right) Why don' you go back upstairs, Randy, 'n' lay down till you feel better.

RANDY. (As THEY reach far stage right, HE turns and addresses the barroom in general) A part of the Old West has died here today and a part of me has died with it. (Resuming his sobbing, HE exits)

BLACK BARB. Pore Randy. He's shore takin' it hard.

BEV. Oh, you know how men are. They're jes' more emotional, is all. He'll be OK after he cries himself out.

SAL. (Coming out from behind the bar) Hey, some a you gals help me move Big Mama back a the bar. It's bad for business havin' her out here. (BEV and BLACK BARB help HER pull the body behind the bar. BLACK BARB then goes back downstage and sits at the table)

ONE-GUN. (Taking BIG MAMA's stool at the bar) Hit me again, bartender!

BEV. (Moving over near ONE-GUN) I jes' wanna say one thing ta you, One-Gun Wanda. When word gets out how you shot Big Mama, that you broke the code of the West, there's gonna be a lotta gals gunnin' fer you.

ONE-GUN. (coolly) I cal'late that's my worry, not yores.

BEV. But you gunned her down afore she even had a chance ta draw! That ain't the way we do things hereabouts.

ONE-GUN. Zat so? As fer me, I allus try ta mind my own business and I get along best with folks that does the same.

BEV. No offense meant. I'm jes' sayin' that, ef'n I was in yore boots--

HEATHER (Entering left) Howdy, Sal. Howdy, Bev. Howdy, Barb. (Beat as SHE looks around) Say, where's Big Mama?

BEV. She cashed in her chips.

HEATHER. No! I'll be dad-burned! I thought she'd be with us fer-ever. (Beat) Well, I'm here, Bev. Let's us talk.

BEV. (Moving downstage to the table) Black Barb, ya mind clearin' out? Miz Harper an' me got some serious talkin' ta do.

BLACK BARB. (Rising) Course not. I'll jes' mosey over ta the bar 'n' have me another White Russian.

BEV. Thanks, Barb. Tell Sal ta put it on my tab. (Black Barb tips her hat to Bev and moves to the bar as Bev and Heather sit at the table)

HEATHER. So somebody finally got Big Mama. I shoulda figured it'd happen sometime. She had more gals gunnin' for her than there are cows in Tumbleweed Flats.

BEV. Cattle.

HEATHER. Cows, cattle. What difference does it make?

BEV. Buy y' a drink?

HEATHER. Thank you. I'd like a Pink Lady.

BEV. (To SAL) Bring us a Pink Lady. An' another Tequila Sunrise. (To Heather) Now, you said you wanted ta talk. So here I am.

HEATHER. It's about that 50 acres of frontage upriver of town. We want to buy it so the town can expand.

BEV. The town kin expand across the river.

HEATHER. But then we'll need a bridge or a ferry.

BEV. Then build yoreselfs a bridge or buy a ferry.

HEATHER. We don't have money like that, and besides you don't need that land.

BEV. Course I do! I cain't water my livestock jes' from wells an' springs. I gotta have the river.

HEATHER. You can buy land upriver from there. I heard tell ole Miz Peters'll sell.

BEV. (Laughing sarcastically) Yeah, at a hundred dollars a foot fer river frontage. (SAL brings them their drinks.)

HEATHER. Besides, your cows make the water all muddy when it gets to town.

BEV. Cattle.

HEATHER. Cows, cattle, what difference does it make? You've got us all boxed in to the west with that great big spread of yours and downriver is Dismal Swamp. There's just no place for the town to grow.

BEV. Who says it hasta grow?

HEATHER. Why, we all do.

BEV. Who's "we"?

HEATHER. All the decent folks who live here in town.

BEV. A passel a dad-burned, citified Easterners! Let 'em all go back ta St. Louis. This here is cattle country.

HEATHER. It is not! This is people country. This is a place where people have come to put down roots and build churches 'n' schools 'n' town halls 'n' firehouses 'n' police stations 'n' grocery stores 'n' butcher shops 'n' hardware stores 'n' banks 'n' barber shops 'n' paved roads 'n' sidewalks 'n' street lamps 'n' trolley barns 'n'--

BEV. Trolley barns!? (Slaps the table) That does it! Dad-gummit, the last thing we want around here is ta have our horses pullin' trolley cars! This is a place fer ranchers 'n' cowpokes 'n' cattle 'n' grazin' land 'n' wide-open spaces 'n' sagebrush 'n' tumbleweed 'n' ropes 'n' saddles 'n' stirrups 'n' Levi's 'n'-- Consarn it, I ain't goin' on! We was here first an' you ain't gettin' our land fer no trolley cars!

HEATHER. Oh, yes we are! And, if you won't sell, we'll take it. I'm aimin' to start up a Homesteaders Association and we'll go to the governor and then we'll see who gets what!

BEV. In case you don't know it, the governor of this territory is a cattle rancher.

HEATHER. If we can't do it legal, there's always other ways.

BEV. (Her eyes narrowing) Meanin' what?

HEATHER. Oh, cows can disappear--

BEV. I'll be hornswoggled! Am I hearin' right? Are you tellin' me yore gonna rustle my cattle? Folks here don't take kindly to rustlers. You know 'z well 'z I do, they string 'em up ta the neares' cottonwood tree!

HEATHER. If they find out who they are. (Beat) Or springs 'n' salt licks can get poisoned--

BEV. Dad-blast it, are you tellin' me yore gonna kill off my cattle? Let me tell you, yore headed fer trouble!

HEATHER. Or barns 'n' bunkhouses can burn down.

BEV. You step outside the law an' I'll get a posse together so fast yore head'll swim!

HEATHER. We'll do whatever we want, 'cause we got right on our side. You ranchers 've gotta go.

BEV. (Rising).You settlers are the ones gotta go. This was great country till you came along.

HEATHER. (Rising) Your sun has set. A new day is dawnin' in the Old West.

BEV. Over my dead body!

HEATHER. If you say so! (Both go for their guns simultaneously, shoot simultaneously and slump to the floor simultaneously.)

BEV. She got me!   HEATHER. She got me!

BLACK BARB. (Running over) By gum 'n' by gosh, they got each other.

BEV. Bury me out on the lone prairie.

HEATHER. Don' t bury me out on the lone prairie.

BEV. The light's fadin'.

HEATHER. It's growin' dim.

RANDY. (Rushing in stage right) I heard shooting! (Beat as he looks around) Oh, no! Not Miz Barton! And Miz Harper!

BLACK BARB. Yup.

RANDY. (Running over, HE kneels down between them, facing downstage) Oh, please, gals, speak to me! (HE starts to sob uncontrollably)

BLACK BARB. Git a-hold a yourself, Randy!

145

RANDY. (Wailing) But it's Miz Barton and Miz Harper!

BLACK BARB. (SHE reaches down and slaps his face) Sorry I had ta do that, Randy.

RANDY. (Rubbing his cheek) You wouldn't dare keep slapping me if I was a woman! (HE sniffles, takes a handkerchief from his pocket and blows his nose)

BLACK BARB. (Kneeling down) Take 'er easy, gals. You got any last words?

HEATHER. There's no place like home. (She falls back dead)

BLACK BARB. Miz Barton?

BEV. Ride tall in the saddle. (She falls back dead)

BLACK BARB. (Rising) Them was both good gals.

RANDY. (Still on his knees, through his tears) So they were. (Impassioned) But, when will you women ever learn? That's your answer to everything -- fighting and gunplay! Why can't you take a lesson from us men and sit down and talk and reason things out? But no! It always comes down to violence! (Melodramatically) But, God willing, someday you'll discover that there is a better way and the world will have a brighter tomorrow!

SLOW CURTAIN

GOT A DATE WITH AN ANGEL

CAST OF CHARACTERS

PERRY BALL. A young male, 18-25. He is warm, friendly, deferential, but confused and unsure of himself.

ANGEL. A female of indeterminate age. She is cold, judgmental, and censorious throughout.

The scene is Perry's bedroom, somewhere in the USA. The room has a masculine flavor but is not distinguished by sports memorabilia, music posters, or anything indicating a surpassing interest in any avocation.

The time is the late afternoon of a spring day.

AT RISE: Perry is kneeling beside his bed, hands clasped in prayer.

PERRY. And please help me. Everything seems to go wrong in my life! I really think I need someone to guide me along the right path! I'm praying you'll send me someone to show me the way! I don't think -- at least I hope I'm not asking too much. If I am--

(There is a tremendous clatter outside the window upstage, the window flies open and the angel blunders into the room, falling inside the window.)

ANGEL. Oh! Oh!
PERRY. (Jumping up and running over to her) Are you hurt?
ANGEL. (Standing up) No. I'm fine thank you. It's just that we get so used to flying around that I'm way out of practice when it comes to climbing anywhere.
PERRY. (Hesitantly and timidly) Are you an angel?
ANGEL. So I am, young man. And I've been sent with orders to help you lead a good and morally fulfilling life until you join us upstairs (She casts her eyes heavenward.), as I'm sure you will.
PERRY. But, if you're an angel, how come you don't have any wings?
ANGEL. I do. what do you think this is? (She points to a lump high up on her back.) Think I've got scoliosis or something? It's a backpack specifically made to store wings. Very convenient if we're not using them.
PERRY. Well, it's just wonderful that you're here to help me. (Pause) How did you know I needed help?
ANGEL. (Sententiously) Up there, they know everything. There's a dossier on everyone here on earth and the system has been computerized for some time, so I got your dossier right away and I read up on you; thus I know all about you. For example, remember that pack of Wrigley's Spearmint you stole from Pop

Carey's store when you were eight?

PERRY. (Embarrassed ad thunderstruck) Gosh, you do know everything!

ANGEL. (Stiffly) Do not say "Gosh." It is merely a euphemism for "God" and we are not supposed to take his name in vain.

PERRY. (Apologetically) Gee, I'm sorry, I —

ANGEL. Do not say, "Gee." It is a euphemism for "Jesus" and so is sacrilegious. Say "shit" instead. It's quite acceptable.

PERRY. Uh-- I-- uh-- (Pause) Since you know all about me, how can I find out all about you?

ANGEL. You can't. My life before I ascended was of no consequence. I got into heaven as an entry-level angel and always followed all the rules, so I got more and more responsibility and eventually got picked as a messenger. I've been back to Earth several times and have helped several figures you may have heard of. I helped a young man named Augustine — he lived in Hippo — to turn his life around — my, he was a sinner! And later I helped Cotton Mather, Cotton wasn't a bad child, but he was overly interested in games like ring-a-rosie and hide-and-seek and other frivolities. But he became especially devout. And there were others who allowed me to aid them. Very gratifying. Incidentally, my celestial name is Star -- Shooting Star.

PERRY. Gee — I mean, wow! And, when you're not being a messenger, what do you do up in Heaven?

ANGEL. Oh, we spend a lot of time in church and we read a lot — all religious books.

PERRY. Of course.

ANGEL. And we listen to music — all the great masses of the great composers. It's very nice. (Pause) And then we have such excellent food.

PERRY. I read that you eat manna all the time.

ANGEL. But that's not as dull as it sounds. The kitchen's been in charge of Brillat-Savarin for years and we all agree that his meals are really heavenly.

PERRY. I see you have a sense of humor.

ANGEL. (Baffled) What?

PERRY. Oh, never mind.

ANGEL. Anyway, to get back to our food. We have manna italiana, manna española, manna à la francaise, just to mention a few. And for dessert we have baked manna, manna profiteroles — you name it.

PERRY. Sounds nice.

ANGEL. Of course we eat small portions of everything. We don't want to be guilty of gluttony, because that's one of the seven deadly sins. The Bible says, "When thou sittest to eat, consider diligently what is before thee. Be not desirous of dainties, for they are deceitful meat" and "Hast thou found honey? eat so much of it as is sufficient for thee, lest thou be filled therewith and vomit it" and we must not "walk in excess of wine, revelling and banquetings." (Pause) I hope you are not gluttonous.

PERRY. Well, the night before last I had two helpings of filet of sole.

ANGEL. Soul! Has depravity on here earth reached the point where there is cannibalism involving the eating of souls? Fie!

PERRY. No, no! Sole is a fish.

ANGEL. (Censoriously) Nonetheless, two helpings is certainly gluttony! (Pause) I'm afraid you are indeed a sinner on that score! For shame!

PERRY. I'm sorry.

ANGEL. Sorry is not good enough! Repent! I'd suggest bread and water for the next month for you to atone. (Pause) Of course you went for a long walk after this banquet.

PERRY. I'm afraid I went to the living room, lay down on the couch and slept for a couple of hours.

ANGEL. Thereby compounding gluttony with sloth! Fie!

PERRY. Well, I was kinda tired and sleepy.

ANGEL. "The way of the slothful man is as an hedge of thorns," says the Bible. "He that is slothful is brother to him that is a great waster" and "The desire of the slothful killeth him: for his hands refuse to labor." And finally, "Give not sleep to thine eyes, nor slumber to thine eyelids."

PERRY. You mean we're never supposed to go to sleep at all?

ANGEL. Of course not. But to sleep at night and to take a nap in the daytime as well is certainly being guilty of the deadly sin of sloth. Once again you are proved a sinner!

PERRY. What should I do?

ANGEL. For the next month sleep only four hours a night and find some productive activity for the other four hours you might sleep. I'd suggest prayer.

PERRY. (Reluctantly) I suppose I could try it.

ANGEL. You almost have to in order to atone for your sins.

PERRY. I wish I could be like those people who don't have all these sins to atone for.

ANGEL. Why, that's a terrible thing to say!

PERRY. Huh? (Pause) Why?

ANGEL. Because you are committing another deadly sin!

PERRY. (Concerned) Am I? I just wanted to be sin-free. Like the people that already are.

ANGEL. That is a clear-cut case of the sin of envy.

PERRY. Oh?

ANGEL. "Envy slayeth the silly man," the Bible says.

PERRY. Oh, not again!

ANGEL. Because "a sound heart is the life of the flesh; but envy is the rottenness of the bones."

PERRY. It's that bad?

ANGEL. All sin is bad. And so any kind of envy is bad.

PERRY. Golly, and I was feeling kinda proud that I was honest enough to admit I was — I am — a sinner.

ANGEL. First of all, do not say, "Golly." It's another euphemism for "God" and it's blasphemous.

PERRY. Sorry.

ANGEL. And, as to feeling proud about anything, another sin! "Woe to the crown of pride," says Isaiah. "Hear ye and give ear; be not proud, for the Lord hath spoken," says Jeremiah. "Talk no more so exceedingly proudly," says Samuel. "Let not arrogancy come out of your mouth; for the Lord is a God of knowledge, and by him are actions weighed."

PERRY. I didn't mean "proud" like in "arrogant." So you're saying, even if I'm proud of being honest about being aware of being humble, that's bad too?

ANGEL. All pride is a sin and that's that. You're convicted by your own words. Young man, you're a sinful wretch.

PERRY. Gee — I mean, gosh — I mean, golly- I mean, I don't know what I mean! I don't mean to criticize, but on TV there are these angels who come down to help people and I thought maybe I could get —

ANGEL. Are you telling me you are coveting other angels? Without even knowing what they are like? Without knowing what they are going to say? (Pause) Don't you realize, young man, that all of us who are sent down here have to take messengering classes to make sure they know what all the rules are? (She lifts her eyes heavenward.) They don't want us to deviate one jot or tittle from the party line. So, even if you get another angelic messenger that you've coveted from afar, let me assure you, you'll get one exactly like me.

PERRY. Oh.

ANGEL. Do not be deceived by what you see on television or in the movies about angels come down to earth as huggable grandmothers or worldly-wise young men all bursting with benevolence! Our job is to point out the right path, for "strait is the gate, and narrow the way, which leadeth unto life." Do you understand?

PERRY. (Chastened) Uh, yes.

ANGEL. And your covetousness is yet another sin. The Good Book says, "he that hateth covetousness shall prolong his days."

PERRY. I thought covetousness meant only about money and other, like, worldly possessions.

ANGEL. Not at all. It means any kind of coveting. "Covetousness, wickedness, deceit, lasciviousness, blasphemy, foolishness, all these evil things come from within and defile the man." So the sin covers a lot more than money, and you are guilty of it, along with all the others!

PERRY. I don't know—

ANGEL. And another thing -- you evidently watch TV and go to the movies. I hope you watch the proper programs and attend the proper movies.

PERRY. I try to—

ANGEL. I hope you devote a lot of time to television early on Sunday morning. There are very fine preachers on those programs.

PERRY. Usually I'm still —

ANGEL. (Harshly) I thought so! Your sloth takes over! I suspected as much! (Pause) What programs do you watch?

PERRY. Uh, *Touched by an Angel*, —

ANGEL. Sentimental hogwash!

PERRY. *The Gospel Hour*, —

ANGEL. Too sectarian.

PERRY. *Hell Lies Ahead.*

ANGEL. That's more like it.

PERRY. And some popular programs, like *Law and Order*, and *Baywatch*, and—

ANGEL. (Thundering) *Baywatch!* Pure lust! So you suffer from that sin, too. I might have known!

PERRY. Aw, it's not —

ANGEL. "Abstain from fleshly lusts, which war against the soul" is my message. We must deny "ungodliness and worldly lusts and we should live soberly, righteously and godly in this present world," for "all that is in the world, the lust of the flesh and the lust of the eyes is of the world and the world passeth away and the lust thereof."

PERRY. But all *Baywatch* —

ANGEL. Enough! Seven varieties of sin and you are guilty of every one! Every single one! I regret to say it, but you are at one with the publicans and sinners —

PERRY. Just a minute! You may be an angel and all that, and I may be a sinner, but you can't call me a Republican! That's too much!

ANGEL. I didn't say a Republican. I said publican. I don't even know what a Republican is. We don't have any of them up there.

PERRY. Figures.

ANGEL. Be that as it may, young man, you are almost hopelessly lost unless you change your life!

PERRY. But that's why I prayed for an angel to come —

ANGEL. Enough! I leave you alone with this message: Repent! Repent before it is too late! Or else your lot will be woe! (She goes to the window and awkwardly climbs out. She repeats off-stage "Woe, woe" until her voice is no longer audible.)

PERRY. (Alone, he sits in the chair right, looking glum. After 10 or 15 seconds, he runs over and kneels beside the bed, hands clasped in prayer.) Dear Satan, please help! If you have a messenger service, I'm praying you'll send somebody! In a hurry, Satan!

Blackout

DR. HYDE AND MR. JEKYLL

CAST OF CHARACTERS

Dr. Henry Hyde, a successful physician
James Jekyll, a philanthropist

Mrs. York, a patient
Mr. Redding, a patient
Ellen, Dr. Hyde's ex-mistress
Miss Dismas, a patient
Voice of Miss Allen, Dr. Hyde's receptionist
Mr. Mountjoy, manager of a soup kitchen
Molly, a destitute woman
Liz, another destitute woman
Bill, a destitute man

With doubling, only six actors will be needed.

The action of the play takes place at two sites in London, the office of Dr. Henry Hyde and a soup kitchen in a slum.

SCENE I

AT RISE: Dr. Hyde stands before his desk and speaks coldly to a weeping Mrs. York.

HYDE. Oh, stop that cacophonous caterwauling! All the tears in the world are not going to change the situation one iota!

MRS. YORK. What's an iota?

HYDE. Don't interrupt me when I'm giving my diagnosis! Not only will the boy never walk, he will never be even faintly normal mentally: he'll be lucky if he gets to be a moron!

MRS. YORK. Oh, doctor, can you hold out even a tiny glimmer of hope?

HYDE. I cannot. Now please leave. My fee is 100 pounds, which you can pay as you depart.

MRS. YORK. 100 pounds?! But, doctor, Bert -- my mister -- don't make but 15 pounds a week! How can we ever pay a bill like that?

HYDE. In installments. You can arrange them with my receptionist as you leave, which I trust will be shortly.

MRS. YORK. (Rising) Oh, doctor! (She is totally broken.)

HYDE. (As she reaches the door) Mrs. York, perhaps a witticism will raise your spirits. What is the hardest part of a vegetable to digest?

MRS. YORK. (Puzzled) I haven't the faintest, sir.

HYDE. The wheelchair. (He laughs as she exits in a paroxysm of sobbing. He goes to the door, which she has left open.) Miss Allen.

MISS ALLEN. (offstage) Yes, doctor?

HYDE. Send in the next patient. (He returns behind his desk and sits.)

REDDING. (A hugely overweight man makes his way into the

room and heads for the chair in front of Hyde's desk.)
Afternoon, doctor.

HYDE. (Coldly) Sit down.

REDDING. (He puts a paper on Hyde's desk and then sits.) Your
girl said I should give you this.

HYDE. (Picks it up and looks at it.) Redding, eh? Well, Redding, I
see you weighed in on the baggage scale in Paddington Station
at 320 pounds. I have no scale on which I can verify that, so
I'll take your word for it. (Pause) What's the problem?
Anorexia? (He laughs.)

REDDING. I don't know what that is, doctor.

HYDE. Of course you don't. Just a private little joke indecipher-
able by the semi-literate and uneducated.

REDDING. Look, doctor, I may not have a lot of fancy schooling,
but I'm as good as the next man --

HYDE. You are of course entitled to that opinion, from which I
dissent. But enough of this nonsense. You are fat and you want
to be thin.

REDDING. A doctor I seen last year said I was suffering from
obesity --

HYDE. In other words, you are fat.

REDDING. He said it might be glandular.

HYDE. He was an incompetent. Have you ever seen any pictures
of people in poorhouses?

REDDING. Yes, once, years ago.

HYDE. See any fat people in those pictures?

REDDING. No, but--

HYDE. Enough said. You're fat because you eat too much. I can of
course give you a diet, but I suspect you have had them before
to little or no avail.

REDDING. Well, I --

HYDE. Silence! The cure, I believe, lies in surgery.

REDDING. You mean you want to cut that fat away?

HYDE. No, I want to do an appendix transplant.

REDDING. I don't understand.

HYDE. It's an operation I've performed more than a hundred times. It is a sure cure for high blood pressure, cancer, tuberculosis, neurasthenia and obesity. Not to mention leprosy and the vapors.

REDDING. What's the vapors?

HYDE. Don't distract me. The operation will cost one thousand pounds, payable 50 percent in advance and 50 percent once the operation is completed.

REDDING. What about a second opinion?

HYDE. No other surgeon will agree with my remedy. It's a pioneering operation and they're all a bunch of supercautious fools.

REDDING. I dunno, doctor.

HYDE. Don't take up space in my office while you engage in what I suppose you would glorify by the term "thinking it over." Go home and let me have your decision on the telephone. But don't delay too long. Carrying all that weight around, you could drop dead at any minute. Pay my receptionist as you exit, if you survive long enough to make your way to her desk.

REDDING. I -- (Hyde withers him with a look. He leaves, closes the door and, a minute later, can be heard offstage, yelling "What?! That's outrageous!")

HYDE. (He is playing with some papers on his desk when the upstage door opens and a woman, her face almost completely concealed by a veil and a cloak pulled up to her nose, enters.) What the hell? What are you doing here, you stupid slut? I told you never to come here.

ELLEN. I had to see you. Your butler won't let me into your house.

HYDE. (A little more self-possessed) Quite so.

ELLEN. (Melodramatically) Oh, Henry, what made the magic go out of our affair?

HYDE. Magic?! A few rolls in the hay in that flea-bitten flat of yours is magic? Be serious.

ELLEN. You were the great love of my life!

HYDE. Then you've had a very barren life.

ELLEN. I would even forgive you for hitting me all the time. And that time you threw me down the fire escape.

HYDE. You put milk in my tea instead of lemon.

ELLEN. I forgot you liked lemon. My hip has never been the same since.

HYDE. I'm surprised. You certainly have enough padding on it.

ELLEN. Oh, Henry! That hurts me when you say that! That hurts me as much as the time you kicked my little puppy and broke his jaw just because he was chewing on your boots.

HYDE. I put him out of his misery, didn't I?

ELLEN. You threw him out the window. Six floors.

HYDE. Look, you didn't come here to go over all your complaints about me. What do you want?

ELLEN. I'm pregnant.

HYDE. So?

ELLEN. So I'm pregnant.

HYDE. I heard you the first time. Why should that concern me?

ELLEN. You're the daddy.

HYDE. What a joke! Let me put it this way: "If you're buried by an avalanche, how do you tell which rock hit you first?"

ELLEN. That's an awful thing to say, Henry. After I met you, I didn't see anybody else.

HYDE. (Unconvinced) Sure. (Pause) But what do you want from me?

ELLEN. I want your advice about the little bundle of joy.

HYDE. Get rid of it.

ELLEN. I figured you'd say that. Can you help me?

HYDE. Sure. I've got some old coat-hangers around somewhere.

ELLEN. No. I mean an operation.

HYDE. I'm not in the "you-rape-'em-we-scrape-'em" business.

ELLEN. Oh, you can do it. I know you can do it.

HYDE. Very well. Next Wednesday at 1 p.m. Here. My fee will be 100 pounds.

ELLEN. Fee?! I thought you'd do it for nothing.

HYDE. Did you. (This is not a question.)

ELLEN. You know, for old time's sake.

HYDE. What a chuckle. 100 pounds.

ELLEN. But I haven't got that kind of money. How will I get it?

HYDE. On your back, the way you always have.

ELLEN. Oh, you have no heart!

HYDE. One of my colleagues remarked that, if I ever had to have a heart operation, it would be micro-surgery. (He smiles.)

ELLEN. I'll tell your wife!

HYDE. Tell away. She's well enough trained not to raise embarrassing questions with me.

ELLEN. Oh, you have all the answers, don' t you?

HYDE. I try to. (Pause) Well, do you want the operation or not?

ELLEN. Fifty pounds?

HYDE. 100 pounds in cash. (He goes to the upstage door and opens it.) Now, get out and start earning the money! (She leaves, he shuts the door and goes to the door stage left.) Miss Allen, send in the next patient. (He returns to his desk.)

DISMAS. (Entering, she is slim, shy, tentative and obviously very nervous. She has a moist handkerchief which she switches from hand to hand.) Hello, doctor. (She hands him a folder.)

HYDE. Come in. Sit down. (She does so and he looks at the folder.) You have consulted a number of physicians, I see. Why?

DISMAS. Uh, you see -- that is -- I mean –

HYDE. Speak up.

160

DISMAS. It's just that -- it's only that -- (She makes a supreme effort.) I'm nervous.

HYDE. Everybody's nervous. What are you nervous about?

DISMAS. Everything. (Pause) And I'm shy.

HYDE. I see. When?

DISMAS. All the time. People scare me.

HYDE. Why?

DISMAS. I don't know. They just do. (She squeezes her handkerchief and sweat drips out onto the floor. Hyde looks disgusted.)

HYDE. (Coldly) Do not repeat that nauseating action. My receptionist has enough to do without mopping up bodily secretions from my floor.

DISMAS. I'm very sorry, doctor. Terribly sorry. I --

HYDE. To return to your problems. If people frighten you, you must have a terrible time at work.

DISMAS. Happily, I don't have to work. My parents left me an income.

HYDE. I see. Which means that most of the time you stay at home suffering and pitying yourself.

DISMAS. Oh, I -- I wouldn't exactly put it that way.

HYDE. Of course you wouldn't. I would. (Pause) I can cure you with surgery.

DISMAS. Surgery? Really, doctor?

HYDE. Surgery. An appendix transplant has been successful in curing paranoia, schizophrenia, manic-depressive psychosis, flatulence, bubonic plague and self-pity.

DISMAS. Really?

HYDE. It never fails.

DISMAS. My, doctor, I just don't know. I--

HYDE. Your choices are clear: Do you want to continue to be a whining, sniveling, contemptible wreck or to become a latter-day Joan of Arc, strong, stalwart, fearless?

DISMAS. A latter-day Joan of Arc, strong, stalwart, fearless.

HYDE. Do you want to go on as a cringing, crawling, groveling excuse for a woman or be transformed into a contemporary Madame Curie, proud, self-reliant, adventuresome?

DISMAS. A contemporary Madame Curie, proud, self-reliant, adventuresome.

HYDE. Do you want to be a pitiful relic of a decaying, dying, dreary, discredited yesterday or the shining herald of a bright new tomorrow?

DISMAS. The shining herald of a bright new tomorrow.

HYDE. Then it's settled. You need the operation. Be at Sestercean Hospital next Tuesday night. I shall operate on Wednesday morning. Now, do not clutter up my office with your continued presence any longer. (She jumps up and scuttles out, leaving the door open. Hyde goes to the door and speaks to someone offstage.) No more patients today, Miss Allen.

ALLEN. But, doctor, there's a man here that's in pain. He's all doubled over and--

HYDE. Tell him to stand up straight and stop malingering. No more patients. (He slams the door.) At last. (He goes to the cabinet beside the door and opens it, revealing beakers, retorts and test tubes, some filled with vari-colored liquids. He mixes some of these, creating pyrotechnic effects and dramatic changes in color as he works. This continues throughout the tape of his voice.)

TAPE OF HYDE. Back to work on my project. I know I can make it succeed! There has to be some magic elixir that will render a subject immobile but not deaden his nerve impulses! Oh, my God, what fun surgery will be then! To see the patient lying there, to know that he is suffering the most horrible agony but is unable to do anything about it! And think of prolonging the surgery so that the pain goes on and on! Oh boy, oh boy, oh boy! I'll have to be awfully careful, though. I don't want to immobilize myself. I just wonder about this blend of acetylsalicylic acid, verapamil hydrochloride, a tiny bit of cerebrospinal relaxant and my supersecret ingredient. Voilà! Now to shake it up and take a sip of it. I wonder if I should mix it with something highly potable and palatable like lemon juice. No, I guess not. That might render it ineffectual. I'll just take it straight. (He takes a large sip, then begins all sorts of facial contortions followed by bodily contortions, twists and jerks. He staggers across the room to his desk, falls into the chair with his head down. When he raises his head, his face bears a look that is positively beatific and he is smiling. The tape resumes.) Oh, my goodness, I feel so good! God's in His heaven and all's right with the world! I want to help others to be as happy and as blessed as I am at this moment! I must go out and be about my Father's business! I can do so much for my fellowman-- comfort the sick, uplift the downtrodden, oh, golly, do so many things! (Smiling, he exits upstage.)

Blackout.

SCENE 2

AT RISE: Mr. Jekyll is talking to Mountjoy, who stands behind the soup kitchen's counter and busies himself with various stirrings of the contents of pots and pans.

JEKYLL. So, you see, Mr. Mountjoy, I'll do anything I can to help out-- scrub floors, wash dishes, anything, anything, anything, anyth--

MOUNTJOY. All right! All right, Mr. --

JEKYLL. Jekyll. Jimmy Jekyll.

MOUNTJOY. For the next few minutes, there's nothing for you to do. But, when we open the doors and the poor unfortunates come in, you can help me serve the potage jardinière, le maca-

163

roni au fromage, the café noir, and les petits gâteaux de la semaine passée.

JEKYLL. Sounds delicious!

MOUNTJOY. They'll complain. They always do. The soup will be too watery, there won't be enough cheese with the macaroni and the week-old cookies will be stale. There's no satisfying them.

JEKYLL. Oh, I'm sure that, in their heart of hearts, they are deeply grateful for your beneficence.

MOUNTJOY. (Flatly) Yeah. (A woman dressed in rags, her face smudged, her hands black with dirt, sticks her head in the door left.) What is it, Molly?

MOLLY. Oh, Mr. Mountjoy, sir, could I talk to you for just a minute?

MOUNTJOY. (Not too kindly) What do you want, Molly?

MOLLY. Oh, sir, I don't have a penny for my room at the Havens Institute for Destitute Prostitutes tonight. Can you help me out with just a little? Please, sir?

MOUNTJOY. You know the rules here, Molly. You can get food and nothing else.

MOLLY. Oh, but, sir--

JEKYLL. (Stepping over to her, he reaches into his pocket and pulls out a bill.) Here, my good woman, maybe this will help you in your hour of need.

MOUNTJOY. Hey, Jekyll, watch that. You--

MOLLY. Five pounds! Wow! A bed and a bottle of rotgut, too!

MOUNTJOY. One thing, Molly. Don't tell anybody where you got that. (To Jekyll) If she does there'll be a stampede in here like you've never seen.

JEKYLL. Then please, Molly, let this be our little secret

MOLLY. (Curtseying) Oh, yes, sir. Don't worry, sir. (Sticking the bill in her stocking, she exits.)

MOUNTJOY. Now, Jekyll, I appreciate that you want to help people, but--

JEKYLL. My friend, what did the good Lord put us here on earth for, if not to do good works?

MOUNTJOY. Well—

JEKYLL. To feed the hungry.

MOUNTJOY. Well --

JEKYLL. To house the homeless.

MOUNTJOY. Well --

JEKYLL. To befriend the friendless.

MOUNTJOY. Well--

JEKYLL. To employ the jobless.

MOUNTJOY. Well --

JEKYLL. In short, to make our planet the terrestrial paradise that love and kindness and benevolence and--

MOUNTJOY. OK. OK. So we're supposed to help other people. That's what we're doing here, so if you --

LIZ. (Entering stage left) Oh, Mr. Mountjoy, I know you don't like to have people interrupt you while you're fixin' dinner, but something terrible has happened! You ain't seen me for two months 'cause my mister came back, right?

MOUNTJOY. Right.

LIZ. This morning he left again and he says he's never comin' back. Never. And me with the two wee ones. What am I gonna do? (She dabs at her eyes with a dirty handkerchief.)

JEKYLL. Oh, you poor woman, my heart goes out to you!

LIZ. (Crying a bit more) Oh, thank you, sir.

JEKYLL. Fate has indeed dealt you a cruel blow.

LIZ. (Crying even more) Yes, sir.

JEKYLL. Your future, alone and with two tiny tots, certainly looks bleak.

LIZ. (Crying even more) I know. I --

JEKYLL. Even though the dole will help, it will barely be enough to keep body and soul together.

LIZ. (Sobbing now) It's cruel!

JEKYLL. And why should this happen to you, you who, I am sure, have always lived a wholesome, upright, Christian life?

LIZ. (Sobbing even more) It ain't fair!

JEKYLL. It makes you wonder if there's any justice in this world.

LIZ. (Sobbing, on the edge of hysteria) I know, sir, I--

JEKYLL. And all you have to anticipate are grim and forbidding tomorrows for years ahead. I do feel terribly sorry for you. (Liz runs out the door and can be heard sobbing and screaming hysterically offstage.) I hope my words of solace brought the poor wretch some comfort.

BILL (Dashing in) What happened to poor Liz in here? Did you do anything to hurt her?

JEKYLL. No, we were only trying to lift her spirits.

BILL. You sure done one lousy job of it. Listen to her out there! (Liz is still sobbing and having hysterics offstage.)

JEKYLL. Perhaps He (He raises his eyes heavenward.) didn't grant us the grace to find the right words to help her. (Pause) But maybe next time.

BILL. Next time! She's prob'ly gonna jump off some bridge unless we can calm her down. Next time!

JEKYLL. Now, my good man, calm yourself.

BILL. Don't "my good man" me! You toffs are all the same, lookin' down on us ordinary folk!

JEKYLL. Just because an inscrutable providence has smiled a bit more on me than on you is no call for you to be upset. You should bend every effort to be happy with the station in life to which God has called you.

BILL. (Balling his hands up into fists) I'll give you 'scrutable providence, you --

166

MOUNTJOY. Cut it out, Bill! Cut it out or it's no food today! Understand?

BILL. (Wilting) Yeah. Jeez, there ain't no justice.

JEKYLL. (Stepping over to Bill and putting a hand on his shoulder) Now, Bill -- for I take that to be your name -- don't be downhearted. You may not have many of the world's goods, but you have your soul and, what's more, you have a strong, healthy body --

BILL. I've got dandruff.

JEKYLL. Well, except for that--

BILL. And athlete's foot.

JEKYLL. And that –

BILL. And hay fever.

JEKYLL. Well, happily, living in the slums here in the East End, you probably don't encounter a lot of hay. So that, too, has its bright side, doesn't it. And I'm sure you must have many, many friends.

BILL. A few people seem to like me.

JEKYLL. There! I knew it! (Slyly) And I'll bet you're quite a man with the ladies.

BILL. I do all right.

JEKYLL. (Not to be sidetracked) -- and God's bright sunlight. So what does it matter that you don't have two pennies to rub together, that you have to come here and choke down watery soup and macaroni and cheese without the cheese and stale cookies, (Bill starts to cry tears of self-pity.) that you have to appear in public dressed in rags, that you probably can't afford medical or dental care, (Bill is crying now.) that you appear to the insensitive outsider to be one of the wretched of the Earth, when actually you have all the things that really matter.

BILL. (Sobbing) Such as what?

JEKYLL. Oh, lots of things.

BILL. Oooh!

JEKYLL. Above all, you mustn't give in to self-pity. I pity you and Mr. Mountjoy pities you, but, if you start feeling sorry for yourself, you're lost.

BILL. Wouldn't you, if you was in my shoes?

JEKYLL. (Softly) Of course I would, but that's beside the point.

MOUNTJOY. (Gently) I would, too.

BILL. Oh, my God! (Shoulders heaving, he runs out of the room.)

MOUNTJOY. Sometimes it's hard to help them.

JEKYLL. I'm sure that, beneath it all, he was happy to hear my uplifting message.

MOUNTJOY. (Skeptically) Maybe so. (There is a great hullabaloo offstage left.)

OFFSTAGE VOICES. Oh, no! No, Liz! No, Bill! Oh, my God! They can't mean it! Come back, Liz! C'mon back, Bill! (There is a loud squeal of brakes.) Jesus! Poor Liz! Poor Bill! I can't believe they did it! Oh, it's awful! I can't look!

MOLLY. (Frenzied, she comes tearing in and runs up to Jekyll.) You done it! You made Liz and Bill feel so bad they joined hands and jumped in front of 'a bus!

JEKYLL. You don't mean--

MOLLY. Yes! They're both dead!

JEKYLL. I hope they have gone to a kinder, better world, where they have found contentment.

MOLLY. They was getting along all right here 'til you started messing with them, you monster!

JEKYLL. I only wanted to help them.

MOLLY. Help! You helped 'em all right! you helped 'em to die! you ain't fit to live yourself! (She looks around wildly, sees a knife on Mountjoy's counter, grabs it and stabs Jekyll repeatedly.) Take that!

MOUNTJOY. No, Molly! No!

MOLLY. (Still stabbing) And that! And that!

MOUNTJOY. Oh, my God! You're killing that kindly man who only wanted to help!

MOLLY. (Still stabbing) And that! And that!

MOUNTJOY. (He runs around the counter and raises the head of the fallen Jekyll, as Molly dashes out, greeted by a cheer off-stage.) How do you feel, Jekyll?

JEKYLL. (Faintly) A bit under the weather.

MOUNTJOY. Do the wounds hurt?

JEKYLL. Just when I breathe, which won't be for long. (Pause) Mountjoy, don't tell the police that I was done in by that lamentable, luckless, miserable, hapless, downtrodden, woeful wretch. Tell them I ran into a knife-rack or something. That poor unfortunate has suffered enough.

MOUNTJOY. You are such a good soul.

JEKYLL. That is what the Lord above put us here for.

MOUNTJOY. Any last requests?

JEKYLL. Inform Dr. Henry Hyde of Harley Street of my demise. Or, rather, his wife. Tell her to destroy everything in his office. And then -- (His face becomes distorted and he makes convulsive movements as he lies on the ground.) Oh, no! The potion is wearing off!

MOUNTJOY. Jekyll -- uh, Jim, are you in pain?

HYDE. Jesus! What kind of a mental defective are you? Stabbed ten times, and he wants to know if I'm in pain! Christ!

MOUNTJOY. Is there anything I can do for you?

HYDE. Put something solid under my head. One of your loaves of bread should suffice.

MOUNTJOY. Do you have any last words?

HYDE. Forget all that hogwash about helping your fellow-man! He isn't worth it. Look what happened to me! Done in by a derelict! Murdered by a mendicant! Slain by a serf! Liquidated by a lowlife! Dispatched by a dreg! I've learned my lesson! In the future I'll never repeat this mistake!

MOUNTJOY. What future?

HYDE. You ghoul! I ought to -- Arrrgh! (He dies.)

MOUNTJOY. (Closing Hyde's eyes.) Sad what happened to this good man at the end. But he must have had a twinge of pain and it was the pain talking. I feel sure that he was always a benevolent soul, a credit to his Creator (The lights start to go dark.), a lover of the Lord, a sweet, charitable, kindly, (As he babbles on--

Blackout

DEAR OLD GOLDEN RULE DAYS

CAST OF CHARACTERS

Miss Flaherty, a teacher, white

Her pupils, all black, all aged 10 or 11

    Betty
    Paula
    Jennie
    Lonnie
    Malcolm
    Martin

A kook

A soda jerk

A man

The play takes place at various spots in Greenwich Village.

The time is the early spring.

NOTES ON THE PLAY

This play is not allegorical. In no way is it intended to convey any impression of whites as teachers and blacks as pupils. It is based on an actual incident.

The children differ considerably from one another, but they have two traits in common: they are tremendously physical and their affection must be expressed in an especially tactile form. Not as articulate verbally as they would like to be, they communicate many of their feelings physically. Above all, they show their affection by touching Miss Flaherty or her clothes very frequently; if she were not aware of this need, she would probably be annoyed by it, but, understanding it, she responds in a highly tactile fashion, patting arms and heads and occasionally drawing a child close to her. The sole exception to this is Martin, who is as physical as the others, but who avoids contact with Miss Flaherty and whom she does not touch.

At rise, there is a large semi-circular bench stage center with a plastic-globe-covered street light to its right. As the lights come up, Miss Flaherty and her pupils start down the right aisle, talking as they move toward the stage.

MISS FLAHERTY. Now, come on, kids! Let's stick together! (The children cluster around her.) Now, just a minute. Betty, Paula, Jennie, Lonnie, Malcolm, Martin, (Pause) OK, we all made it in one piece, Whew! I don't believe it. And as for you, Lonnie, the next time you want to play Tarzan on the subway, you let me know and I'll get you a spot in the elephant graveyard!

LONNIE. (Smiling) You bad, Miss Flaherty.

MISS FLAHERTY. You bet I am. (To the group) Now, the first place we're going to visit is Washington Square. It's called the heart of Greenwich Village. (She sees that Betty is terrified.) C'm'ere, Betty. (She puts her arm around Betty, who seems reassured.)

MALCOLM. It's beautiful.

MISS FLAHERTY. Hold your horses, Malcolm. We're not even there yet.

MALCOLM. (Defensively) Well, I still say it beautiful.

MISS FLAHERTY. (Patting him on the shoulder) You're right, Malcolm, It is nice.

PAULA. How much it cost to live here, Miss Flaherty?

MISS FLAHERTY. Oh, I guess about two or three hundred a month, Paula.

PAULA. You mean-- dollars?

MISS FLAHERTY. (A little sadly) Yes, Paula.

PAULA. You mean they's people who makes so much money they pays three hundred dollars a month for they house? Whoooo-eee!

MISS FLAHERTY. There are some very rich people, Paula.

PAULA. (Looking up at the buildings) They must be a pretty lot of 'em. Miss Flaherty, least down here.

MARTIN. (Defensively) They's rich people in Harlem, too.

JENNIE. (Sarcastically) Yeah, millions of 'em! (Pause.) Only rich people there is pushers and pimps!

MISS FLAHERTY. Now, Jennie! Don't let's spoil our day by me

having to tell you about watching your mouth! (She touches Jenny's shoulder to show she isn't angry with her.)

JENNIE. But I only sayin' the truth, Miss Flaherty!

MISS FLAHERTY. (Wearily) I know it, dear, but let's forget about it for today. Let's try to think about happy things, OK? (By this time, they have reached the stage.)

LONNIE. That's right! Miss Flaherty planned this trip for a long time, so don' you go spoilin' it. You wreck it and ol' P.S. 205 won't never let her take us nowhere again.

MISS FLAHERTY. Thanks for the moral support, Lonnie, but let's just drop it, huh?

JENNIE. (To Lonnie, sotto voce) That oughta hol' you, Mister Sawed-off Kareem Abdul-Jabbar. (She sticks her tongue out at him.)

LONNIE. (Also sotto voce) Wait'll I get you on the block! (As he sees that Miss Flaherty is watching, for her benefit, imitating Jackie Gleason as Ralph Kramden) One a these days-- POW!

MISS FLAHERTY. C'mon, kids, There's a play area over there, If any of you want to climb the jungle gym or one of those towers, go ahead.

MARTIN. (Suspicious) They let us do that?

MISS FLAHERTY. Of course. Why wouldn't they?

MARTIN. All those kids white.

MISS FLAHERTY. Don't worry about it, Martin. Just go ahead.

LONNIE. (Reaching under his sweatshirt) Hey, Marty, I got my frisbee. Catch! (He sails it to Martin, who sails it back.)

MARTIN. You frisbee with Malcolm! I wanna see if they let me climb! (He exits left.)

LONNIE. Here, Mal! (He sails the frisbee to Malcolm, who catches it half-heartedly and launches it back without any enthusiasm.) Jeez, get the lead out! (He throws it back and it sails offstage into the wings. Malcolm walks off to get it, not hurrying.) C'mon, move it! You about as fast as rush-hour traffic!

MALCOLM. (Returns with the frisbee, which he throws to Lonnie with no élan.) Here!

LONNIE. (Puts the frisbee back under his sweatshirt and goes to join Martin.) Man, you the worst frisbee-er of all time!

MISS FLAHERTY. Don't you want to go and play with them on the jungle gym, Malcolm?

MALCOLM. No. Miss Flaherty, I rather just look at all the people.

MISS FLAHERTY. What about you, Betty?

BETTY. (Genuinely alarmed, moving very close to Miss Flaherty) Oh, no! I just want to stay by you.

PAULA. Scairdy-cat!

MISS FLAHERTY. Now, Paula, don't start up. If Betty wants to stay, she wants to stay. (She pulls Betty close.) And it's all right with me.

PAULA. Well, I'm gonna go climb that jungle gym, I show those boys I do better than them! (She goes off left.)

MISS FLAHERTY. (Leading the other three to a bench, where all sit) Why don't we sit down over here and wait for the others?

JENNIE. Can I walk around, Miss Flaherty? They's so many cute boys down here!

MISS FLAHERTY. No, I think you'd better not, Jennie. (Pause) Shall I tell you about the first time I ever came here? It was while I was a junior in high school over in Jersey City and it was the first time my parents ever let a boy take me to New York for a date. We went to a restaurant for dinner and then we came and walked in the park. It used to be different then. These benches weren't here and they didn't have those big lights and there were a lot more bushes.

JENNIE. What was his name?

MISS FLAHERTY. Francis.

JENNIE. That's a girl's name.

MISS FLAHERTY. Not with an I. F-R-A-N-C-I-S. But he called himself Frank.

JENNIE. Was he cute?

MISS FLAHERTY. I thought he was very good-looking.

BETTY. Was you-- was you in love with him, Miss Flaherty?

MISS FLAHERTY. No, I don't think so, Betty. I liked him a lot, though.

MALCOLM. Is he-- you still go out with him?

MISS FLAHERTY. No, Malcolm, I don't. I go out with somebody else. (Pause) But what is this, anyway? The third degree?

JENNIE. What about the cat you goin' out with? Is he real heavy?

MISS FLAHERTY. Now, come on, Jennie. You heard what I said: no more third degree.

JENNIE. (Accepting this for her over-invasion of privacy.) Sorry, Miss Flaherty. I'ze just askin'.

MISS FLAHERTY. (Touching Jennie's shoulder) Of course you were, Jennie. No harm in asking.

JENNIE. (Brightening) You right, Miss Flaherty, The worst they can say is "Shut up," right?

MISS FLAHERTY. Right.

MALCOLM. This place look like it full of weirdos, Miss Flaherty.

MISS FLAHERTY. Well that's one reason I wanted us all to go on this trip, Malcolm. I wanted you all to see a different part of New York and I wanted you to see that you can't judge people by the way they look. You have to wait and find out what they're really like. They may look very kookie, but they may be very nice, Or they may look normal and they may be very kookie. You just have to wait and see,

LONNIE. (Offstage left, from the jungle gym) I see London, I see France, I see Paula's underpants!

PAULA. (Offstage) Oh, you jive dude, you!

LONNIE. I see London, I see France—

PAULA. You shut up, you dirty--

MARTIN. (Mimicking) Or I'm gonna tell on you!

PAULA. I tellin' nothin', but you dirty! You nothin' but dirty!

176

MARTIN. Ah, split, will ya?! Why don' you put an egg in your shoe an' beat it? (He and Lonnie laugh.)

PAULA. (She comes back onstage, looking very sour, and plops herself down beside Betty, who is close to Miss Flaherty.)

MISS FLAHERTY. (Has heard all the byplay, but pretends she hasn't.) Was it fun, Paula?

PAULA. (Sullenly) It was all right.

MISS FLAHERTY. Well, you know how boys are, Paula, when they think a girl's horning in on their special stuff,

PAULA. Yeah, I know, (To herself) The phonies!

MISS FLAHERTY. Well, I guess that's the way it is, dear.

JENNIE. (Suggestively) You got to find a game that only two can play, Paula.

MISS FLAHERTY. (Patiently) Now, Jennie, we're not in school, so I can't give you a lecture, but I want to talk to you anyhow, (She draws Jennie aside.) Jennie, our bodies are like God's holy temples and, if we defile them, we are doing a very sinful thing. We are treating them as less than holy. And we can defile them even with impure thoughts and words. When those impure thoughts come to our minds, we have to be strong enough to think other thoughts, And when those words come to our lips, we have to be strong enough to fight them back and not to say them. That way we are doing what God wants and not falling into the temptations that the Devil in putting into our path. Do you see what I mean, Jennie?

JENNIE. (She realizes the gulf between herself and Miss Flaherty, but likes Miss Flaherty enough not to confront her.) Yes, I sees, Miss Flaherty.

MISS FLAHERTY. Good. (She gives Jennie a hug and leads her back to the bench,) You're a very nice girl, Jennie, and I always want to be as proud of you as I am now. (She sits down, her arm still around Jennie's shoulder. Pause)

KOOK. (A white man of about 40 who moves around a lot as he

talks and has a nervous tic which draws his lips back tight over his teeth from time to time.) Hello, madam. Hello, young people. (Betty draws very close to Miss Flaherty.) Madam, I've been assigned a role in a psychodrama. I've been asked to assume the role of Jesus Christ. Therefore, in that role, I am supreme along with the president of the United States, the premier of Russia and the premier of China. The four of us control everything,

MISS FLAHERTY. (Very unruffled and calm) That's a great honor.

KOOK. Yes, it is, but no less than I deserve. Anyway, back to business. In my new capacity, I'm supposed to ask as many people as I can this question: Is the world any better now than it was in 1901? Think before you answer. Remember, the Boer War was still on! Many peoples of the world were still under the oppressor's heel! All was not sweetness and light! Life was fraught with problems!

MISS FLAHERTY. My, you seem to know a lot about history.

KOOK. You're so right! I know who was at the Congress of Vienna! I know who crossed the Rubicon! I know who were the Commies in 1848! 1 know when Barbarossa will return! I know-- I know many things.

MISS FLAHERTY. It sounds as if you do! Since you asked me, I'd say that things were just as bad 80 years ago as they are now.

KOOK. (Infuriated) That's wrong! You're supposed to say they're better now and I'm supposed to show you why they aren't. You know what I think? I think you're either a Red spy or else you're crazy! That's what I think!

MISS FLAHERTY. Everybody to his own opinion, I suppose. But why don't you go interview somebody else? Surely you want to get answers from as many people as you can.

KOOK. It isn't a question of want to! I have to! My psychodrama assignment demands it! (He lopes off.)

BETTY. Oooh, Miss Flaherty, how could you be so cool? That man was psycho!

MISS FLAHERTY. (Putting an am around Betty' a shoulder) Of course he was, Betty, but you have to be able to tell kooks who are dangerous from the ones that aren't.

MALCOLM. (Admiringly) Miss Flaherty, you something else!

MISS FLAHERTY. Thank you, Malcolm. I'm honored to have a good word from you.

LONNIE. (Running back in) C'mon, Marty! Here goes the frisbee! (Reaching under his sweatshirt, he pulls out the frisbee and launches it offstage.) Cool, man! (The frisbee comes flying back in from off stage and it barely misses those on the bench.)

MISS FLAHERTY. (Loud) Martin! Martin! (She jumps up and walks almost offstage left.) You come right over here! (Martin comes onstage.) Martin, you can frisbee to your heart's contents but let me tell you, I do not intend to be decapitated, Is that clear?

MARTIN. What "decapitated"?

MISS FLAHERTY. It means I do not intend to have my head out off.

MARTIN. You get you head cut off by a frisbee, you head on less tight than I thought!

MISS FLAHERTY. (Sharply) That's enough of that, Martin! Don't you get smart with me or your name will be mud, M-U-D! Understand?

PAULA. That's tellin' im, Miss Flaherty!

MISS FLAHERTY. (She walks back to the bench and speaks quietly) Paula, don't gloat. (She hugs Paula.) He did wrong and he knows it, so it's all forgotten. We don't want to rub it in, do we?

PAULA. (Defiantly) Yes, we do!

MISS FLAHERTY. (Firmly) No, we don't. (Pause) But anyhow,

let's move on, shall we? Now, where did Lonnie go? (Lonnie has run offstage left, back to the play area.) Martin, will you get Lonnie?

MARTIN. I'll decapitate him if he don't come! (He runs offstage left.)

MISS FLAHERTY. (Starts moving) Let's be on our way. I want us to see Eighth Street and look into some of the store windows. (They move up the left aisle in a sort of procession: Miss Flaherty and Betty, Paula and Malcolm, then Jennie. Miss Flaherty turns.) Where are Martin and Lonnie? (They come running up and fall in at the end of the procession.) So, we're off. Stick close by me. (They walk up the left aisle and down the right aisle as the scene on stage is shifted.) It's only a block away. It's full of clothing stores and psychedelic shops where they sell posters and candles and all kinds of interesting things. (They arrive back on stage and stop in front of a psychedelic goods shop.)

PAULA. What that funny smell?

LONNIE. You didn't wash today, ugly.

PAULA. You shut your trap and stop bad-mouthin' me, you skinny so-and-so!

LONNIE. (Rushing at her) I make you sorry--

MISS FLAHERTY. (Intercepting him) Now, Lonnie. (Jocularly) Pick on somebody your own size. (Lonnie forgets his revenge.) That smell is incense, Paula.

PAULA. What it for, Miss Flaherty?

MISS FLAHERTY. Oh, just to make a nice smell. Like, suppose you were cooking and the cooking left a greasy smell in your apartment. You could just light up some incense and have a better smell.

PAULA. I don't like it. I think it smell creepy.

MISS FLAHERTY. They always use it in my church. I think it's lovely.

MALCOLM. You a Catholic, Miss Flaherty?

MISS FLAHERTY. That's right, Malcolm.

MALCOLM. You have to do what the pope say?

MISS FLAHERTY. Well, you might say that, Malcolm, but, you see, we want to, because he's our holy father and we think he knows what's best for us in religion.

BETTY. The Reverend Slade, he say the pope want to take over all the other churches.

MISS FLAHERTY. Of course, the Reverend Slade is entitled to his opinion, but I must say I don't think he's right. I think the pope wants everybody to worship God in his own way.

MARTIN. Muslims, too?

MISS FLAHERTY. Of course. (Pause) But we didn't come to Greenwich Village to talk about religion.

JENNIE. (Who has been studying the window) Hey, look at those beads! They really heavy!

BETTY. Yeah. They nice!

LONNIE. (Who has been looking into the window of an adjoining furniture store) Hey, Miss Flaherty, what that thing?

MISS FLAHERTY. (Moving over to him, accompanied by Betty) Oh, that's a water bed, Lonnie. See, the mattress is filled with water. They say it's a very restful way to sleep.

LONNIE. Suppose it spring a leak while you sleepin'? You could get drowned.

BETTY. And who got a room big enough for a bed like that?

LONNIE. I tell you one thing: I don' want one! (They keep looking into the window, pointing out various objects and talking about them ad lib.)

JENNIE. (Looking offstage right she spots an interracial couple walking by.) My, my, look at that! One of the brothers with a white chick!

MALCOLM. What's the matter with that?

JENNIE. Plenty. Brothers should only go with sisters.

MARTIN. Right on! Brothers oughta leave them honkie chicks
  alone!

JENNIE. (Again looking offstage, she sees two homosexuals walk
  by.) Hey, look at them two!

MALCOLM. Who? Them hippies?

JENNIE. Hippies!? You kiddin'? They ain't no hippies! They faggits. Don't you know nothin'?

MALCOLM. (Slightly awed) Oh, you puttin' me on! (Pause) How
  you know they faggits?

JENNIE. Oh, you can just tell. Look at the way they walk with
  they wrists all funny and swingin' they asses!

MARTIN. Most white cats is faggits anyway! (Pause) Man, I
  never saw so much fuzz in one place. They got more pigs here
  than a pork factory. The bastards.

MALCOLM. They all white, too. How come?

MARTIN. I tell you why. Nobody don't do no bad things down
  here. Pigs that's here got it easy. They put all the black cops in
  Harlem, because they's always trouble up there. I bet these
  pigs here don' have to do nothin' but stand around. The creeps!

MALCOLM. If all they got to do is stand aroun', I think they pretty smart dudes.

MARTIN. Ah, they's pigs! Pigs is nothin' but pigs!

MISS FLAHERTY. (Coming over with Betty and Lonnie in tow)
  What are you all up to over here?

MARTIN. (Pretty sure he's going to got a negative reaction) We
  talkin' about pigs.

MISS FLAHERTY. Pigs? (Suddenly it dawns.) Martin, I've asked
  you, please, not to use that word when you're talking about
  policemen. Why, policemen are some of the most important
  people in society. If it weren't for them, I shudder to think what
  the world would be like! The police represent law and order,
  and law and order are the backbone of any civilized country.
  (Brief pause) You see, if you start criticizing the police, then

you lose respect for law and order and then, the next thing you know, you're undermining the government, and that's terrible! Besides, policemen are so good and kind and helpful. So, Martin, do me a favor and don't use that word. It makes me very unhappy to hear it.

MARTIN. (Humoring her) Right, Miss Flaherty.

MISS FLAHERTY. Did you see anything else interesting?

JENNIE. (With a double-meaning look at the others) Oh, we seen lots of interesting people.

PAULA. (Unable to hold it back) Oh, Miss Flaherty, we seen two faggits!

MISS FLAHERTY. (Discouraging further comment) Did you? Well, let's go over and see what's in the bookstore window over there. (They go over, Malcolm eagerly leading the way.)

MALCOLM. Miss Flaherty, who Hermin Hessey?

MISS FLAHERTY. Hesse, Malcolm. He was a famous Swiss writer but I think his books wouldn't be too interesting for you right now. Maybe in three or four years.

LONNIE. Look, Miss Flaherty! They got baseball books! How much you think they cost?

MISS FLAHERTY. I'm afraid the hardcover ones are pretty expensive. Maybe six or seven dollars.

LONNIE. (Who had been reaching into his pocket, withdraws his hand slowly) Oh.

MISS FLAHERTY. (Touching the back of his neck) Sorry, Lonnie.

PAULA. Miss Flaherty, who (She has trouble with the name.) Throughgood Marshall?

MISS FLAHERTY. Thurgood, dear, Thurgood Marshall.

MARTIN. He a big Uncle Tom.

MISS FLAHERTY. That's not fair, Martin. He was a great lawyer, Paula, and now he's the first black man who ever was on the Supreme Court. He's a very important and powerful man.

MARTIN. (Mostly to himself) Handkerchief-head!

MISS FLAHERTY. Someday, Martin, when that chip falls off your shoulder, you're going to be a very sorry young man about some of the things you said. I can hardly wait. (Pause) Now, boys and girls, how would you feel about a coke? You've all been so good and our trip was such fun, I think you've got a treat coming.

BETTY. (Drawing very close) Oh, Miss Flaherty, you the best teacher that ever was! Except for my mama, you my main lady.

MALCOLM. You out a sight! (He touches her arm.)

MISS FLAHERTY. If I'm a good teacher, that's because I have such nice boys and girls in my class. Come along, everybody. (She moves offstage with the children accompanying her and heads up the left aisle.) Come on, Lonnie! Let's go, Jennie. (As they walk, the children comment.)

MARTIN. Hey, look at that suit, man!

MALCOLM. Yeah, they some heavy threads!

JENNIE. I never seen so many shoes in one store!

LONNIE. (Giggling) Hey, Marty, look at that chick in that picture! She bare-ass nekkid!

MARTIN. Some jugs on 'er huh? (They move back onstage, where the scene is now the interior of a soda-shop. The audience is behind the soda-fountain.)

MISS FLAHERTY. This must be our lucky day! Seven empty seats all in a row.

(There is much scrambling among the children and ad libbing of the "I want to sit by ____" variety. Finally all are seated, Miss Flaherty at the far right, then Betty, then Martin and then the others. A soda jerk appears.)

SODA JERK. Well, what'll it be, everybody?

MISS FLAHERTY. What kind of soft drinks do you have?

SODA JERK. Oh, coke, Tab, ginger ale, And we've got orange drink and grape drink, too.

MALCOLM. I want grape.

LONNIE. I want grape, too.

PAULA. I want orange.

MARTIN. I want orange, too.

LONNIE. I changed my mind, I want orange.

JENNIE. I can't decide if I want coke or Tab,

MISS FLAHERTY. (To the soda jerk) Maybe you'd better wait on somebody else while we thrash this all out. Now, everybody, let's get organized here, so-- (Meanwhile an outwardly affable, heavy-set, middle-aged man has been looking at the group and now comes up to Miss Flaherty. There in an undertone of sadism in his speech that she does not catch.)

MAN. Well, what have we here? An outing?

MISS FLAHERTY. That's right, I'm a teacher in Harlem and these are some of my students. None of them had ever seen Greenwich Village, so I brought them down today to get acquainted with it.

MAN. Well, well! Quite an idea! Yes, sir. Quite an idea!

MISS FLAHERTY. We've been to Washington Square and then we went window-shopping on Eighth Street.

MAN. Did you indeed? I'll bet they think you're mighty nice, Say, ma'am, you know what I'd like to do? I'd like these kids to have a time none of you will forget. Let 'em order whatever they want and I'll take care of it.

MISS FLAHERTY. Oh, no, I couldn't let you do that.

MAN. Sure you could. My pleasure. Wouldn't all you kids like to have a banana split? With three kinds of ice cream and whipped cream and all? And a coke to go with it?

LONNIE. Really? Sure!

MALCOLM. Yeah, me too.

PAULA. Me three.

MAN. Good! (Calling to the soda jerk) Young fellow, give us seven--

MISS FLAHERTY. No, six. I just want a coke, thanks. You know-
- dieting.

MAN. Make that six banana splits and seven cokes. And make it
snappy. We got a lot of hungry young folks here.

SODA JERK. Coming right up.

MAN. (To Miss Flaherty) Now where is the school you teach at?

MISS FLAHERTY. On 136th Street, near Broadway.

MAN. And what grade do you teach?

MISS FLAHERTY. The fourth.

MAN. Well, that's fine. Just fine. And how are all these kids
doing?

MISS FLAHERTY. Very nicely.

BETTY. (Timidly) She a wonderful teacher.

MAN. I'll bet she is. Teaches you all week and then spends
Saturday taking you to other parts of town. (The banana splits
arrive, then the cokes, and the kids dive in.) Eat hearty, everybody! Yes, siree, it's a pleasure to see healthy young appetites.
(Then silence as the kids eat and drink.)

BETTY. (Sitting next to Miss Flaherty, drops a spoonful of ice
cream on her dress.) Oh. I dropped some on my dress! My best
dress! My mother will kill me.

MISS FLAHERTY. Now, Betty, don't go to pieces. (She takes out
a kleenex and starts to mop off the dress. She calls to the soda
jerk.) May we have a glass of water, please? (To Betty) We'll
have it looking as good as new in no time flat. (The water
arrives and she continues the mopping-up operation.
Surreptitiously during this activity, the man sneaks out.) There!
What did I tell you? Good as new! (The soda jerk brings over
the check and puts it down in front of her. She looks around for
the man and at first cannot bring herself to realize what has
happened. She speaks inadvertently.) Oh, no! (Finally it dawns
and she looks at the check and then slips her wallet out of her
purse and counts the bills, looking relieved when she sees she

186

has enough. The only one who has observed this is Martin, seated on the other side of Betty. As she takes the bills from her wallet and puts them on the counter, he comes over to her far side, away from Betty.)

MARTIN. I seen what he done.

MISS FLAHERTY. (Realizing this is a crucial moment for him) What do you mean, Martin?

MARTIN. That honkey! That big spender! I seen what he done! The rat! He walked out and now you got to pay! I could kill him? What he do that for? He do that 'cause we black? That so mean!

MISS FLAHERTY. You're wrong, Martin. He gave me the money. You must have been too busy with your banana split to notice it.

MARTIN. (Unconvinced) That dirty honkey! I'd like to pound him in the mouth! Boy, my brother right. All whiteys is rats!

MISS FLAHERTY. (She knows he knows.) Not all, Martin.

MARTIN. (Realizing what she is doing and why) No, maybe not all. Maybe they's one that ain't. (For the first time in the play, he puts his hand on her arm, not tentatively, but forthrightly, at the same time giving her a look that is not the adoring gaze of a child for a beloved adult, but the strong, respectful look of an adult for someone he likes and admires.)

Slow curtain.

CURTAIN GOING UP

TOMORROW THE WORLD

Today we rule Germany,
Tomorrow the whole world!
               --Nazi Party song

CAST OF CHARACTERS

Mickey

Minnie

Goofy

Donald

Bugs

Daffy

All characters must be dressed in the costumes used in the animated cartoon, although the mouth areas of the masks may have to be cut back to make speech clearer. Obviously all the actors should imitate the speech of the cartoon characters.

The scene is the living room of Mickey's house. There is a door right to the outside and a door left to the kitchen.

The time is the autumn of the present year.

A conventional upper-middle-class living room. Upstage center a fireplace, with a window on either side. Over the fireplace a painting of a figure in a military uniform; the figure has a mouse's head a la Disney, with large round ears. Stage left, the door to the outside. Stage right, the door to the other rooms in the house. In the room left are two chairs with a small lamp table between them, while right is a sofa with a coffee table in front of it. Stage left and right refer to the audience's left and right.

AT RISE: The stage is empty. The sound of a key turning in the lock of the door left is heard. The door opens and, after a pause, a laughing Mickey enters, carrying a laughing Minnie. He sets her down and, joining hands, they whirl in a circle center stage, still both laughing. They move toward the sofa and both fall down onto it, out of breath.

MICKEY. Whew!

MINNIE. Whew is right!

MICKEY. I can hardly believe it. After all these years it's Mr. and Mrs. Mickey Mouse! Think of that!

MINNIE. (Sweetly) No, dear. I told you I wasn't going to give up my maiden name. So it's going to be Mickey Mouse and Minnie Mouse-Mouse. Besides, I think hyphenated names sound extra-classy.

MICKEY. Whatever you say, honey. I'm just so happy to be married to you!

MINNIE. Me, too. And what I like best is that we've agreed to have a companionate marriage.

MICKEY. Yes. That way we won't have to do any of those dirty things that most married couples do.

MINNIE. I feel so good about it because I don't ever want to do anything that a four-year-old couldn't watch.

MICKEY. (Patting her hand) Me either. After all, we still have to be role models for all good little boys and girls.

MINNIE. We certainly do. And for children of all ages. It's really quite a responsibility, but we've been up to it for 70 years, so there's no reason we can't go on being the symbols of everything that's good and sweet and pure.

MICKEY. (Rising, he paces around the room) You know, when you stop to think about it, it's wonderful the way things have changed mouse-wise since we were born. Why, 70 years ago, all people thought about was sicking cats on us or setting out those barbaric traps that broke our backs or using us in their cruel and vicious laboratory experiments. And now look!

MINNIE. You're right, dear. It's wonderful!

MICKEY. Why, we control the theme-park business all over the world now that we've made those depraved Frenchies knuckle under and--

MINNIE. Heavens to Betsy, Mickey! What a way to talk! Remember, we must love our neighbors, even if they get mad because we won't let them have wine in their theme park.

MICKEY. It's not their theme park. It's our theme park and we know that soft drinks are best for them. Alcoholic beverages are a device of the devil! (Pause) But anyhow we've also got the animated film business sewed up--imagine, *The Lion King*, *Pocahontas*, the revival of *Snow White*--all in the same decade. And we've had lots of flicks with people in them, too.

MINNIE. And all of them with those messages of happiness and goodness and purity, and all those other great things.

MICKEY. And of course we've bought a television network, but the best is yet to come!

MINNIE. (Leaning forward in anticipation) What's that, Mickey? Oh, do tell me!

MICKEY. Well, you know we've bought up lots of property on 42nd Street--

MINNIE. Yes?

MICKEY. And a hunk of Rockefeller Center--

MINNIE. Yes?

MICKEY. Don't you see the pattern? It's like a pincers movement. We're going to move from the North and the South and take over the whole New York theater district and we won't put on anything but uplifting shows like *Beauty and the Beast.* No more dirty plays about depraved and unhappy people.

MINNIE. That was such a beautiful show and it made me so joyous! I'd always felt self-conscious about my outsize (Her hand goes to one of her ears.)--about being aurally challenged, but *Beauty and the Beast* made me realize that things like that don't matter if I have a pure mind and a sweet soul.

MICKEY. I've always felt that my ears are special because they make my hearing so much more acute. And I see the theme of *Beauty and the Beast* as postmodern neo-Platonism. I mean, in *The Republic,* Plato makes the distinction between accident and essence and I see the identical message in this play--the physical appearance is the accident and the psychic condition is the essence.

MINNIE. (Very concerned) Oh, Mickey, you're not turning into an elitist, are you? One of the things that's always drawn me to you is that you're so down-to-earth, so folksy. I'd be awfully unhappy if you got--well, kind of uppity.

MICKEY. (Going over and patting her on the shoulder) Never fear, honey, I'm not going to change now. Forget what I said about Plato. I promise never to mention his name again.

MINNIE. (Reaching out and taking his hand) Oh, you just don't know how relieved I am. I mean, if you and I are going to control the entertainment business for the whole country from cradle to grave, we've got to remember that an awful lot of the children of all ages can't deal with that deep stuff like Plato.

191

MICKEY. Of course you're right, Minnie. We have to keep in mind that they're just simple people.

MINNIE. Folks.

MICKEY. Folks. (He sits down beside Minnie.) But talking about Plato makes me think about poor Pluto.

MINNIE. (Patting his hand) Now, Mickey, I've said it before and I'll say it again: even cartoon characters aren't immortal.

MICKEY. (Dabbing at his eyes) I know, but it still hurts.

MINNIE. Just think of him on his own cloud in a pearl-covered doghouse outside a golden palace with God inside, munching on a dog biscuit.

MICKEY. (Looking alarmed) God is munching on a dog biscuit?

MINNIE. No, no. Pluto!

MICKEY. Anyway, I'm sure he's in heaven and I'm sure he's happy.

MINNIE. I'm sure he is, too. (Rising) I suppose I should go and start unpacking. You know, we were so busy dancing around that we didn't even bring in our suitcases! (She is moving toward the door, when the doorbell rings.) Now who can that be? (Mickey rises as she goes to the door. She opens it and Goofy enters, bearing a tray covered with gift wrapping and a bottle, also gift-wrapped.) Why, it's Goofy! Hello, Goofy!

MICKEY. Hello, Goofy!

GOOFY. (Entering) Congratulations, Mr. Mouse and Mrs. Mouse!

MINNIE. (Softly and gently) Not Mrs. Mouse. Ms. Mouse-Mouse. I'm adding my name to Mickey's.

GOOFY. Oh, sorry, Ms. Mouse-Mouse. Anyhow, my congratulations. (He puts down the tray and bottle and shakes their hands.) I knew you were back from your honeymoon when I saw the suitcases on the porch and I said to myself, "We've got to have a roostertail party (This is not a consciously clever locution, but his standard word.) to celebrate their return." So I bought over something to drink and some hors d'oeuvres.

MINNIE. Oh, how wonderful! (She sits on the sofa and unwraps the gifts.) Oh, look, Mickey! Grade A pasteurized homogenized milk and--what are these, Goofy?

GOOFY. I made 'em myself. They're cheese spheres--cheddar rolled in chopped pecans.

MINNIE. (Sampling one) Oh, Goofy, they're delicious! (She holds out the tray.) Try one, Mickey.

MICKEY. (Sampling one) Fabulous!

MINNIE. (Rising) I'll get some glasses so we can have a drink together. (She exits right and returns with three wineglasses, sits down and fills each one with milk.) There! (Mickey and Goofy come over and each takes a glass.)

GOOFY. (Raising his glass on high) To the happy couple!

MICKEY. (Raising his glass) And to the nicest neighbor in the world!

MINNIE. Santé!

MICKEY. Cin, cin!

GOOFY. Prosit! (All drink.)

MICKEY. Boy, I needed that!

MINNIE. My, there's nothing like a nice cold drink of milk on a nice autumn day.

GOOFY. Yeah. It's nice, all right. And we mustn't forget who brought it to us.

MINNIE. (Looking at the bottle cap) Fenland Farms?

GOOFY. No, no! (Raising his eyes heavenward) He from Whom all blessings flow!

MICKEY. Gee whillikers, Goofy, it's so nice to know we have somebody living nearby who's so devout!

GOOFY. "Every thing that may abide the fire, ye shall make it go through the fire, and it shall be clean: nevertheless it shall be purified with the water of separation: and all that abideth not the fire ye shall make go through the water."

MINNIE. (Looking as baffled as Mickey) Yes, indeed.

GOOFY. "If they say thus unto us, Tarry until we come to you; then we will stand still in our place, and we will not go up unto them."

MICKEY. (Looking as baffled as Minnie) Mmm-hm.

GOOFY. "And ye came near and stood under the mountain and the mountain burned with fire into the midst of heaven, with darkness, clouds and thick darkness."

MINNIE. (Still puzzled) Well, if that's what the Good Book says.

GOOFY. "And the people stood up all that day and all that night, and all the next day and they gathered the quails: he that gathered least gathered ten homers; and they spread them abroad for themselves..."

MICKEY. What's a homer, Goofy?

GOOFY. I don't know. I just memorize the scriptures, I don't try to interpret them, because that would show the sin of pride.

MINNIE. And you're right, Goofy.

GOOFY. Would you like to hear more from the Good Book?

MINNIE. Oh, I wish we had time, but we simply have to start unpacking.

MICKEY. Perhaps later.

GOOFY. Fine. I'll come back later. In the meantime, I'll go down to P.S. 40. There's a protest going on down there. They're going to picket until the authorities allow prayer in the public schools.

MINNIE. Fine, Goofy. And thank you so much for the refreshments. It was nice of you to bring them over.

GOOFY. (Heading for the door) Just simple Judaeo-Christian charity. (He exits.)

MINNIE. (After a pause) Mickey, I wonder what you think. Do you think Goofy was stereotyping us when he brought cheese over?

MICKEY. Oh, no. He's not that kind of person. You're just so sensitive. But it's one of the things that's nicest about you. (Pause) I'll go out and get the suitcases.

MINNIE. Let's wait a minute and have another cheese sphere. What Goofy said was very inspiring, but I'm afraid I didn't understand much of it.

MICKEY. (Grabbing a cheese ball) Like he said, we're not supposed to understand it.

MINNIE. I guess. But I have to say-- (There is a thunderous pounding on the door left.) Now what?

MICKEY. (Going to the door) We'll see. (He opens the door and Donald rushes in, jumping up and down and yelling.)

DONALD. So you're finally back from your fornicating honeymoon! It's about fornicating time!

MINNIE. (Rising) It's a good thing your articulation is so fuzzy, Donald, so I can pretend I didn't catch every word you said.

DONALD. I don't give a pile of excrement if you caught every fornicating word or not, but you'd better catch this: that fornicating maple tree on your side of the fornicating property line is shedding its fornicating leaves all over my fornicating lawn and you'd better come over and rake them up!

MICKEY. I'm real busy right now planning to conquer the world entertainment-wise.

MINNIE. Don't you think, Donald, that your temper would improve if you were to undertake a course of speech therapy so you'd become more articulate?

DONALD. I don't need any fornicating advice from any fornicating busybody neighbor about my fornicating speech! Open those fornicating satellite-dish ears and listen!

MICKEY. Now, Donald, that's not very nice. Suppose we were to say something about those dinner-plate lips of yours--not that we would, of course, but wouldn't that hurt your feelings?

DONALD. Those aren't lips, you stupid illegitimate rodent! That's a fornicating bill! Jeez!

MINNIE. Donald, you came perilously close to taking the name of the Lord in vain, and that's something we simply don't tolerate in this house.

DONALD. Will you stop the fornicating moralizing and answer my question about the fornicating leaves?

MICKEY. It has occurred to me that you have three stalwart young nephews and that perhaps I might pay them to pick up the leaves on both sides of the property line.

DONALD. (Mollified) Hey, not a bad idea! Not a bad idea at all. Keep 'em out of the video arcade and teach 'em the value of a buck. OK, how much?

MICKEY. I think I could manage a quarter an hour for each of the lads.

DONALD. (Furious, jumping up and down) A quarter? Whaddaya think? They're fornicating wetbacks that do fornicating stoop labor for fornicating peanuts?

MINNIE. Now, Donald--

DONALD. Don't "Now, Donald" me! You offer those poor kids a fornicating two bits an hour when you've got enough fornicating dough to buy Rockefeller Center?

MICKEY. There's a big mortgage on it that has to be paid off.

DONALD. Pay it off with the fornicating profits from fornicating Epcot Center, but don't pay it off on the fornicating backs of three little kids!

MICKEY. OK, OK. Three bucks an hour--each. How's that?

DONALD. (Completely settled down) That's more like it. I'll have 'em do it tomorrow. (Pause) So how was your honeymoon?

MINNIE. Very nice, thank you. And nice of you to ask.

DONALD. It's nice that your honeymoon was nice. (To Minnie) I think you'll like it in this neighborhood. It's full of good people. Lots of children of all ages.

MINNIE. That's what Mickey tells me. He says there are African-American cats, Hispanic-American jaguars, Native American coyotes and Asian-American pandas all living in harmony. That's heart-warming.

DONALD. I'm beginning to feel kind of sorry I disturbed the peace and quiet of the neighborhood by coming in here and yelling and making a scene.

MINNIE. You know I'm the last person on earth to interfere in other people's lives, Donald. I always say, "Live and let live," except when it comes to people who smoke or drink or use drugs or swear or have sex or look at Calvin Klein ads. Like I say, except for those people, I never even criticize, but I do worry about you, Donald. I wonder if it might not be a good idea for you to undertake a course of therapy to control your temper. If you keep blowing up, people might think that you're not a nice, sweet, kind person and that would be too bad, because we know you are.

MICKEY. That's right, Donald.

MINNIE. Sometimes the stresses of modern life put a lot of pressure on us all, so we have to understand when they seem to get too much for people to bear.

DONALD. (Dabbing at his eyes) You're real understanding.

MINNIE. We're all God's little children and we have to be nice, don't we? (She takes his hand.)

MICKEY. That's right. (She takes Donald's other hand.) We're working to make the world one great big Disneyland, filled with happy, happy, smiling people, all scrubbed and neat and clean and nice. Then it'll be a perfect world, won't it?

ALL THREE. (Dancing in a circle stage center) Happy, happy, happy, happy (The doorbell rings while they are chanting, but they don't hear it.)

ALL THREE. (Dancing in a circle stage center) Nice, nice, nice, nice! (There is another ring of the bell, but they don't hear it.)

BUGS. (Entering the room, followed by Daffy) What's up, doc?

DAFFY. Sparklin' sarsaparilla! It's a sex orgy!

BUGS. (To Daffy) Not this crew! (To the trio downstage) We rang, but I guess you didn't hear us, so we came in.

MICKEY. (Not happy to see him as the trio downstage breaks up) Hello, Bugs. Hello, Daffy. What do you want?

BUGS. We just wanted to talk to you. About Midtown Manhattan.

MICKEY. (Flatly) Oh. (Pause) What's there to talk about?

BUGS. Oh, come off it, Mike!

MICKEY. Please don't call me Mike. You know my name is Mickey.

BUGS. I know. It appeals to the little kiddies. And Mike sounds too tough, right?

MINNIE. Oh, really, Bugs! You're too much!

BUGS. Come off it, Min. Don't play demure with me.

MINNIE. And stop calling me Min. It makes me sound like some kind of washerwoman.

DAFFY. Sparklin' sarsaparilla! What're you? A princess or something? Now you're just a suburban housewife!

MINNIE. (Coldly) With a good stake in Manhattan real estate! (Mopping her face) I see you still have your malocclusion and are still drowning everyone you talk to with your saliva.

DONALD. Right! Why don't you shut your fornicating trap?

DAFFY. You're just the one to talk about speech defects, Don. You practically have to have a translator every time you open your mouth. (Pause) At least I've been taking speech classes.

DONALD. (Cynically) Sure!

DAFFY. I have! I even get special exercises. "She sells seashells by the sea shore." "Sister Susie's sewing shirts for soldiers."

DONALD. Get your fornicating money back!

BUGS. (To the two ducks) Enough, you two! Give it a rest! (To Mickey and Minnie) You been on 42nd Street recently?

MICKEY. Of course. Checking out the profits of our stores.

BUGS. Look across the street? At the old Times building?

MICKEY. Of course not. Everything that's happening is happening west of Seventh Avenue and 42nd. Anybody who's cool knows that!

BUGS. That so, Mike? (Mickey winces.) Take a look across the street next time you're at forty-deuce and Seventh. It's your future, You're going down, doc.

MINNIE. You're whistling in the graveyard, Bugs. Mickey and I have a whole gallery of supporting players who are all famous.

BUGS. And you think I and my crew are chopped liver? We can match you character for character and we don't reek of sanctimoniousness.

MICKEY. We're in tune with the times, Bugs.

BUGS. Listen. Right now you've got some prude running the city and pushing erotic cleansing for all he's worth. But that's gonna end soon and you're gonna be left high and dry with your "nice, nice, nice."

MINNIE. We'll just see about that, won't we, Bugs?

BUGS. You bet we will! And while I'm here to visit, I might's well congratulate Mike because he's boinking you honestly now--

MINNIE. (Falling back on the couch) Oh! Oh!

BUGS. And to warn you both it's war to the death! When I'm through with you, there'll be no more Vermont cheddar and French Roquefort! You'll be glad to get Velveeta! (To Daffy) C'mon, Daf. Let's go wipe some of this purity off! (They exit, leaving the other three stunned.)

Quick blackout

CURTAIN GOING UP

GOING UP!

CAST OF CHARACTERS

Cynthia

Diane

Ken

Bob

Black

(The Hansens' living room. A door to the kitchen and the bedrooms upstage left and a door to the entrance foyer upstage right. Stage left, a couch with a cocktail table in front of it on which are an ashtray and a teacup with saucer; upstage center is a large overstuffed chair facing front with an end table beside it on which are a lamp and an ashtray; stage right, two chairs in a group with an end table between them on which are an ashtray, an African wood carving and two coasters; far right, a bar. Everything indicates opulence and good taste, although the effect of the room is to suggest a magazine advertisement for an opulent living room. At rise, Bob is standing at the bar, just having finished making himself a drink, which he is sampling. Cynthia and Ken are seated right, each with a drink, and Cynthia is laughing in a subdued fashion at something either she or Ken has just said. She stops and assumes a serious expression as Diane enters upstage left, closing the door behind her very carefully and quietly.)

CYNTHIA. How is she, Diane?
DIANE. She's finally sleeping a little, thanks to the tranquilizers. (She moves to the couch.)
CYNTHIA. (Without deep sincerity) Good. I say, that's fine.
KEN. I'm glad. She certainly is all torn up.
BOB. (Crosses to Diane and draws her down beside him on the couch, putting his arm over her shoulders.) The important thing now, honey, is how are you?
DIANE. Tired, Bob, if you want to know the truth. Damned tired! (She holds out her teacup, which she has picked up from the cocktail tables to Cynthia, who looks first surprised, then angry, but finally rises, crosses, takes it and exits to the kitchen upstage left. Diane then leans back and closes her eyes.)
BOB. (Holds her tighter.) I know, honey. I know.
KEN. Diane, Cindy and I have been meaning to tell you how

much we appreciate what you're doing for Helen. You've been just great!

DIANE. (Opening her eyes at this) Thanks, Ken. But you know that, even for sisters, we've always been awfully close. And then, when Bob and I were starting out, Helen and Ray gave us a lot of help. So I guess I'm the logical one to hold her hand.

KEN. Even so, not everyone would do what you're doing. I mean, flying three thousand miles, leaving your kids and everything.

DIANE. We do what we have to do, Ken.

KEN. Which brings me to something we have to talk about, (Cynthia returns with a cup of tea, which she puts down on the cocktail table with obvious ill grace. She then crosses right and resumes her seat, but paying attention to the conversation as she does so.) Did Helen say anything to you and Bob about any instructions that Ray gave her for the funeral? Or did he leave any letter or anything about what he wanted done?

DIANE. I did ask her. She says he never said a word about it. She says he wouldn't even talk about it.

CYNTHIA. I'm not surprised. Ray had a thing about death: he didn't like it.

KEN. So he didn't leave any instructions?

DIANE. She's certain he didn't.

KEN. Well, then, I suppose it's up to us. I mean, Helen doesn't seem in any shape--

DIANE. I wish you were wrong, Ken, but I agree. She just couldn't cope, I'm afraid,

CYNTHIA. (Still not deeply sincere) Poor dear. I say, poor darling.

KEN. The man from the funeral home should be here soon, so I'd like to suggest that we get organized before he gets here.

CYNTHIA. I think everything should be in keeping with Ray's position, so I don't think we should stint. I say, we shouldn't scrimp.

DIANE. Oh, I agree, but on the other hand, we don't want to go overboard and be ostentatious. Ray had his simple side, too. I mean, besides the Bentley he did have a Continental,

CYNTHIA. (A bit stiffly) My brother was the president of the one hundred and forty-sixth largest corporation in America and I think we should bear that in mind. I say, I don't think we should forget that.

KEN. Now, Cindy, keep cool.

CYNTHIA. I'm keeping cool. All I'm saying is that Ray was an important man and I don't think we should forget it. I say, that's all I'm saying.

BOB. Right, Cindy. I'm sure we all buy that.

KEN. Naturally.

DIANE. Of course. It's only that I don't want us to be too lavish. We have to consider poor Helen, too. She's going to have to tighten her belt quite a bit now, you know.

CYNTHIA. (Half to herself) I'd like to try living with my belt that tight! I say, I'd like to give it a try,

DIANE. Well, Ray did have a little insurance-- half a million, I think-- but the income from that won't be anything like his salary.

CYNTHIA. I could struggle by on it. I say, I could make do.

KEN. Come on, now, girls, lets get back to the business at hand. Obviously the service will be at St. David's, and I suppose we'll have to have the invitations phoned out. Ray's secretaries can take care of that.

CYNTHIA. Reverend Vaughan will handle it?

KEN. Yes, he was in this morning, while you were out shopping,

CYNTHIA. I'm so glad. He has such good taste. I'm sure he won't drag in a lot of things about death and all that morbid stuff. If there's one thing I hate it's a depressing funeral. I say, depressing funerals make me feel so uncomfortable. I always think

203

back to my father's funeral. It was so grim it was absolutely unforgettable. Remember, Ken?

KEN. I always remember unforgettable things.

BOB. I know what you mean. But how will we get a list of people to invite?

DIANE. I think we should wait until Helen wakes up and talk it over with her. Then at the graveside we should have just the family.

CYNTHIA. Graveside? Just a minute! You don't mean to say, Diane, that you're thinking of sticking Ray in some run-of-the-mill grave with a little two-by-four headstone?!

DIANE. We could have a larger monument, if you like those big, ugly, showy hunks of stone with all that tasteless sculpture.

CYNTHIA. But you can't be serious! Of course Ray has to have a mausoleum!

DIANE. Don't you think that's a bit much, Cindy? I mean--

CYNTHIA. No, in all honesty, I don't. I think it's the least that Helen can do for Ray. I know he'd want it that way. I say, I'm sure that's how he'd want it done.

DIANE. But wouldn't a mausoleum be frightfully expensive?

KEN. I assume they're not cheap, but I agree with Cindy: Helen really owes it to Ray.

DIANE. I don't know. It seems to me that a small stone in quiet good taste--

CYNTHIA. Please, Diane. How would Ken ever be able to hold his head up at the Downtown A. C., with all Ray's friends knowing we'd stuck him in some kind of a pauper's grave? Why, it's--- it's inconceivable! I say, I think it's unthinkable!

BOB. Yes, dear, I have to say I think Cindy's right. I mean, considering Ray's position and all, it strikes me--

CYNTHIA. Well, as long as we're all agreed on that, what would be really nice is something out of the ordinary. I've heard that mausoleums have been done as miniature replicas of famous buildings. I say--

DIANE. Oh, really, Cindy, you can't--

CYNTHIA. No, I mean it, Why not a miniature House of Parliament? You know how Ray loved London when he was over there setting up the British office. Or a smaller copy of the Lincoln Memorial. After all, there was something Lincolnesque about Ray.

DIANE. (Aroused) Yes. They were both Republicans. Cynthia, I can hardly believe what I'm hearing. Why something like that will absolutely bankrupt Helen!

BOB. Right!

KEN. Yes, Cindy, I do think you're going overboard a bit. When you said "mausoleums" I thought you meant one of the regular ones, with those pillars out in front-- Doric or Colonial or whatever you call them-- and I think we should stick to something more along those lines.

CYNTHIA. (Defeated, but not happy about it) I seem to be outvoted, but if that's the way you all want it-- I say, if you don't want Ray's monument to be monumental-- (The doorbell chimes, off stage right.)

KEN. That must be the man from the funeral home. I told Mavis to send him right in. (A pause, after which Black enters stage right. His hair is black. He wears a black suit, a black tie and black shoes. He carries a black attaché envelope under his arm.)

BLACK. Good afternoon. (Ken and Bob rise. Both cross to him, Ken gets there first and shakes his hand.) My name is Mortimer Black. I'm from the Lyman Homes.

KEN. Yes, so we assumed, Mr. Black. I'm Kenneth Gresham, Ray's--- the late Mr. Hansen's brother-in-law. That's my wife, Cynthia, that's Mrs. Johnson, Mrs. Hansen's sister, and this is her husband. (He is still holding Black's hand, which, while not looking like a dead fish, seems utterly inanimate. He does not appear to know what to do with it, and finally hands it over to Bob.)

BOB. (Taking the hand, he has to clasp, rather than shake it.) Glad to meet you, Mr. Black. (He walks back to the couch, wiping his hand across his chest.)

KEN. Please sit down, Mr. Black. (He indicates the chair upstage.)

BLACK. (A curious combination of the glad-hander and Uriah Heep) Thank you. I wish that we might have met under different circumstances. (He sits down.)

KEN. (Dryly) Yes.

BLACK. (As if by rote) At this dolorous hour, when our fragile mortality—

CYNTHIA. (Only partly to herself) Jesus!

BLACK. I'm happy that you have the consolation of religion to sus—

KEN. Please, Mr. Black. We deeply appreciate your words of comfort, but we'd really prefer to get on with the arrangements, if you don't mind.

BLACK. Of course, of course, Mr. Graham--

KEN. Gresham.

BLACK. Yes, of course, Mr. Gresham. You know, it's peculiar. I find it awfully difficult to remember people's names if they're not-- uh, deceased, (The others smile stiffly.) But enough of my idiosyncrasies. Now, as to the arrangements. (He takes out and lights a black cigarette.)

CYNTHIA. We want the best, that's all. I say, that sums it up.

DIANE. How much will that cost?

BLACK. Would you wish something in the range of, say, $25,000? If so, we could furnish the departed with something modest and tasteful, yet appropriate to his status as a business and community leader. Bronze and satin, and all the proper accoutrements.

DIANE. $25,000?! That sounds modest enough!

BOB. I think that would be fine, (Meaningfully) Don't you, Diane?

DIANE. If you say so, Bob.

KEN. Now, Mr. Black, as far as we know, the depar-- Mr. Hansen had made no funeral arrangements, purchased no burial plot or mausoleum or anything like that.

BLACK. Now, of course, Mr. Grissom—

KEN. Gresham.

BLACK. Sorry, Mr. Gresham. As you know, we are funeral directors and, as such, would not be able to suggest any preferred final resting-place.

KEN. But. (This is a declarative, not a broken, sentence.)

BLACK. (Unctuously) As you say, sir, "but" we have an interesting suggestion to present to you. (Pause) I don't suppose you read Memorial Park Monthly?

CYNTHIA. You're psychic.

BOB. No, Mr. Black, we don't,

BLACK. A pity. (Short pause) Well, in the November issue of last year, a challenging notion was put forth, one that my firm has been quick to act upon, I'm proud to say.

KEN. Well?

BLACK. Just bear with me, please. Do you know what the major problem in our metropolitan cemeteries is today?

CYNTHIA. Corruption?

BLACK. No. It's a terrestrial version of the space race. We're running out of land because there's been such a de-population explosion. It's just that too many people are dying.

CYNTHIA. Speak to the medical profession. I say, talk to the doctors.

BLACK. (Chuckling, but not very heartily) Yes, you have a point, Mrs. Grantham.

CYNTHIA. (Rather sharply) Gresham!

BLACK. Quite so. Sorry, Mrs. Gresham. Were you no longer among the living--

CYNTHIA. That seems quite a price to pay for being addressed by the right name. I'd just as soon live with your mistake, thank you, I say, thanks all the same.

BLACK. (Again laughs not very sincerely) Yes. But, anyway, what are our burial-places going to do? I assure you, what's going on in our cemeteries is no laughing matter.

BOB. I believe you.

BLACK. As I suppose you are aware, there has been some-- uh, what might be called "doubling up"-- husbands' coffins interred atop their wives--

CYNTHIA. What does Women's Lib have to say about things like that? I say, how do the militants--

BLACK. But that has only been like sweeping the problem under the sod, so to speak. No, a whole new approach was called for. We simply had to breathe new life into the burial business. So we asked ourselves, what could we do? There was just no more land to be bought. Finally we figured out there was nowhere for the deceased of this world to go but up.

BOB. I think you might be able to get an argument from the theologians on that.

BLACK. Uh? Oh. (Laughs.) Yes, yes, very good, Mr. Jackson.

BOB. Johnson.

BLACK. Johnson.

BOB. Johnson.

BLACK. Johnson. So, an ingenious idea has been proposed and we're working on it now: high-rise mausoleums. (On this last, he rises slowly.)

KEN. You mean, like apartment buildings?

BLACK. Yes, indeed. (Getting carried away) They're the coming thing in the burial field. Before long, you'll see them springing up all over the place. And my firm is building one of the first, if not the first, in the United States. We bought a large plot at Celestial Serenity Cemetery and we've already started work on it. (Lyrical) It'll be 24 stories high, with sixteen-- uh, "residents" to a floor and on top of it will be twin penthouses. (Pause) Actually, it was one of these penthouses that I had in mind for Mr. Hansen.

KEN. Just how will this work, Mr. Black?

BLACK. It'll be just like a condominium. There'll be an initial payment to buy in and then regular monthly-- or, if you prefer, yearly-- carrying charges. Frankly, at this point we're not sure about the tax picture, but there may be some abatement.

BOB. (Unable to credit what he is hearing) I can't believe it! (Rises and crosses to the bar, where he puts ice cubes into his glass, facing downstage as he does so.)

BLACK. (Crossing to stage left) Oh, yes. Although, as I say, the tax picture is cloudy. Now, as to the appointments, they will be the last word in luxurious-- uh, resting. I might even say they are sumptuous. (He crosses right.) All the halls and each room will offer wall-to-wall carpeting, there will be elevator service, central heating and air conditioning and (At this point he is right behind Bob, with his downstage hand raised above Bob's shoulder. Bob does not realize he is so close.) of course 24-hour doorman service. (He lowers his hand heavily onto Bob's shoulder.)

BOB. (He is starting to pour his drink. When Black's hand comes down onto his shoulder unexpectedly, he jumps and pours the liquor not into his glass, but onto the top of the bar. He speaks to cover his embarrassment.) Incredible! (He takes out his handkerchief and mops up the spilled liquor.)

BLACK. Yes, isn't it, though. No one could want a finer resting-place. And very reasonable, too.

DIANE. What's the rate for the-- what do you call them-- "rooms"?-- on the floors below the penthouse?

BLACK. For the Leisure Lounges, as we call them, the initial payment is $10,000 and the carrying charge we estimate will be in the vicinity of $100 a month.

DIANE. That seems about what we had in mind. (Bob recrosses to his seat on the couch.)

CYNTHIA. What, putting Ray way down on the street floor or something? I think that's awful! I say, I think it's mortifying!

KEN. Now, honey.

CYNTHIA. Well, I do! What kind of privacy will he have down there? (Pause) How much are the penthouses?

BLACK. The basic payment for the Eternal Eyries will be $50,000 and the carrying charge in the vicinity of $500 monthly. Actually, it may sound like a lot, but it's really most reasonable.

DIANE. For Donald Trump, maybe.

BLACK. Now, now, Mrs. Jansen, we're all overwrought during a lugubrious period like this, but I must impress on you that the present time is a very propitious occasion to get in on the ground floor for this penthouse deal.

DIANE. Well, it's just that it seems a very large amount of money to me. Suppose Helen commits herself to it now and then decides that it's too much. What happens then?

BLACK. I don't know, but I suppose eviction proceedings are begun.

BOB. Are you kidding?

BLACK. I'm not sure. It sounds like the logical thing.

BOB. I suppose so.

CYNTHIA. Oh, Mr. Black, there is one more question that has to be raised.

BLACK. Yes?

CYNTHIA. Let me preface this by saying that I yield to no one in my liberalism on matters having to do with minorities, I mean, when I hear about a mugger or a rapist, I'm not one of those people who automatically assume he's black. I say, I always wait to read it in the paper. But, even so--

BLACK. Ah, yes, Mrs. (He mumbles something indistinguishable that sounds faintly like "Gresham.") Now, obviously, state law requires that we do not practice discrimination. (The others nod assent.) But there are means of discouraging prospective-- uh, tenants. And rest assured that we have made plans to use those methods. So, if you are concerned about any possible deterioration of-- uh, property values on that score, please don't be. You'll also be interested to know that there is no chance for any low-income high-rise mausoleums to spring up in the-- uh, neighborhood. Thus I can give you my strongest assurances that you have no cause for any apprehension.

KEN. (After a pause) Well, what do you say, all? Shall we take one of the penthouses?

DIANE. I don't know. It sounds awfully expensive.

CYNTHIA. I feel we should go ahead. I think Ray would like it. And, after all, what we're really doing is just recommending it to Helen. She'll have to make the final decision. I say, she's the one who'll have to decide.

BOB. Then why don't we say tentatively that we'll advise her to do it? OK? (He looks at Diane, who nods reluctant assent.) Fair enough,

BLACK. Splendid, Mr. Judson.

BOB. Johnson.

BLACK. Sorry, Mr. Johnson, But you have made a wise decision. The late Mr. Hansen would have applauded it, I feel sure. These penthouses are remarkable. The view will just take everyone's breath away,

DIANE. (A bad loser. Half to herself, half to Bob) It won't take Ray's breath away.

BOB. (Sotto voce) Cut it out, Diane.

BLACK. (Rising) Then I'll have the proper papers drawn up and see that they're delivered to Mrs. Hensgen—

KEN. Hansen.

BLACK. Hansen. My apologies. And, oh, yes, I almost forgot. (He sits down, opens his attaché envelope, takes out a contract, takes out his fountain pen and fills in the amount.) Here is the contract for the funeral arrangements, including the best of everything. But tasteful. (Rises.) I'll leave it and you can give it to the widow. (He hands it to Cynthia.) Please accept my condolences on your grievous loss. (He moves toward the door upstage right.)

KEN. (Rising) Here, I'll see you out. (They exit right.)

CYNTHIA. (After an awkward pause, where she senses that Diane and Bob want to talk) I'm going to freshen up, (She rises, crosses to the cocktail table holding the contract and smiling triumphantly. She drops the contract onto the table. She exits left.)

DIANE. (She picks up the contract between thumb and forefinger and holds it at arm's length.) Well, our grievous loss is Skyscraping Sarcophagus's gain.

BOB. Now, come on, Diane. I think it's best for us to go along with Cindy and Ken on this to keep peace in the family.

DIANE. (She drops the contract and puts her arm around him) Bob, promise me one thing?

BOB. What's that, honey?

DIANE. When I die, don't bury me in a penthouse. You know how deathly afraid I am of heights.

Quick curtain.

FAMILY VALUES

or

AMERICAN DRAMA 1990 – 1999

CAST OF CHARACTERS

John Panament

Mary, his wife

Johnny, his son

Marianne, his daughter

Jenny, his daughter

.

The scene is the kitchen of the Panament railroad flat in the Clinton section of Manhattan.

The time is the present.

All actors are on roller skates throughout.

Upstage center is a kitchen sink, with a drainboard to the left on which are a few cheap dishes and metal-doored cabinet under the sink. In front of the sink are a dining-room table, cheap and worn, and four kitchen chairs. Upstage to the left of the sink is a medium-sized refrigerator in rather bad shape. The door to the outside world is on the left and the door to the other rooms in the apartment is on the right. If the floor is covered, it should feature cheap and much-worn linoleum.

AT RISE: John and Johnny are seated at the kitchen table, drinking beer.

JOHN. I tell ya, she's against me, like all a yez.

JOHNNY. Geez, pop, I think you got her all wrong.

JOHN. No I ain't. She hates me. And after all I done fa her!

JOHNNY. Nah, pop. I'm sure she likes you a lot.

JOHN. Don't tell me! My own daughter and she can't stand me! I think she's a dyke just ta spite me!

JOHNNY. Nah, pop. That's just the way she is.

JOHN. You're just stickin' up fa her because you hate me too. Don't think I don't know! You 'n' her 'n' yer mother 'n' Jimmy 'n' Jenny--all a yez!

JOHNNY. No, pop. That ain't true.

JOHN. Don't you contradict me, you goddam faggot! (He slaps Johnny across the mouth.)

JOHNNY. (Brightening) Oh, pop, you ain't done that fer a long time! Pop, whadda ya say we go inta my bedroom an' I'll strip an' you can use the belt on me. Huh, pop?

JOHN. Nah. I'm tired.

JOHNNY. Please, pop? Please?

JOHN. Maybe this weekend.

JOHNNY. I'm takin' that as a promise, pop.

JOHN. We'll see. (Pause) Get us another beer.

JOHNNY. Sure, pop. (He rises, crosses to the refrigerator, gets two beers and returns to the table.) Here, pop.

JOHN. I s'pose your mother ain't makin' dinner tanight.

JOHNNY. I guess not. I don't think she's been outa your bedroom all day.

JOHN. Jesus, what is it? Five days this time? I mean, five days so far.

JOHNNY. Yeah.

JOHN. I hate it when she gets these here spells. I mean, she don't say nothin', she don't do nothin', all she does is sit in that room with the shades down and sometimes she cries. It's depressing, ya know what I mean?

JOHNNY. Yeah. Well, maybe she'll snap out of it soon.

JOHN. So you gonna make dinner?

JOHNNY. I'm waitin' fa Marianne ta get home so she can do it.

JOHN. Whatsa matta? You crippled or somethin'?

JOHNNY. Nah, but I did it last night an' Wednesday. It should be her turn.

JOHN. Go ahead an' do it. You cook better than her anyway. You know she don't like ta cook.

JOHNNY. I keep tellin' her about how all the great chefs are men, but she still don't like ta cook.

JOHN. All she wantsa do is go in her room an' look at all them pitchers a Marilyn Monroe 'n' Candice Bergen 'n' Madonna.

JOHNNY. So she's got a thing fer blonds.

JOHN. Jeez, I dunno where I went wrong wit' you kids. I mean, I got a good job wit' Con Ed, I pay my taxes, I go ta church on Christmas 'n' Easter, I'm in the VFW an' the lodge--I just don't know. An' there's her--an' you, goin' down on every guy in New York, an' Jimmy in the slammer an' Jenny peddlin' her ass up an' down Eighth Avenue! Christ, what a life I got! And another thing—

(Marianne enters the kitchen, carrying her purse and a package. She looks around the kitchen.)

MARIANNE. Whatsa matta? (to Johnny) You didn't start dinner yet, Julia Child?

JOHNNY. Drop dead. It's your turn.

MARIANNE. (Walking over to him, she stands beside his chair, her downstage hand balled up into a fist.) Don't mouth off ta me, you fuckin' fairy! Do you want another black eye this week?

JOHNNY. (Intimidated) No.

MARIANNE. Then get crackin' an' get dinner.

JOHNNY. (Rising) I'll heat up a couple cans a chili. That'll be quick. (He busies himself getting dinner, while Marianne sits.)

MARIANNE. Good. I got a date tonight.

JOHN. What's in the package? Somep'n fa me?

MARIANNE. (Snorting) That'll be the day, you old fart!

JOHN. Don't talk ta me like that. I'm your father.

MARIANNE. Don't remind me. (Pause) No, I got somethin' fa mama. It's a sweater. Sweaters are in this year.

JOHN. So give it ta her.

MARIANNE. Yeah. Why not? (She rises and heads for the door upstage right.) I'll bring her out here. (She exits.)

JOHN. Get me another beer.

JOHNNY. Sure, pop. (He does so.)

JOHN. I dunno why she treats me that way. After all I done fa her.

JOHNNY. That's just the way she is, pop.

JOHN. Hmph!

(Marianne appears, steering Mary, who is in an almost catatonic state and whose face bears an expression of deep sorrow. She leads Mary to a chair and sets her down.)

MARIANNE. There, mama. (She picks up the package.) I got

216

somethin' for ya, mama. (She opens the package and pulls out the sweater.) It's a sweater.

MARY. (Showing a glimmer of interest) Nice.

MARIANNE. Yeah, ain't it? I got it at Macy's.

MARY. (More interested) Real nice.

MARIANNE. Here, let me help ya put it on. (She does so.)

MARY. (Stroking the sweater) I like it. I really like it. (She stands up and starts pirouetting around the room.) It's great!

MARIANNE. Glad ya like it, mama.

MARY. (Moving faster, growing wilder) I don't just like it! I love it! I adore it!

JOHN. Christ! Here we go again!

MARY. (Touching her hair) But I must look like a mess. I'm gonna go fix myself up. (She tears out upstage right.)

JOHNNY. (Putting three bowls of chili and a plate of crackers on the table) Soup's on. (He, Marianne and John start eating.)

MARY. (Tearing in) There! Don't I look better? Oh, how many days have I gone without cleaning the livingroom? I gotta get busy right away! (She dashes out.)

JOHN. (Throwing down his spoon and rising) Jesus! I can't take it. I'm gettin' outa here. (He puts on his jacket, which has been on the back of his chair.) I'll be at Dooley's. (He exits upstage left.)

JOHNNY. So ya got a date tanight.

MARIANNE. Yeah. Me an' Helen's goin' ta the dance at the Sapphic Sisters Society.

JOHNNY. Great.

MARIANNE. You?

JOHNNY. Yeah, me an' Bob's goin' ta the Gay Caballero.

MARIANNE. You goin' in drag?

JOHNNY. No. Bob don't like me in drag. Besides, there is too much bashin' goin' on around there lately.

MARIANNE. Mm.

JOHNNY. Last Saturday Carl 'n' Vince 'n' Miss Lee all got beat up.

MARIANNE. It's rough.

JOHNNY. I dunno why they won't leave us alone. All we want is to just lead our lives. I mean, it ain't as if we was hurtin' them. I mean, we got feelin's like everybody else. All Bob 'n' me want is ta go out every Friday 'n' Saturday until we get enough money saved ta get an apartment and then get married 'n' live happily ever after.

MARIANNE. I know whatcha mean. That's what me 'n' Helen want, too. Just ta go out every Friday 'n' Saturday until we get enough money saved ta get an apartment and then get married 'n' live happily ever after.

MARY. (She rushes in, goes to the cabinet under the sink and rummages through it, tossing bottles and cans on the floor in front of it.) Where's the Windex? I gotta get the Windex. Them windows in there is filthy. (She grabs a bottle and holds it up.) There it is! (She dashes out.)

MARIANNE. But what I wanna know is, why da you faggots stand fer all this bashin'? If guys come after me 'n' Helen, we'd beat the shit outa them. I mean, we'd punch 'em in the mouth 'n' kick 'em in the balls--

JOHNNY. Yeah, but there's always five or six guys.

MARIANNE. What the hell! I mean, ya gotta stand up fa your rights! You gotta make 'em pay fa their fun! Am I right or am I right? (She is picking up the mess in front of the sink.)

JOHNNY. (Dubiously) I s'pose so.

MARIANNE. Sure! Kick 'em in the balls! That's the answer.

JOHNNY. Well, I never forget to remember that I'm gay an' I'm proud!

MARIANNE. An' I'm gay an' I'm proud!

JOHNNY. I'm prouder than you are!

MARIANNE. You are not! I'm prouder!

JOHNNY. No! Me!

MARIANNE. No! Me!

JOHNNY. (Yelling) You are not!

MARIANNE. (Yelling) You're not either!

(Jenny enters upstage left, carrying a white box, which she puts atop the refrigerator. She crosses to the table and sits.)

MARIANNE. Hiya, Jenny.

JOHNNY. Hello, sis.

JENNY. (Flatly) Hello.

MARIANNE. What brings you here?

JENNY. It's too early fa business ta start so I thought I'd stop in an' kill a coupla hours.

JOHNNY. So, how's business?

JENNY. Shitty. The cops got another crackdown on.

MARIANNE. Rough!

JENNY. Yeah. It's as much as ya life is worth ta go near the Lincoln Tunnel. It's practically a sure bust.

JOHNNY. Too bad.

JENNY. But one good thing. I made a coupla extra bucks this week. I mean, good bread. I was on two talk shows on TV. One was called "Recovering Alcoholics Who Are Hookers" and the other was "Hookers Who Are Recovering Alcoholics." I was the only one who was on both a them.

MARIANNE. Great!

JENNY. I met some real nice people. Of course, I already knew some a them from Eighth Avenue, but I met a couple a gals that don't work there. (Musing) Yeah. One a them was real inneresting. Just imagine! She graduated college, but she don't like ta work in an office with all the guys tryin' ta cop a feel or pinch her ass at the water cooler.

MARIANNE. Bastards! They should get a kick in the balls!

JENNY. So she decided ta be a hooker. An' she makes real good money, too. (Pause) But I gotta say she's got a lot a wacky ideas.

JOHNNY. Yeah?

JENNY. Yeah. Like, she says that when guys are little kids, they wanna kill their father 'n' marry their mother.

MARIANNE. *Guys!?* That's just more a that male chauvinist crap! Why not gals, too? I mean, I always wanted the old man to check out 'n' leave me alone with mama.

JOHNNY. I think the whole thing is sick! I never wanta ta kill nobody! Maybe I thought it would be nice if mom went away 'n' left me with pop, but I sure didn't want nobody dead!

JENNY. Well, anyhow, that's what she said.

MARIANNE. It's bullshit! Ain't women as good as men, fa Chrissake?

JENNY. Sure, but I don't know if that's what she was sayin'.

MARIANNE. (Not mollified) Hmph!

JENNY. An' she said you can tell a lot from what you dream.

JOHNNY. Like what, f'rinstance?

JENNY. Like, if you dream about a cigar, you're really dreamin' about a dick.

JOHNNY. (Given pause) Yeah?

MARIANNE. More bullshit! I don't dream about no dicks.

JENNY. An' if you dream about a doughnut, you're really dreamin' about a pussy.

MARIANNE. (Given pause) Really?

JOHNNY. That's a laugh! Who ever dreams about doughnuts?

JENNY. I'm on'y tellin' ya what she said. I don't know if it's true or it isn't true. An' she told me a lot a stuff about myself. (Pause) Where's the old man? Dooley's?

MARIANNE. Yeah.

JENNY. I thought he didn't like it there no more.

JOHNNY. He don't. He thinks Dooley waters his whiskey an' he thinks all the other guys at the bar are talkin' about him.

JENNY. Why don't he go some other place?

MARIANNE. Where? They kicked him outa Kerrigan's after that fight he started an' O'Connell told him not ta come back ta the Shamrock after he said that pebble he found in the salted peanuts was put there on purpose so'z he'd choke on it.

(Mary comes rushing in, Windex in one hand, cloth in the other. She looks quickly around the table.)

MARY. OK, OK. Outa here, all a yez! I gotta scrub the kitchen floor now. It's real dirty!

JOHNNY. Oh, ma!

MARIANNE. Not now, mama. We're all talkin'. Whyncha go an' clean up your bedroom. An' I bet the windas in there is all dirty, too.

MARY. Good idea! (She rushes out upstage left.)

JENNY. Still nutty as a fruitcake.

MARIANNE. I dunno what's better, when she's sittin' in her room lookin' at the wall or when she's runnin' around like crazy. She gets worse all the time.

JENNY. (Shaking her head) Too bad. (Pause) Ya hear from Jimmy?

JOHNNY. Yeah. We got a letter this week. He got in trouble again. They kicked him outa his therapy group.

JENNY. Whad he do now?

JOHNNY. Well, ya know, it's hard ta tell, the way he writes. I mean, he don't write too clear.

JENNY. So what happened?

JOHNNY. It seems he was gettin' along real good. They could show him a pitcher of a nine-year-old kid an' he could handle it. You know what I mean. He didn't get all turned on or nothin'. An' they was startin' on eight-year-old kids, like workin' their way down, ya know? An' they was havin' their therapy group in the TV room in the jail an' some guy comes in an'-puts on Sesame Street, ya know? They got all these four- 'n' five-year-old kids there on the program 'n' when the camera shows them, Jimmy, like, goes crazy, along with a couple other guys. An' the head a the therapy, he says for them to turn it off an' they won't do it an' they start beatin' up on him and they get kicked outa the program--so he won't get no more therapy. So he says in his letter, like, what do they expect him ta do when they're showin' him dirty movies like *Sesame Street?*

JENNY. The poor kid.

MARIANNE. Yeah. I dunno what's gonna happen. He'll do his time 'n' they'll let him out 'n' he'll see some kid 'n' he'll get in trouble all over again.

JENNY. Maybe they could get him a job in a retirement home or something. He ain't no threat ta them old people.

MARIANNE. Yeah. If they could keep him there all the time.

JENNY. It's a helluva mess, all right.

JOHNNY. Yeah. It's real sad.

JOHN. (Entering upstage left, he takes off his jacket, puts it on the back of a chair and starts to sit down, when he sees Jenny.) What're you doin' here?

JENNY. I'm sittin' an' talkin'. Dya mind?

JOHN. Whatsa matter? The Johns all on strike on Eighth Avenue?

JENNY. I'm sittin' an' talkin'.

JOHN. I heard ya. Well, fer a change you ain't on your back. (He sits. Pause) That Dooley's gets worse 'n' worse.

JOHNNY. Whatsa matter, pop?

JOHN. What's it to ya?

JOHNNY. Nothin'. Just askin'.

JOHN. Ah, all a them lousy bastids in there is a bunch a creeps. I'd like ta punch 'em in the mouth.

JOHNNY. Whad, they say somethin' to ya?

JOHN. Nobody said nothin'. It's just they all got an attitude.

They're always lookin' at me. You know, funny. They look at me funny. I can't even enjoy a beer in peace.

JOHNNY. Aw, pop, they prob'ly--

JOHN. (Drawing back his hand) Shaddup! You want another one in the face?

JOHNNY. (Brightening) Yeah, pop.

JOHN. Ahh, shaddup!

JOHNNY. Yes, pop. (Long pause)

JOHN. So what was youze talkin' about when I come in? (Hard and suspicious) Me?

MARIANNE. Jimmy.

JOHN. That moron! Nothin' but trouble!

MARIANNE. He ain't no moron. They said he's got a 75 IQ.

JOHN. He ain't smart enough ta keep his hands offa little girls. He's a sicko! A stupid sicko!

JENNY. Oh, Jeez! Leave the poor guy alone.

JOHN. I mighta known you'd throw in your two cents' worth. You always stand up fa him.

JENNY. I got my reasons.

JOHN. Like what?

JENNY. None a your business. Just I got my reasons, that's all.

JOHN. No, no. Clue me in. I wanna know.

JENNY. You don't wanna know.

JOHN. I tole ya, I wanna know.

JENNY. You never treated Jimmy 'n' me the same as you treated them two. (She gestures toward Marianne and Johnny.)

JOHN. That ain't true! I treated yez all the same! I yelled at yez all when ya done something wrong and I whipped yez all when ya done real bad stuff!

JENNY. Yeah, but you never whipped us the way you whipped them!

JOHN. That ain't true!

JENNY. Yes, it is. You wuz whippin' them all the time an' you hardly ever whipped us!

JOHN. (Defensively) Well they deserved it more. An' if I would've knew that this sicko (He gestures toward Johnny.) was gettin' ta like it, I wouldn't a touched him.

JOHNNY. Now, pop, I--

JOHN. Shaddup! You loved it an' ya still love it! You're one sick kid! Why couldn't ya be just a normal faggot?

JENNY. You neglected Jimmy an' me. That's what you done.

JOHN. I did not!

JENNY. (Darkly) An' that ain't all.

JOHN. What's 'at s'posed ta mean?

JENNY. Tell ya som'p'n, pop. Yestaday I met this girl, see, 'n'--

JOHN. Whatta, you gone lezzie on me, too?

JENNY. Leave me finish, will yez? (Pause) See, this girl graduated college an' she took a course in psychology, 'n'--

JOHN. That bullshit! I had enough a that when yer mother started havin' her spells. The psychologists give me all this doubletalk 'n' mumbo-jumbo when anybody could tell what was wrong wit' her. She was crazy. An' they couldn't fix her up, so she's still crazy. Only worse.

MARIANNE. (Interested) Let her go on, pop.

JENNY. So this girl says I'm a hooker because I didn't get enough love from you. She says every guy I'm takin' on it's because I'm payin' you back.

JOHN. That's bullshit! I don't know why you listen ta garbage like that!

JENNY. It ain't garbage. An' while we're at it, there's one more thing.

JOHN. (Uneasily) What's that?

JENNY. Listen, will you deny that you started screwin' Marianne 'n' Johnny when they was both kids?

JOHN. Who tole ya that?

JENNY. Marianne tole me--years ago.

JOHN. (To Marianne) I tole ya ta keep ya mouth shut, ya little-- (He catches hold of himself.) They wasn't kids! She was 13 an' he was 11.

JENNY. An' you was screwin' them fa years!

JOHN. What was I supposed ta do? Yer mother was crazy 'n' half the time she wouldn't let me get near her 'n' the other half it was like she was dead!

JENNY. So how come ya screwed them two an' never screwed me 'n' Jimmy?

JOHN. Fa Chrissakes! What was I, Superman?

JENNY. I'll tell ya why. You loved them an' you din't love us.

JOHN. That's bullshit!

JOHNNY. (To Jenny) You're just jealous, that's all.

JOHN. Listen, I had my hands full wit' them two. How could I take on two more?

JENNY. Where there's a will there's a way, like gramma usta say.

JOHN. (After a pause) Ya know what I think? I think you oughta stay away from them broads that graduated college. They don't know what the hell they're talkin' about.

JOHNNY. Hmph!

JOHN. Keep talkin' ta them an' you'll be as nutty as yer mother. (Pause) by the way, where is she?

MARIANNE. She's cleanin' up your bedroom.

JOHN. On another cleanin' jag?

MARIANNE. She's been in there a long time. I better see if she's OK. (She exits upstage right.)

(There is a lengthy silence at the table.)

JOHN. (To Johnny) Get me a beer.

JOHNNY. Sure, pop. (He does so. To Jenny) You want one? (She nods assent. He serves the beer and sits down.)

MARIANNE. (Entering upstage right, she steers Mary, who is catatonic again.) She wuz just sittin' there.

JOHN. Jeez!

(There is silence at the table again as Marianne sets Mary down in a chair.)

JENNY. Ya know, I didn't really come here just ta kill a couple a hours. (There is silence from the others.) Doncha wanna know why I come? (More silence) Well, I'll tell yez anyway. Know what day today is?

MARIANNE. Friday.

JENNY. Nah, that ain't what I mean. Know what special day it is? (More silence) It's my birthday.

JOHNNY. Yeah? Happy birthday.

JENNY. (Looking at John and Marianne) Ain't youze two got somethin' ta say?

MARIANNE. Happy birthday.

JOHN. OK. Happy birthday.

JENNY. (Rising) I figured youze wouldn't remember. (She crosses to the refrigerator and picks up the white box atop it.) So I bought a cake. (She carries the box to the table and opens it.) Nice, huh?

JOHNNY. Real nice.

MARIANNE. Yeah.

JENNY. I s'pose youze ain't got no candles.

JOHNNY. Nope.

JENNY. Ah, what the hell. Gimme a knife an' I'll cut it up.

JOHNNY. Sure. (He goes to a drawer and returns with a knife.)

MARIANNE. It's Jenny's birthday, mama. (No reaction from Mary.)

JOHNNY. (As Jenny is cutting the cake) Just gimme a little piece. I gotta watch my figure.

JENNY. (Handing him a small piece) Here. This OK?

JOHNNY. Great.

JENNY. (Handing pieces to John and Marianne) Here. Here ya go.

JOHNNY. Hey, we gotta sing "Happy Birthday." (He starts to sing and is joined by Marianne and a half-hearted John. It is a ragged rendition.)

JENNY. (Gesturing toward Mary) Think she wants a piece?

MARIANNE. Nah.

JOHN. She's outa it again.

JENNY. I would of liked fa her to of joined the party. (Pause) Ya know, so'z we'd all be together again like a family. Except fa Jimmy, I mean. (Pause) Because that's the most important thing there is, ya know? The family.

JOHNNY. Yeah, that's true. I mean ya go out inta the world an' ya meet otha people, but they ain't family. They're, like-- otha people.

MARIANNE. That's right, People come inta ya life an' go outa ya life, but they ain't like family, because the family is always there and they gotta act nice ta ya--or at least they gotta pretend ta. (She goes and gets herself a beer.)

JOHN. Yeah. It's like I always usta tell ya when ya was kids. It's a hard, cold world out there. There's people that'll rob yez an' beat yez up an' kill yez an' do anything ta yez. They're a buncha lousy bastids an', take my word fer it, they all hate yez. All they wanna do is hurt yez an' make ya feel rotten an' lousy an' they try ta make ya think they like yez, but they're lyin'. They always got some bad thing up their sleeve, like how they're gonna screw ya. An' it's the same thing in the family, except ya can keep an eye on everybody all the time 'cause yer all packed in like a bunch a fuckin' sardines.

JENNY. That's right, pop. I mean, whydja think I moved outa this goddam crazy house?

JOHNNY. Right! Howdja think I can explain ta my friends I got a sister that hates men?

MARIANNE. *YOU?* Whaddaya think I gotta tell my friends I got a brother that won't go near a woman?

JENNY. Well, Johnny, you got one sister that likes men.

227

JOHNNY. You're only competition, an' I don't like competition. God knows how many blow jobs you took away from me! I can't hardly wait till I can move outa here.

JOHN. You wanna leave? What about me? I gotcha mother an' she's just nothin' but trouble an' she's no goddam good ta anybody, but I still gotta look out fa her 'cause no nuthouse'll take her.

JENNY. Serves ya right. About time you took a little responsibility 'stead a drinkin' all the time an' screwin' your kids.

JOHNNY. Some family.

MARIANNE. What the hell. It may be shitty, but it's the best we got.

THE OTHERS. (Raising their beers, as Marianne raises her mother's arm on high, all speak dully and flatly.) The Family.

Curtain

THE BARGAIN

CAST OF CHARACTERS

Emily Leighton, over 40, preferably over 50

Quinn Marker, 24

The scene is the opulent living room of the Leighton apartment on upper Fifth Avenue in Manhattan.

The time is the present.

AT RISE: Emily Leighton is alone, seated on the sofa. On the coffee-table in front of her is a silver coffee service. On the sofa beside her is a copy of the NEW YORK TIMES, which she picks up from time to time between drinks of coffee from a bone-china cup.

The doorbell rings and she crosses to the door right, ad admitting Quinn Marker, who carries a copy of the TIMES.

MARKER. Mrs. Leighton?

LEIGHTON. Mr. Marker? (He nods.) Do come in. (She gestures toward a chair.) Sit down. (He does so.) Coffee?

MARKER. No, thanks. I had some earlier.

LEIGHTON. All right. To business, then. You called about the ad, you said.

MARKER. Yes. To tell the truth, I almost didn't. I mean, it didn't seem possible. I thought there was some kind of misprint when I read it.

LEIGHTON. Evidently you are not alone. Believe it or not, yours is the only call I've had.

MARKER. I was sitting at my desk in the city room and reading the paper--at the TIMES they expect us to read the paper every day--and I saw the ad and I didn't believe it, so I called down to classified and they said there were no typos or anything.

LEIGHTON. So there weren't. The ad ran exactly as I had dictated it.

MARKER. I don't get it. (He takes his paper and reads.) "For sale. 1996 custom-made Rolls-Royce limousine. Radio, TV, bar, phone, A/C, all power. $1. Call 555-1272 before noon!" (He puts the paper down and pauses.) One dollar?

LEIGHTON. One dollar. (Marker pulls out a reporter's pad and starts to flip through it, looking for an empty page.) Just a moment, Mr. Marker. Kindly put that pad away.

MARKER. But--

LEIGHTON. If you are here as a potential buyer, then you are not here as a reporter. Do I make myself clear?

MARKER. You mean, this is off the record?

LEIGHTON. That is precisely what I mean.

MARKER. (Putting the pad away) If you insist.

LEIGHTON. I insist. Unlike your generation, Mr. Marker, my generation has some regard for privacy. We don't want the world to know about our doings in the boardroom or the bedroom or (She smiles.) even the garage.

MARKER. OK. I see. Off the record it is. (Pause) But back to the car. Was it totalled in a wreck?

LEIGHTON. It is in perfect condition and hardly driven at all. There are less than 500 miles on it. It's only four months old.

MARKER. I don't get it.

LEIGHTON. There is nothing to "get," as you put it.

MARKER. I'm puzzled. Why would you order a car like that, which must have cost a bundle—

LEIGHTON. $200,000 or thereabouts, I believe.

MARKER. --and keep it just a few weeks and sell it for a buck?

LEIGHTON. In the first place, I didn't order the car. My husband did. My late husband.

MARKER. Oh! Reginald Leighton of Leighton Industries, Ltd.?

LEIGHTON. That is correct.

MARKER. If you don't mind my asking, did the car have some unhappy association for you? I mean, did your husband--uh, pass away in it or something?

LEIGHTON. I do mind your asking, but I suppose that kind of crudity goes with being a good reporter. Anyway, it has no such unhappy association for me.

MARKER. Your husband passed away about two weeks ago, if memory serves. The TIMES had a huge obit.

LEIGHTON. That is correct.

MARKER. And you are disposing of those things he had that you don't want?

LEIGHTON. In a sense, yes.

MARKER. I'm still baffled.

LEIGHTON. I am selling the company under an arrangement he made before his death.

MARKER. And firing all the employees?

LEIGHTON. Only one of them.

MARKER. And that is?

LEIGHTON. His private secretary, Miss Austin.

MARKER. I'm sure she'll be able to get another good job. She must be very competent.

LEIGHTON. (A trace of hardness in her voice) She must be. She lives on Sutton Place.

MARKER. On Sutton Place? How much was your husband paying her, if you don't mind my asking?

LEIGHTON. I have had the figures looked up. She was making a salary of $60,000 a year.

MARKER. That's a very nice salary.

LEIGHTON. (sourly) Yes. Isn't it though. (This is not a question.)

MARKER. And she lived on Sutton Place? How could she-- (Suddenly he gets an inkling and looks a bit embarrassed.) Oh.

LEIGHTON. As you say, Mr. Marker, "Oh." (Pause) Don't be embarrassed. I would have thought your profession rendered you impervious to embarrassment. In any event, I had suspected for some time.

MARKER. (Still embarrassed) I see.

LEIGHTON. My husband's will was read the day before yesterday. In the will he left Miss Austin the proceeds from the sale of the Rolls-Royce limousine.

MARKER. (It dawns.) Ah! (Long pause) Uh--uh--can I have that coffee now?

LEIGHTON. Of course. (She pours a cup and looks at him inquiringly.)

MARKER. Black, please. (He crosses and picks up the coffee.)

LEIGHTON. Now, Mr. Marker, do you wish to purchase the car? (He gulps the coffee.)

MARKER. Of course I do.

LEIGHTON. I should prefer to have a check in the event there is any question about the selling price. I assume you don't have your checkbook with you.

MARKER. No, I don't.

LEIGHTON. When I receive the check, I'll mail you all the proper papers. (She rises.) And now, Mr. Marker —

MARKER. (After gulping down the rest of his coffee, he rises.) Mrs. Leighton.

LEIGHTON. (Ushering him to the door) Thank you. (She opens the door and he stands in the doorway.) You simply have no idea what a pleasure it has been doing business with you. (She closes the door and smiles.)

CURTAIN

CURTAIN GOING UP

THE HERO

CAST OF CHARACTERS

Pvt. Young

Sgt. Powers

.Lt. Berry

Maj. Mabry

Col. Quail

Gen. Harrison

Offstage Voice

The time is early November, 1944.

The place is a U.S. Army camp in Northern France. The five scenes take place in the offices of the sergeant and four officers. Every office is furnished in the same way: there is a desk slightly left of center with a metal chair with arms behind it and a plain metal armless chair in front of it. On each desk is a wooden or metal nameplate bearing the name of the occupant. There is a telephone on each desk.

It is essential that each scene end in a blackout to indicate the passage of time, however brief.

THE HERO

SCENE I

AT RISE: It is the office of Sgt. Powers. He is alone, seated behind his desk when a crowd noise is heard offstage right. He crosses to the door right, opens it and yells.

SARGE. What the hell is--? Hey, who the hell are all the Krauts? What're they doin' here? Are they tryin' to capture-- Hey, they're all tied up!

VOICE. Sarge, you're not gonna believe it! Youngie captured 'em all! Single-handed! An' then he brung 'em in!

SARGE. Bullshit!

VOICE. No, Sarge, it's true! Eight of 'em! An' he brung 'em all in!

SARGE. Private Young, come in here! And you other guys, take the Krauts to the stockade!

YOUNG. (He enters and Sarge closes the door behind him.) Sarge?

SARGE. C'min here, Young. (He motions to the chair in front of the desk, while he sits in the one behind the desk.) Now, what's all this, Young? What's goin' on, anyhow?

YOUNG. Ain't much to report. I got separated from my squad an' then the artillery started an' I run into this farm building--it was a long, narrow buildin'--an' I was at one end and then them Krauts run into the other end of the buildin' an' I heard 'em yellin' an' then this shell fell at their end of the buildin' an' that whole end fell in an' they all got knocked out an' I pulled 'em out of the wreck an' I took their guns an' I tied 'em up with their own stuff, like belts an' stuff, an' I marched 'em over here an' here we are an' here I am. An' that's the story.

SARGE. Well, I'll be dipped in shit! That's amazin'! Oh, by the way, good work, Young.

YOUNG. Thanks, Sarge.

SARGE. (After a pause, stroking his chin) Hey, you know, we

235

gotta let the lieutenant know about this.

YOUNG. Aw, gee, Sarge, it wasn't no big thing.

SARGE. That ain't for you to say. (Rising) We're gonna go see Lieutenant Berry. Let's go. (They exit.)

Blackout.

SCENE 2

AT RISE: Berry is seated behind his desk. Sarge is seated in the chair facing the desk, Young standing behind him.

SARGE. --so he took their guns an' he tied 'em all up an' then he marched 'em right into camp! Ain't that something, sir?

BERRY. That's some story, Sarge! And I'm telling you, it isn't gonna stop here! No, siree. I'm thinking, what're they going to say back at the Point when they find out that little old "Razz" Berry had the first real hero in France in his platoon only a year after he got his bars! "Razz," huh? I'll razz them, the bastards! (Pause) Tell you right away we've got to get this to Major Mabry. He'll know just how to play this thing up-- you know, he worked for a newspaper and a magazine in Philly before he went to work for Connie Mack.

SARGE. Pardon, sir. Maybe I shouldn't say nothin', but what about Captain Brown? Won't he get pissed--I mean, mad-- if you skip over him?

BERRY. Good point, Sarge, and I appreciate that--I mean, thinking about what's best for me. But Captain Brown is off at SHAEF headquarters kissing Ike's ass or whatever ass gets in his way. He won't be back for a week. Serves the bastard right! He'll miss out on the biggest thing that's happened around here since we set up camp. (Smiling) I love it! Tell me I'm wet behind the ears, will he? Worthless shit! We'll see who's wet behind the ears now! (Pause) Oh, yeah, Good work, Private--uh--

SARGE. Young, sir.

BERRY. Private Young.

YOUNG. Thank you, sir.

BERRY. You won't have any trouble telling your story to the major, will you, Young? He's a very nice guy--uh, I mean, a very good officer. All for his men.

YOUNG. No, sir. I'll just tell the story straight out.

BERRY. Good. (He picks up the phone and dials three numbers.) Major Mabry? Lieutenant Berry, sir. Sir, I have something very, very important that I think you ought to know about right away! (Pause) Huh? Oh, very good, sir! It's of major importance! Can I come right over? Good, sir. Be right there. (To Sarge and Young) OK, men, let's roll! (All exit.)

Blackout

SCENE 3

AT RISE: Mabry is seated at his desk. Berry occupies the chair in front of the desk, with Young and Sarge standing behind him.

YOUNG. --and that's just how it happened, sir.

BERRY. And that's exactly the way he told it to me, sir. (Pause) I've been wondering, sir. What do you think about the bronze star?

MABRY. You're young, lieutenant and that's why you think small. Bronze star, nonsense!

BERRY. Yes, sir!

MABRY. Let's think silver star! You got a hero and all the world loves a hero! Tell you a story. When I was working for the Philadelphia Journal, I had this young roommate. Well, one day he was walking past a row house when fire broke out on the second floor and this young mother was leaning out the window with a baby in her arms and she was screaming, "Save my baby!" Well, she tossed him the baby and later she was saved, too. Well, sir, it was before the firemen arrived, so, when I wrote the story she was on the fourth floor and the kid weighed 30 pounds instead of 10 pounds. So Bruce, my roommate, won a city medal and a $10,000 prize. So maybe a little license can help here, too. Oh, incidentally, I won the Press Association prize for the best breaking news story of the year. Not bad, if I do say so myself.

BERRY. No, sir!

SARGE. No, sir! (He looks at, then nudges Young.)

YOUNG. No, sir!

MABRY. And I made it clear to her she should say my story was 100 percent accurate or the guy wouldn't get the 10 thou. So she kept her mouth shut.

BERRY. Great, sir!

MABRY. Then there was another time I dressed up a story about a guy who had two woodchucks in his backyard and he killed 'em with a hoe and some rocks. And it turned out the woodchucks had rabies, they said, and he protected his two little kids by killing the woodchucks.

SARGE. Jeez, did they really have rabies?

MABRY. Who knows? I sure as hell didn't know. The point is, it made a great story! I won a prize for that one, too. A big plaque!

BERRY. Great, sir!

MABRY. But back to Private-- uh, Private--

YOUNG. Young, sir.

MABRY. Right! Young! Where're you from, Young?

YOUNG. New York City, sir.

MABRY. Not Fifth Avenue or Madison Avenue or one of those ritzy places?

YOUNG. No, sir. The Lower East Side, sir!

MABRY. Lower East Side? And your name's Young?

YOUNG. Yes, sir!

MABRY. That's a real American-sounding name. I thought the Lower East Side was all Jews and Italians. Especially Jews since Hitler.

YOUNG. My folks moved to New York a couple years ago. My father works for the New York Central.

MABRY. This gets better and better. Where do they live, your folks?

YOUNG. Second Avenue and Seventh Street, sir.

MABRY. (After a long pause, when he is obviously thinking) Wrong! (His voice becomes loud and intimidating.) You were brought up at the corner of First Avenue and First Street. Got that?

YOUNG. Uh, yessir!

MABRY. And you went to P.S. 1!

YOUNG. But, sir, I don't think P.S. 1 is even on the Lower East Side!

MABRY. Nobody's going to check that. You went to P.S. 1!

YOUNG. Yessir.

MABRY. And you were first in your class when you graduated.

YOUNG. But I wasn't all that smart in school, sir.

MABRY. First in your class! Got that?

YOUNG. Yessir.

MABRY. See, the story I've got in mind, the theme of being first being the best, runs through your whole life. It's great! It's great! Old Hemoglobin Harry's going to eat it up with a spoon!

SARGE. Hemoglobin Harry?

MABRY. General Harrison. That's what the officers all call him- not to his face, of course.

BERRY. I see.

MABRY. See, he wanted to be "Old Blood and Guts," but GeneralPatton got that first. He pretends he doesn't know

239

about the "hemoglobin" bit, but we think he does and we think he really likes it.

BERRY. Very good, sir!

MABRY. We have to go through channels, so we'll have to see Colonel Quail to get to the general. I'll call him. (He picks up the phone on his desk.) Stevens, this is Major Mabry. Please ask the colonel if I can see him right away. It's vitally important and it'll be good for him! (Pause) I know, but you'll just have to interrupt him! I mean, it's very vital. (He turns to the others, holding his hand over the mouthpiece.) I'll bet he's doing a crossword puzzle, as usual, or doing something else to kill time. (He uncovers the mouthpiece. Short pause.) No, I assure you we won't be wasting his time. (Pause) Thanks, Stevens. Lieutenant, Sergeant, please wait here while I take Young in to see the colonel.

BERRY. Yes, sir.

SARGE. Yes, sir.

(Mabry and Young exit.)

Blackout

SCENE 4

AT RISE: Colonel Quail is seated at his desk. He is flipping playing cards toward his hat, about five or six feet off to his right on the floor. The floor around the hat is covered with cards. Mabry enters, followed by Young, both saluting.)

QUAIL. Yeah?

MABRY. I've got a big development for you and I'd like to ask your permission to tell the general about it. He'll love it!

QUAIL. Just a minute. (He launches another card toward the hat; it misses.) Shit! (To Mabry) I'm trying to unwind. I had all kinds of trouble with the crossword this morning and I couldn't finish it! A bad day!

MABRY. Too bad, sir.

QUAIL. What's a six-letter word for a fruit generally considered a vegetable?

MABRY. Tomato.

QUAIL. Wrong. That's seven letters.

MABRY. Whatever you say, sir.

QUAIL. OK. What do you want, major? (He waves his hand.) Siddown. (Mabry sits, with Young standing behind him.) Yeah?

MABRY. Private Young here has captured eight Germans single-handed and brought 'em all in. They're in the stockade right now.

QUAIL. Yeah? Sounds like a DSC to me.

MABRY. Yes, sir.

QUAIL. So you want me to call the general and alert him? Why not? (He picks up the phone on his desk and dials three numbers.) This is Colonel Quail. Please tell the general that I have something really big to relay to him. I mean, even national publicity. (Pause) OK. I'm sending in Major Mabry and some private. (Pause) OK. The major will explain it all to the general. (He hangs up and speaks to Mabry and Young.) Down the hall to your left.

MABRY. (Rising) Yes, sir. Thank you, sir.

QUAIL. (As Mabry and Young are leaving) And don't forget who got you in to see the general. Just remember the key figure in this whole story! (As Mabry and Young exit, he goes back to tossing his cards.)

Blackout

SCENE 5

AT RISE: General Harrison is seated behind his desk, smiling and interested, as Mabry keeps speaking and Young, obviously terrified, stands stiff as a ramrod. Not so incidentally, the general's voice is loud and powerful. If the actor playing this role wants to essay a Southern or Southwestern accent, so much the better.)

MABRY. --and they're all in the stockade now!

GENERAL. Wonderful! Wonderful! Congratulations, private!

YOUNG. (Saluting) Thank you, sir.

MABRY. But there's a fascinating sidelight, sir!

GENERAL. Well? Go ahead, major.

MABRY. The number one runs like a theme through his whole life. His folks live at the corner of First Street and First Avenue in New York.

GENERAL. Yes?

MABRY. And he went to Public School One in Manhattan.

GENERAL. Yes?

MABRY. And he graduated number one in his class! You see, air, it's almost as if destiny marked him as the first, the best, all through his life!

GENERAL. I like that, major! I like it! (Pause) There's no need to say anything more. (He looks closely at Young.) Like to get the Congressional Medal of Honor, private?

YOUNG. (Saluting) Yes, sir!

GENERAL. Well, that's what's gonna happen. I'm putting you in for it today! Major, you take care of the paperwork and you take care of arranging a big press conference for tomorrow at 9 a.m. (Pause) You may know, my sister is married to Senator Brausen. Get in touch with his office and with her and tell him I'd take it as a great favor if he could expedite this thing. (Pause) By the way, don't just get the Stars and Stripes at this press conference. Get all the correspondents for all the big papers in the states. And the press associations. (To Young) By this time tomorrow you're going to be famous, private.

YOUNG. (Saluting) Yes, sir!

GENERAL. All your home folks in New York are gonna be talking about you, private! (To Mabry) 1 assume they've got home folks in New York.

YOUNG. Yes, sir!

MABRY. Yes, sir!

GENERAL. The first Congressional Medal winner in my army! I guess I'll show Omar Bradley and George Patton and all the rest of them! (Smiling) They'll be green with envy!

MABRY. Yes, sir!

GENERAL. This is great! (Pause) Major, get this private assigned to your office toot sweet and keep him there!

MABRY. Yes, sir!

GENERAL. He talks to nobody until tomorrow, get that? Nobody!

MABRY. Yes, sir!

GENERAL. I see something really big coming out of this! I mean, after he gets the medal! What part of New York are you from, private?

YOUNG. (Saluting) Manhattan, sir!

GENERAL. Interesting. In all the war movies all the guys from New York are all from Brooklyn.

MABRY. He's from the Lower East Side of Manhattan. It's what some people call the ghetto.

GENERAL. (Worried, quizzical) You're not a Jewish fella, are you, private?

YOUNG. (Saluting) No, sir!

GENERAL. Good. You had me worried there for a minute. (Pause) I bet they never had a real war hero from your part of New York, am I right?

YOUNG. Yes, sir. (Salutes)

GENERAL. (Rising and pacing downstage) I can see it now. After the war's over and you're back in New York with your Congressional Medal, I'm gonna devote all my time and energy and money to getting a park near your home, a park to commemorate your heroism and the quick recognition it got from your commanding officer and the army that was proud to have you as part of it!

YOUNG. (Saluting) Yes, sir!

GENERAL. (He is now front and center) Yup. Mark my words. You can depend on it. In a few years there's gonna be a new garden spot on the Lower East Side: General Harry Harrison Park!

Blackout

THE PEOPLE STORE

CAST OF CHARACTERS

Martha, aged 60 to 70

Harry, 30 to 50

Brad Smith, 30 to 50

Vivian Kimball-Smith, his wife, 30 to 50

Jason Smith, their son, age 10

The scene is a hardware store in a small American city.

The time is Spring, 1995.

AT RISE: A Smiling Martha enters the store and a smiling, glad-handing Harry hurries over to greet her, holding out his hand, which she shakes warmly.

MARTHA. Hi, there, Harry!

HARRY. Howdy, Martha.

MARTHA. And how are things going at Harry's Helpful Hardware? (Looking around) Things look about the same.

HARRY. You didn't look at our new sign out front. We're not Harry's Helpful Hardware any more--not that we're not still helpful. (She smiles and nods assent.) I changed the name to Harry's--The People Store.

MARTHA. You've always been just folks as far as we're all concerned.

HARRY. And I've got to step that up. It's tough competing with the big chains, so I figure I've got to add more of the personal element. I want to make everybody who comes through that door feel like family.

MARTHA. Some of us already do. Of course I always felt this was a real friendly place.

HARRY. But you haven't been here for--what, a couple of months?

MARTHA. I didn't get out much during the winter. I really was housebound. I dunno, the cold seemed to bother me more this year than it ever did before. So I didn't get out much, what with the temperatures down in the 20's half the time. I don't mind telling you I had a bad case of cabin fever by March. But now I've started going out a couple of times a week, so you'll be seeing a lot more of me than you did this winter, because I sure didn't get out much then.

HARRY. (Semi-sincerely) Glad I'll be seeing more of you, Martha.

MARTHA. Course it wasn't only the weather that kept me in all winter. I had a bad cold in December that just hung on and hung on and hung on--you know how persistent those colds can be. (Harry nods assent.) Lots of folks say a cold is harder to shake in the summertime, but I don't agree. For me they're all the same--summer or winter they just hang on and hang on. Well, anyhoo, all Christmas and New Year's time I was hacking away, bringing up gallons of phlegm (Harry looks unwell.) and gulping down Robitussin by the quart. It's a wonder I didn't get tiddly from drinking so much of it. (Harry smiles.) Anyhoo, it was some ordeal, let me tell you!

HARRY. I'll bet.

MARTHA. And then of course the cold didn't help my arthritis very much. You know, with that bad knee I worry all the time about falling and breaking a hip. Before Elmer passed, it wasn't such a concern, but now that I'm alone, well, you know. Ann calls every day--I'm so lucky to have a daughter like that-- (Harry nods.) but even so, if I got badly hurt, it'd be a whole day of lying there in pain until she couldn't get me on the phone and realized something was wrong and drove over from Somerset. And God knows Bowser wouldn't be any help. That dumb mutt would probably hide under the diningroom table and whine. I love him, but he's no help at all. Anyhoo, I've got all kinds of thick rugs all over the livingroom in case I take a spill.

HARRY. (Glassy-eyed by now) Uh-huh.

MARTHA. Bertha tells me I'm babying myself, but I tell her I'm only playing it safe. Bertha's on the phone to me every other day or so, but God, how she does babble on! It's kinda sad, you know, to see those older folks who are so lonely that they just talk and talk and talk. I pity people who are at the mercy of older folks who can kinda trap them and talk their ear off. I watch Bertha at the bank and I see the tellers kinda wince when she comes up to their window. All she's there for is to cash a check, but she's good for 15 minutes. It's kinda sad.

HARRY. Yeah, it is. (Pause) Was there something you wanted today, Martha?

MARTHA. I came in to price 60-watt bulbs. The one on my porch gave out and I can get the Simmons kid to put a new one in for me --he's a nice, helpful boy--he helped me put up my storm windows last November and he shoveled my walk every time we had a storm all winter. He's not like so many of those kids today, always mouthing off--you know they just have no respect for anything--but don't get me started on that.

HARRY. (Quickly) No, I won't.

MARTHA. Where was I?

HARRY. The bulb.

MARTHA. I don't really have to buy it this minute. How much are they, Harry?

HARRY. They're 59 cents each, Martha.

MARTHA. My, the price never goes down, does it? Well, like I say, I can do without it for the time being. Maybe I can stop back tomor-- (At this point, the Smiths enter.)

HARRY. 'Scuse me, Martha. Looks like I've got some customers.

MARTHA. Well, I'll be on my way. It's always a treat to have a conversation with you, Harry. (She exits, smiling at the Smiths as Harry moves over to them.)

HARRY. (Once again the smiling, hearty, extroverted glad-hander) Howdy, folks. Gee, am I glad to see you! My friend Martha was kinda talkative today. Anyway, howdy again.

BRAD. Hello.

HARRY. I'm Harry.

BRAD. Hello, Harry.

HARRY. I'm the owner.

BRAD. I see.

HARRY. I don't know if you've seen any of our ads on TV (Brad shakes his head in the negative.) but we used to be called Harry's Helpful Hardware. Then one day I heard an ad on the radio. It was from Western University Hospital, and they said, "We don't treat diseases; we treat people." And it got me to thinking about my business. See, I don't deal with hardware; I deal with people. That's why I changed the name to The People Store.

BRAD. I suppose it's all in your point of view, but if I went to a hospital I think I'd want them to treat diseases. Anyhow, I think your new name is a nice idea. Now, we came in--

HARRY. And I'm delighted you did, because we here at Harry's always like to meet new folks, Mr.--uh--

BRAD. Smith. Brad Smith.

HARRY. (Holding out his hand, which Brad shakes perfunctorily.) Pleased ta meetcha, Brad. And this attractive lady is Mrs. Smith, I'll bet.

BRAD. Yes. My wife, Vivian.

HARRY. Pleased to meetcha, Viv. (He holds out his hand and she puts her hand in his with no enthusiasm.)

VIV. Mmmmm.

HARRY. And, unless I miss my guess, this sturdy young fella is your son. Right, son?

JASON. (Sourly) Yeah.

BRAD. That's Jason.

HARRY. (Tousling Jason's hair) Glad to meetcha, son--Jason. Bet you're a football player, right?

JASON. (Still sour) Squash.

HARRY. (Taken aback, he evidently doesn't know what squash is.) Oh, what's that?

JASON. It's a game.

HARRY. Golly. You coulda fooled me. I always thought squash was a vegetable. (He laughs heartily.)

JASON. (Flatly) It is.

HARRY. Whaddaya do in the game? Try to squash the other team? (He laughs again as Jason gives him a dirty look) Just kidding,

Jason. Gotta show folks I've got a sense of humor, right? (He laughs again.)

BRAD. We're here--

HARRY. Do you work, Viv? Or are you a homemaker?

VIV. (Flatly) I work.

HARRY. And I bet you do a good job with whatever it is you do, right?

VIV. I teach.

HARRY. Really? Well, if I'da had teachers like you, I'da done a lot better in school, and that's no lie! I bet all your kids love to learn their ABCs and four-times table!

VIV. I teach at the community college

HARRY. Wow! High-powered, eh? I never went to college myself. I had to go to work.

BRAD. Look, we want--

JASON. Pop, I got soccer practice at one.

HARRY. Soccer, too? Jeez, you're quite the little athlete, huh?

JASON. I'm not a little athlete.

VIV. Jason, be respectful.

JASON. OK, mom, but keerist!

BRAD. Harry, we--

HARRY. I have two kids. My boy--that's Don--he's named for Don Mattingly--I'm a big Yankee fan--he plays baseball-- my son, I mean. Of course Mattingly does, too. (He laughs.)

BRAD. Look, Harry--

HARRY. And you should see my daughter Cheryl. She's named for Cheryl Tiegs. Prettiest little girl you ever did see! She can cook, too. (He focuses on Vivian.) What do you teach, Viv?

VIV. (Curtly) French.

HARRY. That's a real pretty language. Real--uh, feminine, you know what I mean?

VIV. No.

HARRY. It's not a rough, tough language like German. That's a man's language, right?

VIV. Brad, can't we--

JASON. C 'mon, pop.

BRAD. (Sternly) Harry-

HARRY. Oh, yeah. Gee, I guess I just let myself get carried away. I mean, you're just such nice folks and folks are what make the world go 'round. (Pause) So, what can I do for you?

BRAD. I'd like one of those sets of wrenches you advertised in the Journal for $79.95.

HARRY. A great set of wrenches--and a real bargain, too. I can see you're a real smart shopper, Brad.

BRAD. The wrenches?

HARRY. Sure. I'll go get 'em. (He exits.)

VIV. Jesus!

JASON. We ever gonna get outa here? I got soccer practice.

BRAD. (Dryly) So you said.

HARRY. (Entering with a box) Here ya go. (He opens the box.) Wanna take a look? Beautiful set, huh?

BRAD. Very nice.

HARRY. Good for around the house or to put in your car if you do any repairs yourself.

BRAD. I do and that's what I wanted them for.

HARRY. Lemme see. If I'm any judge, you drive a Lincoln and the little lady drives a Ford Taurus.

BRAD. Exactly right.

HARRY. Myself, I've got a Pontiac.

BRAD. (Perfunctorily) Nice car. Now, I'd like to put this on my credit card. (He takes out his wallet and holds it.) MasterCard OK?

HARRY. Fine as silk. (He takes the card which Brad hands to him.) Myself, I've got MasterCard and Visa and American

Express. Can't have too many credit cards, I always say. (He laughs.) Course I gotta be careful to dole 'em out one at a time to my better half. She's a menace with impulse buying. Lotta gals are like that, right? (Viv glares at him.)

BRAD. Can I sign the slip?

HARRY. Surest thing you know, Brad. Just come with me over to the register and I'll fix you up. (They exit.)

VIV. (To Jason) This had better not last too long. A couple more minutes and I'll grab that chain saw over there, plug it in and go to work on Harry.

JASON. He sure talks a lot, but he seems like a nice enough guy.

VIV. (Acidly) So he does. Just folks.

JASON. Aw, mom--

VIV. You're a very kind judge of people, Jason. That's one of the things I like best about you. Actually I could take lessons from you in that area. (She hugs him.)

JASON. (Embarrassed, he ducks out of her hug.) Aw, c'mon, mom!

BRAD. (Returning with Harry, he is carrying a bag.) All set?

VIV. All set.

JASON. All set.

HARRY. Well, Brad, Viv, Jason, it's been real nice meeting you and getting to know you. We'll have to get together over at my place some Sunday for a barbecue. Look me up. I'm in the book. Harry Harding. (Short pause) Say, you free for this coming Sunday?

VIV. (Very quickly) Sorry, we're supposed to drive over to Elmwood.

HARRY. Too bad. Maybe some other time. (He holds out his hand to Brad.) Have a good-- (The phone rings offstage.) Guess I'll have to get that. (He exits and yells from offstage.) Have a good day!

VIV. I'll have a good day once we get out of here.

BRAD. Now, Viv--

VIV. Do me a favor, Brad. Next time we want hardware, let's go to a hardware store. No people store, OK? (They exit.)

Blackout

CURTAIN GOING UP

THE ROBBERY

CAST OF CHARACTERS

Stephanie Simmons, a dazzlingly beautiful movie actress,
   age 20-30
Giovanni, an Italian-American robber, under 40
Sean, an Irish-American robber, under 40
Juan, a Puerto Rican immigrant robber, under 40

Each of the robbers has a very slight accent.

The scene is the living room of the suite occupied by Simmons in
an expensive Manhattan hotel.

The time is the spring of 2000.

THE ROBBERY

AT RISE: Simmons, in an expensive peignoir, is talking on the phone.

SIMMONS. (Her voice is cloyingly sweet, her enunciation careful, sounding faintly upper-class.) Oh, no, my dear, I don't mind at all. After all, any actress considers it an honor to be interviewed by Nancy Brown and I think it's just wonderful of you to lead off your column tomorrow with a story about me. (Pause) *And* a picture! It's just wonderful of you and I'm sure it will help *A Holiday from Marriage.* (Pause) Yes, it did get wonderful reviews in L.A. (Pause) Mm-hm. The *Times* said it was wonderful. (Pause) Oh, aren't you sweet! (Pause) I can hardly wait to see your column tomorrow. I know it'll be wonderful. (Pause) Oh, I will! I will! (Pause) I hope so, too, love. And do let me know the next time you're going to visit the Coast. (Pause) Byeeee. (She hangs up, her expression changes and she quickly punches in a four-digit extension number, tapping her foot impatiently as the phone rings. As she speaks again, her voice is harsh and strident and the careful enunciation has vanished.) Byron, you stupid son of a bitch, what the fuck do you think you're doing? (Pause) Whaddaya mean, what do I mean? I mean, what's the big idea of telling Nancy Brown it was good enough to interview me on the phone instead of coming here? (Pause) I don't give a good goddam what that dopey dyke said! (Pause) If she's too busy to come here, then fuck her — that's what you shoulda said! I know she's in 245 papers, you feeble-minded faggot! Suppose she writes that she interviewed me on the phone — I'm fucked! (Pause) I don't give a shit if Marla Meryl Mayberry's in town today! She's just some has-been piece of ass! I'm in a hit flick! (Pause) What am I paying you a hundred thou a year for? (Pause) Don't crawl to me, you mealy-mouthed motherfucker! (Her tone changes and her voice becomes exceedingly cold.) Now, you listen to me. I want to be left absolutely alone for two hours. No phone calls, no visitors, no security guards rapping on the door every 15 minutes and asking if I'm OK, no nobody, no nothing! And if I don't get two hours of absolute peace and quiet, you'll be out on that lard ass of yours and you can go peddle it on Christopher Street! (She slams the phone down, looks around the room, walks over to the lavishly stocked bar, surveys the bottles and makes herself a drink, mixing water and ice in it. She takes it over to the sofa center, puts it on the coffee table, sits and picks up a copy of the *Hollywood Reporter*, which she starts to read. From the door upstage right emerge three men in ski masks, all wearing suits, ties and gloves and one carrying an attaché case, all trying to make as little noise as possible. Nevertheless, there are a few sounds, she turns and then jumps up, facing them, undecided as to whether to be afraid or angry.) What the hell!?

GIOVANNI. (Advancing on her) Don't be scared, Miss Simmons. And don't scream. We don't want to have to hurt you.

SIMMONS. (Now frightened) No, please don't hurt me. Who are you? What do you want? I'll do whatever you say. Just don't hurt me.

GIOVANNI. No need to worry, Miss Simmons. We wouldn't think of hurting you if you just let us go about our business and don't make any trouble.

SIMMONS. How did you get in here?

SEAN. That's our secret, Miss Simmons. (Pause) But we did hear you say you're gonna be left alone for a couple hours. That's nice for us. We won't have to hurry.

SIMMONS. What do you want?

GIOVANNI. That ought to be clear. But first of all, we're gonna have to tie you up and gag you, just in case you decide not to cooperate.

JUAN. Don't worry, we won't tie you up too tight and we've a gag so we won't have to use duct tape.

SEAN. Just put your hands behind your back. (She does so, and he ties them with a rope he takes from his pocket.) Now sit down. (She does so, he kneels and ties her ankles together with another piece of rope.) And now the gag. (He takes a cloth gag from his pocket and ties it around her mouth.) There. All set.

JUAN. And now we get to work. (Pause as he looks at her more closely) Hey, you know, you're one beautiful chick. Even more beautiful in real life than in the movies. (Ingratiatingly) You know, I seen all your movies. (She nods.)

GIOVANNI. OK. Let's go. (To Juan) Look in her purse.

JUAN. (Looking around the room he spots it on the small table near the door to the hall left. He walks over, grabs it, takes it to the coffee table and turns it upside down to dump the contents. He picks up the wallet, pulls out the cash and counts it.) Shit! Only 250 lousy bucks!

GIOVANNI. That's what I figured. These big people never carry much cash. Only plastic.

JUAN. Should we take the cards?

GIOVANNI. Why not? (Juan picks them out and pockets them.) Maybe we can find a use for them.

SEAN. (Who meanwhile has wandered over to the bar) Jesus, Mary and Joseph! Will you look at this bar! Nothing but the best! I mean the very best! (Picking up bottles one after the other) Looka this: Royal Salute scotch--that goes for about 175 a bottle!--and Delamain and Pierre Ferrand brandy—top of the line! And Stoly Cristall (He pronounces it *crystal*.)--you can't do no better than that for vodka. (Pause) Hey! Oh, my God! (Holding up a bottle) This here's Middleton!

GIOVANNI. What's Middleton?

SEAN. It's Irish whiskey and it goes for, like, a hundred a fifth! I always heard about it from my old man but I never tasted it! I gotta try this! (He lifts the bottle and takes a long pull.) Jesus, Mary and Joseph, smooth as silk! (He takes another long pull.)

JUAN. How can you be thinking about booze when you got a red-hot broad like her sittin' there? Man, I'd like to show her what I can do! She'll forget every maricón in Hollywood when she gets it from a real man!

GIOVANNI. Forget it! We don't want no kidnap or rape charge hung on us!

JUAN. But shit! We got her here and I know she likes to fuck. I seen in the Enquirer where she dated Dexter Gordon and Greg Lawrence and Rod Jackson and I bet those guys don't take no bitch out unless they get some. But she needs to know what a real man's like in bed! Give her a little Puerto Rican cock and she'll go crazy!

GIOVANNI. Look, I told you to lay off, so lay off! Nobody's screwin' nobody! And, by the way, why don't you give her your life story so she can identify us later? (Pause) C'mon, you guys, we gotta get down to business.

SEAN. Just a minute!' I gotta try this Royal Salute.

GIOVANNI. Christ, will you get away from that bar!

SEAN. Just a minute, willya? (He takes a long pull from the bottle.) Like Father O'Rourke usta say, "nectar of the gods"! Man, that's something to remember! That's a killer drink!

GIOVANNI. I'll give you a killer drink if you don't get cracking! Now, you remember the plan: I stay here and keep an eye on the broad and you guys go through the bedroom. (He points to Sean.) You take the bureaus and dressers and (He points to Juan.) you go through the closets and check all her clothes. Check all the suits that got pockets and see if there's anything there.

JUAN. Yeah, yeah! (He moves toward the bedroom door right.)

GIOVANNI. (Looking at Sean, who is taking another long pull from the Royal Salute) will you put that fuckin' bottle down! Get goin'!

SEAN. Awright, awright. Fuckin' dictator! I'm goin', I'm goin' (He exits right.)

GIOVANNI. Now, Miss Simmons, don't get nervous. The last thing we wanna do is hurt you--or anybody. We don't want no trouble. We're just here to do a job and, if nobody gets in our way, it'll all be real smooth. So lay back and relax. I'd say, "Smile," but I know you can't with that gag. But you can smile in your heart because you're safe with us. (She nods assent, too vehemently. Long pause) Ya know, I seen that last movie you made--that one about Samson and Delilah--*Pillar Talk*--yeah, that was the name of it--you was great! (She attempts a smile.) I mean great!

JUAN. (Entering in a state of some agitation) I can't do it!

GIOVANNI. What're you talkin' about? You can't do what?'

JUAN. I can't go through all them clothes. All them slinky dresses and them silk nightgowns! They give me a hard-on! All I can think about is comin' in here and fuckin' the broad!

GIOVANNI. Forget it, Charlie! No sex!

JUAN. Ah, c'mon! Anyhow, who died and left you president?

GIOVANNI. (Moving closer to him, threateningly) I got elected president! By me! You got a problem with that?

JUAN. (Backing down) Nooo. It's only that--Jeez! Have a heart, willya? I mean, here's one a the most beautiful broads in the world and we got her and we can do whatever we want with her.

GIOVANNI. You got that wrong! Like I said, we're here to do a robbery and we ain't gonna get involved in no rape. (Pause) Tell ya what. (He gestures toward the bedroom door.) Whyncha go back in there and tell Sean--I mean, our friend, that he should go through the closets and you take the bureaus. Maybe rings and bracelets won't give you no hard-ons.

JUAN. Oh, all right. (He exits.)

GIOVANNI. So, what was I sayin'? Oh, yeah. Your flicks. The one I liked best was the Irish girl with your brother was in the IRA and your boyfriend was, like, a British GI and they shoot each other. What was that called? (Pause) Oh, yeah. *Dublin in Brass.* That was one of the best ones you was ever in. (She shakes her head violently in assent. Sean enters from the bedroom.) What're you, through already?

SEAN. Yeah. I looked over everything in the closets. Not too much. She must be travelin' light. I didn't find a fuckin' thing. (He walks over to the bar.) Guess I'll have me another sip of that Royal Salute. (He takes a long pull at the bottle.)

GIOVANNI. Hey! Watch that! We gotta get outa here and I don't want you staggerin' all over the place.

SEAN. Don't worry, me bucko! If there's one man who can hold his liquor, it's me. I remember one time I put away a whole fifth in two hours and I was still sober as a judge. And another time--

JUAN. (Entering, holding a large jewelry box) We hit the jackpot! There's a real big necklace-- (Simmons moans.)

GIOVANNI. Sorry, honey, but that's what we're in business for.

JUAN. And a couple big diamond rings and some bracelets and--

GIOVANNI. Great! (He opens the attaché case.) Just dump 'em all in here and we can split.

JUAN. (Dumping the jewels into the attaché case) A real nice haul.

GIOVANNI. A good day's work, huh, men? (They both say, "Yeah.") Well, Miss Simmons, thanks for being such a good hostess. We'll never forget our visit with you. (She struggles and tries to speak.) No, I don't think we wanna hear what you've got to say. After listening to you lay out that poor bastard on the phone, I bet you got some choice words for us. But we ain't got time to stay and listen. Maybe next time, huh? Just remember, three a your fans laid out plenty a bread to see your flicks and now you paid us back, right? (She struggles as the three exit to the bedroom.)

Blackout.

TWO MONOLOGUES

Left Face

Right Face

CURTAIN GOING UP

LEFT FACE

The monologue was first produced by the Impact Theater Company on July 19, 1994.

(The Speaker is wearing a dress that is fashionable, if a bit conservative. She may also be wearing a hat. She wears a corsage. Her manner is pleasant and terribly earnest.)

Mr. Chairman, Madame President, members of the Bronxville League for Expanded and Awakened Democracy:

Let me tell you first how honored I am that you have chosen me as your Citizen of the Year. It is flattering beyond words, but as those of you who know me are well aware, I am hardly ever beyond words. (She laughs self-consciously.)

At the outset, I want to say that I would never have been able to earn this honor if it were not for my husband Stanley. Unfortunately Stanley is away on a business trip, as he is much of the time, but, if it were not for his success as president of Stanley Enterprises, I would not have the opportunity to devote myself to good works. I try to keep Stanley up to date on my activities, but that is not always easy. Last Monday evening, for example, I spent almost four hours detailing to Stanley my plans for the SOS program-about which more later--when he suddenly remembered that he had a breakfast appointment the next day and decided it would be better if he spent the night in the city, so, even though it was late in the evening, he had the chauffeur take him to the Waldorf. This is the type of dedication that has made him such a prominent figure in the industrial world.

Our president has asked me to say a few words about the projects I am currently working on.

The first area in which I am involved with some of you involves our feathery, furry and finny friends.

The forces of good have triumphed over the forces of evil in the battle to protect the whale and the dolphin. But, let me ask you, how much thought have you given to the squid? You may on occasion have ordered calamari in an Italian restaurant, but it probably did not cross your mind that squid is a staple of the diet in both Italy and Japan. Now, let me say at the outset that I intend no slur against residents of those two countries. Our Italian-American friends have enough crosses to bear already, what with names like John Gotti in the news, so I have no wish to add to their burdens. And I have met so many nice persons from Japan here in Bronxville--that nice Mr. Yakimoto, whose firm bought Yankee Doodle Products, and that nice Mr. Fujimara, whose company purchased Uncle Sam Foods, and so many others.

But I'm sure you're eager to get back to the squid. In a word, the squid population is being decimated. As the demand for seafood increases, I am sure that every squid must feel threatened. We must take steps! So a few of us are setting up the SOS program-- Save Our Squid--and, if you're interested in joining us, please see me at the conclusion of my little talk.

And, as those of you who have walked on the picket line with me are well aware, we are continuing our protest against those fiends in human form, the monsters who are running Marquis Labs. The latest atrocity to come to our attention is this: they have developed a medicine to expand human veins and arteries and so facilitate blood circulation. Now, admittedly a few lives may have been saved by this medication, but at what cost, I ask, at what cost? To develop this product, several hundred white rats were cruelly exploited: first, their veins and arteries were constricted, and then they were given the product to expand these vessels. Imagine the pain! What must those poor animals have thought and felt? And, although their lives were not taken in the experiment, what a shadow must have been cast over what should have been their golden years! This must not go on! If you wish to join our picket line, please see me at the conclusion of my little talk.

The second area in which I've been very active involves our African-American fellow citizens. Many of you are aware of our drive to bus students from the Bedford-Stuyvesant section of Brooklyn to schools here in Bronxville. It is true that this would involve a long bus ride--perhaps two hours each way--but, in the first place, travel is broadening, and, in the second place, our schools have so much more to offer than theirs do. I mean, where else would they have the opportunity to have fellow-students who drive BMW's and Jaguars to school? Could they start Latin in the sixth grade in Bedford-Stuyvesant? But, sad to say, we've been encountering opposition on both sides. I can understand the attitude of our friends in Brooklyn who want to keep their children in schools there. We have to remember that they have been denied many of the advantages that we have enjoyed and so must be educated to those advantages. What I can not understand, however, is the opposition here in Bronxville. Honesty compels me to say that it smacks of racism, reluctant as I am to use that word. The fact that a prominent African-American neurosurgeon who lives here also opposes this busing should not be allowed to obscure the issue. Even a neurosurgeon can be misguided.

But, to show that our hearts are in the right place, we did hold a poetry/music contest open to all African-American students in New York City, with a top prize of $1,000, quite a large sum to youths of that background. And I am happy to announce that we judges have selected a winner, a rap song by Rasheed-al-Shabazz-al-Jamal of Lenox Avenue in Manhattan. I have it here and, with your indulgence, I'd like to read it to you:

We stood outside beneath the moon
We felt so good 'cause it was June.
I suddenly began to croon
Because I knew I'd fuck you soon.

We both felt great and that's no shit.
I knew that I would score a hit.
I kissed your lips a little bit,
And then I grabbed you by the tit.

You were my chick, you were my lass.
No need for coke, no need for grass.
My tempature was rising fast,
And then I grabbed you by the ass.

And so we spent a perfect night.
To see you I would risk a fight.
It wasn't fair, it wasn't right
We had to see dawn's early light.

Isn't that just splendid? It has feeling and power and, in that last line, an echo of patriotism. We are very happy to have such a talented prize-winner. We gave a couple of honorable mentions to another young poet, but we all agreed that his work was too sophisticated, too white, if you will. The poem we chose seemed to us a better attempt to capture the soul of a people.

And a footnote: a group of us wrote a letter of protest to Texas Senator Burnside. It seems Texas bee-keepers have been conducting forays into Mexico and using flame-throwers to destroy beehives there on the grounds that they contain bees "contaminated" by intermingling with killer bees. You will recall, of course, that killer bees originally came from Africa, so we see this as racially motivated. It's the old Southern fear of miscegenation all over again. We haven't yet had an answer from Senator Burnside, but I will let you know when we do.

Finally, our legal subcommittee, of which I am proud to be a member, has been very active.

We have filed an amicus curiae brief in the case that the

municipality has brought against the two gay gentlemen who stand accused of having sexual relations on one of the tennis courts in our park on Sunday afternoon. While it is true that the police claim to have a dozen or so alleged witnesses, we all know how fair and objective our local Gestapo can be when they are trying to make a case against anyone. I can only say that, if the couple involved had been a heterosexual pair, I'll bet there would have been no arrests and no court action. We view this as a clear-cut bias case, bias against the two gentlemen's sexual orientation, and we will fight it with every ounce of energy we can summon.

The same holds true of the challenge being mounted to the local ordinance we succeeded in getting passed last month banning smoking in all restaurants. Our organization has always taken pride in our support of the rights of the individual and our willingness to battle for those rights against the power of the government. But sometimes it becomes necessary to save people from themselves and that is why we backed this ordinance in the first place. After all, if we had heroin addicts shooting up at the tables in our restaurants, we would surely take action. Well, we say that nicotine addiction is exactly the same thing. When the price of cigarettes goes to $5 a pack, as it surely will, we will have crazed cigarette junkies mugging us and robbing our homes to get money for a True Blue fix. Besides, our experts told us that a non-smoker sitting in a closed room 50 feet from a smoker is consuming the equivalent of one cigarette every three years. Well, I don't know about you, but I for one don't want to die of lung cancer. Enough said. To those restaurant owners who assert their business has fallen off by 30 percent, I can only say that we must all make sacrifices for the general welfare. And besides, they no longer have to hire employees to scrub ashtrays and repair burns in their tablecloths, which should make up for the losses they say they are sustaining.

Last but not least, we are continuing our struggle to close the Indian Point nuclear power plant. We have suffered a setback recently in the petition submitted to the state supreme court by physics professors at the various branches of the State University of New York. They claim that more than 80 percent of their colleagues in physics departments across the country believe atomic power to be a safe and environmentally sound form of energy. I say, look at Chernobyl. And I also say, let's not forget that these very same physicists have a vested interest in nuclear power.

After all, who get all the consulting contracts at these plants? And experts can be wrong, too. What about those scientists in ancient times who said the earth was flat? Our feeling--if I may use an indelicate phrase-- our gut feeling is that it is only one step-- maybe half a step--from splitting atoms to create electricity and gas to dropping atomic bombs on those we disagree with. Some weeks ago, I gave my ideas on the subject to Stanley over the course of several hours, but unfortunately he had to go and study a couple of merger proposals before taking another business trip the next day. However, I am sure he is with us in our struggle.

Yet, busy as we are, friends, there are many other areas that must be approached. We must put an end to the burning of fossil fuels, which create acid rain. We must re-do our traffic signs so that they give instructions not only in English, but also in Spanish, Japanese, Italian, French, German and Portuguese, so that newcomers to our land will not feel we are insensitive to their ethnic heritages. We must continue to back dedicated teachers like Mr. Walters, under attack because he assigned *Last Exit to Brooklyn* and *Tropic of Cancer* and showed *Debby Does Dallas* in class. We must protect our toddlers from sugar-laden cereals and child molesters.

There is much to do, but we must find the time and energy to do it. As Shakespeare so ably put it, "Eternal vigilance is the price of liberty" and, as he wrote somewhere else, "Liberty means responsibility." We must assume responsibility. As The Bard also said, "We shall not flag or fail." I know I shall not and I have every confidence you shall not.

Thank you.

RIGHT FACE

The monologue was first produced by the Impact Theater Company on July 19, 1994.

(The Speaker is wearing a dress that is obviously expensive, but in quiet good taste. She may also be wearing a hat. She wears a corsage and carries a large and obviously rather heavy purse, which she plops down on the table. Her demeanor is a bit severe.)

Madame Chairman, Mr. President, members and guests of the American Awareness and Alertness Association of Yonkers.

May I begin by thanking you for having selected me as your AAAA Patriot of the Year. It is an honor I shall always cherish and my only regret is that my late husband, Fillmore, is not here to share it with me. But, even though he has gone to that last big Conservative Club caucus in the sky, I feel sure he is looking down on us this evening, smiling and saying, "To you I pass the torch! Be yours to hold it high!"

And hold it high we shall. I take particular pride in your award because it seems to me a vindication of a decision I made some years ago which cost me the friendship of several of my conservative associates. About 15 years ago I resigned from the John Birch Society on the grounds that it was too liberal and was filled with all manner of leftists. They laughed when I stood up to leave, but who is laughing now? (She gives a forced and hollow laugh.) I'm laughing now because they are past history and I am still fighting the good fight.

The good fight is what we must indeed carry on with renewed vigilance. Given my long and careful study of Marxism-Leninism-Stalinism-Gorbachevism-Yeltsinism, I do not doubt for one second that the so-called perestroika-glasnost movement is nothing more than a vast charade played out on the stage of Red

Square. And recent developments have only strengthened my views. Its aim of course is to lull us into a false sense of security, to make us scrap our A-bombs, H-bombs, B-2 bombers, F-111 jet fighters, Patriot missiles, tanks, trucks, jeeps, machine guns, rifles, pistols, submarines, aircraft carriers, battleships, destroyers, PT boats, landing craft, uniforms, boots, tents, pillows, pillowcases, sheets, Star Wars defense system--you name it.

Then, once we have denuded ourselves, they will strike. Hordes of fanatic Russians or Chinese will land on our shores and sweep through our cities and towns, raping and pillaging and laying waste our countryside! But I, for one, will not be caught napping. (She reaches into her purse and pulls out a pistol, which she waves around.) If any Communist attempts to storm my house, frothing at the mouth and screaming Marxist slogans, I will give him an appropriate greeting! (She fires the gun into the air. Pause.)

But this need not happen. As Shakespeare said, "Eternal vigilance is the price of peace." Forewarned is forearmed. We must not allow ourselves to be deceived and we must not believe for one second that the zealots in the Kremlin sincerely want a rapport with those of us who believe in peace, freedom, democracy, justice, honor, tolerance, humanitarianism, kindness, decency and all other virtues for which our forefathers fought and died. These are the very things that they want to destroy and we must guarantee that these enduring values remain.

Which brings me to an allied subject. Those who have been taken in by the propaganda from Moscow--(Her eyes narrow.) and some whose links with the Kremlin may be more than just philosophical-- want to insure that American citizens have no way to defend themselves. To this end, they have been agitating and continue to agitate for gun control. They begin by seeking to outlaw machine guns and automatic weapons like Uzis and AK-47s. But of course they do not plan to stop there. Next will come pistols and rifles and shotguns, so that law abiding citizens will have no means of protecting hearth and home.

But, even if the Red-pinko-leftist-liberal lobby does succeed in taking away our guns, we will still have other ways of defending ourselves. (She reaches into her purse and extracts a long and very formidable-looking knife, which she waves around.) As long as the Hoffritz cutlery company remains in business, we need not despair: we will have the means of insuring that our lives and our property remain safe.

The subject of property brings up a very ticklish question, one of interest to us all. We who live in and near Yonkers have had first-hand experience with the pressure to integrate housing in our fair city. Now, I yield to no one in my firm conviction that this country belongs to all its citizens and, further, that all those citizens should have the right to live where they wish to live.

Yet I have to ask myself if the configuration of our housing here was caused by some mysterious outside force or by the inclination of residents to do the very thing just mentioned--to live where they wish to live.

In the town in which I grew up--in another state, which shall remain nameless--there were white people and there were colored folk and we all lived in perfect harmony. The white people had houses in that section of town logically called Hilltop, because it embraced the sides of the hills which rose from the river. The colored folk lived in that part of town bisected by the railroad and logically called Riveredge, because it bordered the river. No white people of my acquaintance expressed a desire to live in Riveredge and no colored folk I knew ever told me that they wanted to live in the Hilltop section.

This is not to say that either section was a problem-free paradise on earth. Those whose homes were in the Hilltop area faced the difficulty of getting their cars up the very steep hills after winter snowstorms. Those who lived in the Riveredge area were sometimes troubled by the presence of rats and by floods every spring, when the river often overflowed its banks. But all the citizens were able to cope with their difficulties: in winter, many of the white people drove their cars as far uphill as they could and walked the rest of the way home, many times in snow up to their knees. The colored folk were even able to joke about their aqueous difficulties: I remember Uncle Rufus--we called him "uncle" although he was a boy of only 35 or so--observing with a chuckle one spring, "Why, in my house we got both running water and rushing water," which I found an entertaining witticism.

And yet, as I say, no one wished to leave his or her neighborhood, surely because he or she wanted to be with people of similar interests from similar economic backgrounds with similar educational experiences. I cannot conceive, for example, that Uncle Rufus would have been happy at one of our soirees, where we handled such recondite literary topics as whether *On the Waterfront* presented an accurate picture of American unionism; nor would we from the Hilltop have fitted in at a Riveredge barbecue, trying to enter into a debate as to whether Little Richard or Chubby Checker was a more important contributor to musical history.

And it must not be forgotten that, in that bygone era, we were fortunate in what we lacked: first, we did not have outside agitators roaming the countryside spreading their poison and trying to create chaos and dissension where only happiness and contentment existed; second, we did not have the media as the spokesman for the Eastern liberal establishment, filling our homes with the warped views of insular New Yorkers like Walter Cronkite, Eric Sevareid and Dan Rather; third, we did not have leftist federal judges with their bleeding hearts and iron fists, obsessed with changing residential patterns to suit their personal, preconceived notions, determined to mix oil and water, wheat and chaff, gold and dross, insistent that a welfare mother with 15 children must live next to a millionaire industrialist, that an ex-convict must dwell in the same neighborhood as a philosophy professor, institutionalizing injustice.

And, speaking of injustice, we must all be concerned about the defeats in the last two statewide elections of bond issues to build new prisons. The lack of prison space means just one thing: our streets are filled with vicious and predatory criminals who laugh at our courts, which set lawless fiends loose on the decent members of society. We must be ready to ward them off and I for one am prepared. Of course, for us women, rape is a constant threat, but even more ominous is the possibility of being snatched up off the street and sold into a life worse than death--the world of white slavery. This will not happen to me! (She reaches into her purse and pulls out a can.)

This is Disperse, a disabling spray effective at a distance of 7 to 12 feet and I know from personal experience that it works. I had occasion to use it once when a suspicious-looking man approached me on the street; unfortunately it turned out that he was soliciting funds for a summer camp for handicapped children. But, after the half-hour it took to re-orient him, he quite forgave me and accepted my 25-cent donation with touching gratitude.

But, if the suspicious individual gets closer then 7 feet (She reaches into her purse and pulls out another can.) there's always good, old reliable Mace. I am certain that it is effective. A man who grabbed me by the arm on the sidewalk, allegedly to pull me out of the way of some urchin on a skateboard, was completely incapacitated by a spray of Mace. Although he presented the police with credentials that appeared to indicate he was a stockbroker, these days anyone can get any documents proving anything. I remain convinced that he was the agent of a white-slave ring who would have spirited me away had it not been for my trusty Mace.

Ah, my friends, there are so many areas in which work-- good work--remains to be done.

We must keep up our fight to restore capital punishment. I am convinced that the death penalty does not go far enough, but it is still a weapon society can use.

We must continue to battle abortion. The taking of a human life, even in the form of a fetus, is an abomination. After all, the abortionist may be snuffing out the life of a Socrates, Newton, Mozart or Ronald Reagan.

We must stamp out sexual permissiveness, which attempts to equate all manner of sexual perversions with healthy, normal adjustments to life. Obviously a prison term is not a suitable punishment, since these warped souls would find it a kind of earthly paradise. Society must devise some sort of chastisement that will convince these sick individuals to abandon their sinful ways, to marry and have children--in short, to be fruitful.

So, let me repeat in closing, there is work to be done, but with firmness in the right as God gives us to see the right, we shall win through and witness the triumph of good over evil.

Thank you.